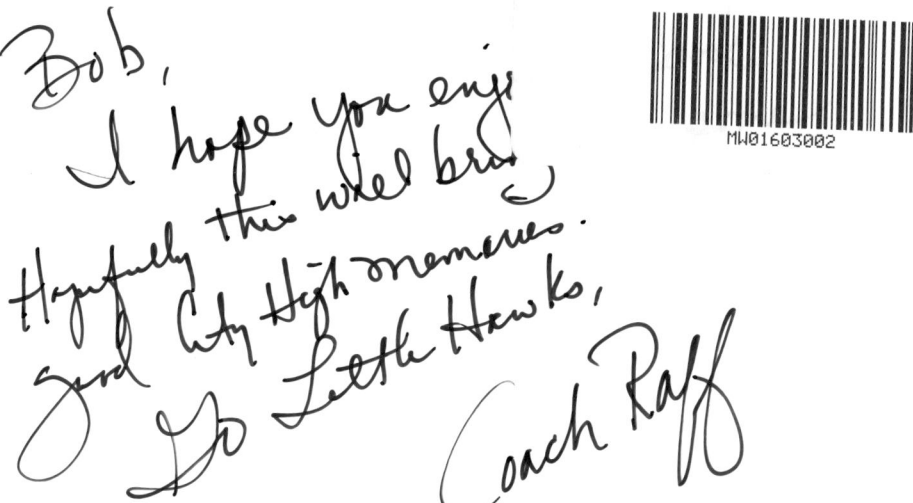

Bob,
I hope you enjoy
Hopefully this will bring
good City High memories.
Go Little Hawks,
Coach Raff

# Dedication

### *To my family:*

*To my dad Leonard the original Coach Raff, and the man who modeled not only how to coach but more importantly how to be a father and how to treat other people.*

*To my mom Leone with that wonderful sense of humor that she passed on to her children.*

*To my sons, Michael and David, whom I had the privilege to both coach and coach with at City High.*

*Most of all to my wife Sharon, who has been at my side for over 40 years and who always gave me the strength to stay positive, to pursue my dreams and who has been as much a part of any success I've had as any athlete I've coached.*

# Preface

Writing this book has given me the opportunity to combine two of my main interests, history and City High athletics, and gives me the chance to give back to the school that has given so much to me.

I chose to write this book because there is truly something special about City High. There is a strong feeling of City High pride that goes beyond winning games. Joey Woody, world-class track performer, said, "We were always reminded from the first day my freshman year to the day I graduated, it's all about Little Hawk pride."

That feeling stays with you long after you leave City High as a competitor or coach. Christine Skelly Weber, class of 1979 and a member of the basketball, softball and track teams, states, "My time at City High on sports teams are some of my most cherished memories and I still follow, with pride, the accomplishments of the Little Hawks. I sincerely hope my children have such an enjoyable and satisfying time playing high school sports as I was able to do at City High."

Many City High alumni continue to stress the values they learned as Little Hawks. Dan McCarney, current football coach at Iowa State University and former football, wrestling and track standout at City High, says, "...at the heart of my approach to life are things I learned from coaches and teachers at City High. The coaches at City High impacted my life way beyond any victories on the field, mat, or track."

I have so many wonderful memories of my 36 years at City High and I hope you enjoy reading this book as much as I have enjoyed writing it.

John Raffenpserger

# Acknowledgments

Thanks to the many people who have contributed in some way to the completion and publication of this book.

Thanks to my brother Gene, a career writer for the <u>Des Moines Register</u> and the real writer of our family. Gene gave me much advice, encouragement, and guidance to get me started and to finish my book.

To Ken McCaffrey, a long-time friend and a writer in his own right, for his editing of this book.

Special thanks to my wife Sharon for the many hours of typing, encouragement and support needed to complete this book.

To the City High Alumni Association and Jim Sangster, in particular, for their help in publicizing this book.

Thanks to Steve Holland and Steve Semken for their advice and support.

Thanks also to the many people who responded to my pleas for anecdotes and memories of their days at City High.

Thanks to Bud Legg, of the IHSAA office, and to Mike Henderson at IGHSAU for opening their files to me.

Thanks to the City High Publication Department for the use of the many yearbooks, Little Hawk newspapers and photos used in completing this book.

To Terry Coleman for his help with the women's sports, especially women's track and field, and for scanning photos used in this book.

Thanks to Bill Bywater and Tru Art® for publishing my book.

A special thanks to the many athletes, students and staff I have been associated with in my 36-year love affair with City High.

*"As a kid I couldn't wait to be a City High Little Hawk......being a Little Hawk was so much more than winning titles. Being a Little Hawk is about lifelong friendships and memories."*

*Michele Conlon, class of 1983, Iowa State University tennis coach*

# INTRODUCTION

Officially it's Iowa City, City High School. But along Dubuque Street in Iowa City or in cities like Dubuque, Atlantic, Ankeny or Ft. Dodge it's known simply as *City High*. Actually it proudly carries this slogan, "City High, the school that leads."

City High's first graduating class was in 1874, with the first athletic squads showing up in the late 1890's. The first real documented athletic squads were found in the 1905-06 school year. The 1906-07 <u>Red and White</u>, the school newspaper at the time, states the following: "For several years athletics were forbidden in the high school due to the abuse by the students of the privileges granted them. In the spring of 1905 we were again granted athletics to be governed by certain stringent restrictions." That would indicate the presence of athletic squads of some nature prior to 1905.

Football was not recognized by the Board of Education until 1907, although there is documentation of games being played prior to that including reference to the fact that the 1907 season was the first allowed <u>since</u> 1900.

In a 1906 issue of the <u>Red and White</u>, reference is made to a new gym. "The first basketball game played on the new floor was also the first game played at home since we were granted athletics again." The dimensions of this new gym were 55' x 39', which was quite large for that time. This would be the gym in the building later called Central Junior High.

Track and field and baseball were the other sports recognized during the 1905-06 school year. Results were found for the track team as early as the late 1890's, but 1906 appears to be an organized team. A.F. Siepert is listed as basketball, track and baseball coach in 1906. No coach's name was listed for the football team, but in all probability it was also Siepert, as usually the same individual coached all sports. It should be noted that in the early years, only last names of coaches were used in most cases. This was common for reporting by newspapers of the time.

Although exact starting dates for other sports may be in question, three sports apparently got their starts in the 1920's. Swimming results were found starting in 1921 and cross country in 1922 with H.C. Soucek as coach. He was also listed as football, basketball and track coach.

City High was represented in tennis tournaments starting in 1928, but research has not turned up a name for a coach until Howard Orvis in 1931, who was listed as a freshman at the University of Iowa.

Golf was added in 1939 with Francis Merten as coach. He also coached three other sports at City High during a nine-year career with the Little Hawks.

The final two boys' sports to be added were wrestling, which had its inaugural season in 1954 with long-time football and baseball coach Frank Bates at the helm, and soccer, which was added in 1984 with Tim Zweiner as the first coach.

# Women's Sports

Although girls at City High had taken part in some form of athletics since the early 1900's, it was in the form of class competition rather than interscholastic athletics. This evolved into the Girls' Recreation Association (GRA) where intramural type competition took place.

Girls in smaller school systems were regularly taking part in interscholastic athletics and eventually pressure was applied to do the same in the large systems.

In 1966, Mona Schallau, an outstanding tennis competitor, petitioned the Iowa City Board of Education to allow her to play in the Girls' District Tennis Tournament. This request was approved and Mona won both the District and State Singles titles. Girls' tennis was then added the following year in 1967 as the first official girls' sport at City High.

In the 1968-69 school year, a group representing the Iowa City Swim Club also petitioned the Iowa City School Board to enter a team of City High girls in the District Swimming Meet. The results were similar to Mona Schallau's, as the City High team won the State Meet and became the first Little Hawk State Team Champion in girls' athletics. In the spring of 1968 Kandy Kellow won the Sectional Golf Tournament but golf was not officially added as a sport until 1972.

The 1970's saw six girls' sports added to the City High athletic program. Volleyball, gymnastics and golf were added in 1971-72. Gymnastics was later dropped, following the 1988 season, by the state because so few schools had programs and there were high insurance costs. Track and summer softball began in 1973, and basketball, six-on-six variety, was added in 1973-74. The traditional 5-on-5 game began with the 1984-85 season. Cross country was added for the girls in the fall of 1979 and in 1985 the final girls' sport, soccer, was added, bringing the total number of girls' sports to 10. The number was reduced to the current total of nine when gymnastics was dropped.

Information for this book was obtained from City High yearbooks (the first published in 1910), the school newspaper <u>Red and White</u> (published every six weeks starting in 1906), microfilm of the <u>Iowa City Press-Citizen</u>, interviews conducted, and questionnaires obtained from City High athletes, the IHSAA and IGHSAU archives, and the author's personal memories of 36 years as a coach at City High.

I apologize for any spelling errors. When first names are not included, they were not known, especially in the early years when in yearbooks it was common to use just last names.

Information in this book includes all sports up through the fall season of 2004.

Some of the proceeds from the sale of this book will go to the John Raffensperger Scholarship Fund. If you would like to contribute to this scholarship or any other scholarship mentioned in this book you could send a contribution in care of City High School.

# CONTENTS

## THE SEASONS

# Football 1907-2004

City High has a heritage of outstanding football teams, individual standouts, Conference Champions, and State Champions.

The 1917 team, under Coach F.J. Voight and captain and All-State performer George "Zip" Kloos, was the first of nine teams to be either voted by newspapers or actually winning a State Championship in football. That early championship was followed by teams of 1936, 1946, 1950, 1953, and 1960 in winning "poll" or newspaper-voted championships.

The Iowa State High School Athletic Association in 1972, introduced a statewide playoff series to determine the State Champion. The Little Hawks won state titles in 1993, 1994, and 1996 with the '93 and '96 teams recording perfect 13-0 seasons. The Little Hawks have had eight unbeaten seasons and 15 one-loss seasons in their long and successful history.

The Mississippi Valley Conference, which has had several major changes in membership, had its official start in 1929, with City High as a charter member. The first season a football champion was recognized was 1931 and the first City High MVC champion was the undefeated team of 1936, with Hall of Fame Coach Herb Cormack at the helm. That team was also selected as State Champions and gave up just 12 points in recording a record seven shutouts.

## *Pre-1920's*

In 1907 the Iowa City Board of Education removed the ban from football and sanctioned the sport at City High. The board took action because it was thought better to control football than to let it go uncontrolled as it was.

The team had a sad debut playing Cedar Rapids, on the Iowa Field, as junior tackle Leo Stohmeyer received a severe neck injury while making a tackle. He was taken to University Hospitals where an operation to set the vertebra was performed. Unfortunately pneumonia and

*First official Football team, 1907*

meningitis developed and he died four days later. The football program survived that incident and continued.

In the pre-1920 era, some rules were different. Touchdowns were worth five points, field goals, which were almost always drop kicks, scored four points.

In 1906 the forward pass was made legal, although not many teams used it mainly because the ball was much fatter.

The kick back was a common play, where you received a kick off or punt and punted it back to your opponent. You could then fall on the ball and it would be your ball. This was true of any punt at that time. Teams often punted on second down as a result of this.

Substitution rules have changed frequently over the years. Early rules said that if a player was taken out for an injury, he could not return until that quarter was over.

Transportation was difficult in the early years because roads and highways were mostly unpaved. Most trips were made by train, or interurban in the case of Cedar Rapids. Most people who lived in Iowa City up to the mid-1950's are familiar with the CRANDIC or Cedar Rapids and Iowa City Railroad that operated an interurban between the two cities up to at least 1955. The CRANDIC provided transportation to Cedar Rapids games into the 1920's. In this timeframe games at Tipton, West Liberty, and Davenport were reached by the Rock Island train. In 1909 the team traveled by train to Davenport, then changed trains to travel onto Clinton for a game.

In a 27-0 defeat at the hands of Clinton in October of 1912, Clinton threw several TD passes to players who had been lying down in bounds on the other side of the field. This was known as the "Sleeper Play" and was used quite frequently in both high school and college games of this period and was later ruled illegal.

During the 1910 football season the team got new uniforms donated by Coast & Sons, a local clothing store. In 1910 due to increased attendance at home games (a reported 5,000 attended a Thanksgiving game vs. Clinton), the school cleared the grand total of $900 on football.

In 1911 Fred Kinney won the Rock Island game with a drop kick field goal and he also set a state record with a kick from the 46-yard line in a game against North Des Moines. This 1911 team had four athletes make the All-State teams: Kinney (FB), Swisher (QB), Goetz (T) and Munkhoff (HB), who was also named the captain of the All-Iowa team.

The year 1913 produced the record scoring total for one game as Iowa City defeated Marshalltown, 106-0. Harrison made 14 of 15 PAT in that game. Another record may have been set as the Little Hawkeyes (as they were known then) defeated Dubuque, 56-0, with all points coming in the second half.

The 1916 and 1917 teams combined for a 15-1-1 record with the 1917 team accorded the State Championship. They outscored their opponents, 229-13. The 1917 team recorded six shutouts. The 1916 team won games 48-0, 55-0, 35-0, and 33-0.

*1917 State Champions*

George "Zip" Kloos was All-State halfback in both years. In 1916 his stat line included at least one 45-yd. run in all eight games plus a 95-yd. punt return TD. The following season he had a 100-yd.-interception return and an 85-yd. punt return. Dr. Von Lackum coached the 1916 team and F.J. Voight led the 1917 State Champion team.

In 1918 a nationwide influenza outbreak closed school for five weeks, cutting the football season to just three games. The spring of 1919 saw the introduction of spring football practice. Workouts were held on Monday, Tuesday and Wednesday.

## 1920's

The 1920's was not a particularly outstanding era for City High football as the Little Hawks won just 57% of their games.

For an interesting side note, in 1920 Elmer Layden, later to be immortalized as one of Notre Dame's famed four horsemen, played for Davenport High against City High, and Duke Slater, later a famed All-American tackle for Iowa, played for Clinton High the same year.

The 1922 team recorded a 7 -1 season with six shutouts, giving up just 24 points. H.C. Soucek returned from WWI to coach six teams in the 20's. Coach Soucek also coached cross country, basketball, track and swimming during his tenure at City High.

The 1923 season was scheduled to be the inaugural season for Shrader Field located at Longfellow School, but the new field was not completely sodded so it could not be used. Locker rooms were ready and weather-permitting practices were held there and at City Park. Games would continue to be played on the Iowa Field.

Starting with the 1924 season, games moved to Shrader Field. Games remained there until the current field opened with the 1948 season.

The only player from the 1920's to be named All-State was Howard Moffit (QB) in 1929. Howard was also a two-year All-State performer in basketball and MVC Champion in track. He returned to City High to coach track (1947-49) and basketball (1950-53) and served as Athletic Director from 1947 to 1953.

## 1930's

The mid-1930's started a "Golden Age" of sorts for City High football that extended into the early 1950's. Much of that can be credited to the coaching regime of Herb Cormack who arrived at City High in 1935 and in a nine-year career accumulated a record of 63-10-5 with two State Championships (1936 & 1946), three unbeaten teams (1936,1942 & 1946) and three seasons with just one loss.

His 1936 team had a school record, seven shutouts and gave up just 12 points all season. Included in the victims was the first win in 22 years over state power Des Moines East. Cormack-coached teams produced 18 All-State players in that nine-year run.

Several firsts were recorded in the 1930's. The first night game ever played by the Little Hawks occurred at Clinton in 1930, Clinton winning, 7-0. In 1932 the first night game in Iowa City was a 6 -6 tie with University High. This was just the second game ever between the cross-town schools, the first was played in 1919. Eight poles provided the lighting for that game with two reflectors and eight 1500-watt bulbs.

In the 1930 season two records were set. Tackle Charles Crawford scored three touchdowns with fumbles and Eldred Vestermark intercepted five passes in one game against Columbus Junction. That remains a record as of the 2004 season.

The 1932 season would not rank with the other Golden Age years of the 30's. The 1932 team had a record of 1-9-1. The Little Hawks scored just two touchdowns and were shut out in nine of the 11 games. Included in those losses was a record 95-0 defeat at the hands of Waterloo West.

The 1938 Homecoming game was postponed twice because of bad weather and was finally played 13 days later.

3

The 1939 season was the first that students attended classes in the current City High building on the far (at that time) east side of Iowa City. There was much controversy when the site was chosen since it was actually outside the city limits. Superintendent Iver Opstad 's decision has certainly stood the test of time as the city has far outreached the school's location. An interesting sidelight to that first year in the new building was that the Homecoming Queen selected was June Williams who later married long-time coach and Athletic Director Bob White. Bob was also a member of the football team that season.

## *1940's*

The 1940's continued a run of success in football. Herb Cormack coached four years in the decade and had a record of 29-4-1 with a State Championship and two MVC titles. The State title came in 1946 when Coach Cormack returned from a four-year stint in the Navy in WWII. This was Herb's last season as he took an assistant job on the Iowa State University football staff following the 1946 season. He left with a 63-10-5-career mark in nine seasons. Among Herb's honors was the State Coach of the Year in 1946, induction into the Iowa Football Coaches Hall of Fame in 1968 and the Herb Cormack Scholarship awarded to a City High senior each year.

Dave Danner (class of 1943) summed up the feeling of many that played at City High in this era: "Just being a Little Hawk and coached by Herb Cormack was a gift."

In 1944 the first Dad's Night was the Burlington game. This began a tradition that continues to the present although it has been known as Parents' Night since the early 70's to honor both mothers and fathers.

*Herb Cormack - Hall of Fame Coach*

Evan Smith, All-State end in 1945, recalls, "Our class was there for nearly the four full years of WWII. The school had air raid drills. There was rationing, including gasoline. One athlete's dad owned a gas station and came up with gas for traveling to events."

The undefeated 1946 State Championship team had numerous honors. Coach Cormack was named State Coach of the Year by the <u>Des Moines Register</u>; four players, Jim Sangster (QB), Don Fryauf (E), Jack Evans (G), and Leo Ziethamel (T), were named All-State. Following the season a postseason charity game was proposed with the Nebraska State Champs, Boys Town, for Thanksgiving. This offer was turned down because school officials felt the weather would not be good enough to allow for good practices or playing the game. They also felt it would disrupt the basketball early season.

Leo Zeithamel, a member of the 1945 and 1946 squads, remembers two events from the 1946 season. "In the game with Dubuque there were just a few seconds left and we were behind 13-12. It was our ball and Sangster completed a pass to Fryauf. Sangster yelled so everyone could hear it, including the Dubuque players, 'Same play!' He completed it with thirteen seconds to go and we won."

Leo also recalls, in practice that season Coach Cormack made the statement, "Remember you have no friends on the football field." "So the next play, I knocked out Bill Roth. Herb jumped me for doing that and I said, "You just told me that we have no friends on the football field."

Don Fryauf had 16 TDs in 1946, including four versus Cedar Rapids McKinley and three versus Burlington. Seven of his touchdowns came from 40 yards or more.

## *Little Hawks Became Big Hawks*

The 1946 and 1947 teams combined to send five players to the1950 University of Iowa football team. Four of these were backs. It is highly unlikely that any other high school had the potential to have the entire backfield on the field for a Division One college football squad. Although they never played at the same time it could have happened. Jim Sangster (QB), Don Fryauf (HB), Chug Wilson (HB), and Bill Reichardt (FB) all were on the 1950 Iowa squad. Holger Christensen (center), was the fifth Little Hawk on the 1950 team. Reichardt went on the following year to be named the MVP of the Big Ten Conference and later played briefly with the Green Bay Packers.

Recalling these years, Hank Rate said, "As a junior, during the 1947 season, I played a little football when Bill Reichardt was a senior and was in total awe of him. Trainer Bill Frye would tape him from head to toe…ankles, knees, thighs, and ribs, then he'd go out and demolish the opposition.

"My senior year I played behind All-State End Gene Hettrick. Before the Dubuque game, Gene developed a nasty boil under his arm and couldn't raise it, so I got the starting call on offense. Gene played defense. During the first series, he made a solid hit on Dubuque's wingback and popped the boil. This released the pain and he went back in on offense. Thus ended my first and last role as a starter.

"Athletics were a huge part of my life, although I feel a little like George Plimpton. My glory was in association with some great guys."

In September of 1947, a red and white school bus was given to City High.

## *New Football Field*

The 1948 season was 7-2 under second-year coach Frank Bates. One important happening was the highly anticipated opening of the new field on the campus of City High. This ended a 24-year run of games played on Shrader Field. The opening game vs. Davenport drew an estimated 7,000 fans. Davenport won 13-0. The following season a new scoreboard was added, donated by area businessmen. This field is still being used and in 1969 was named Frank Bates Field in honor of Coach Bates.

The 1948 squad produced a couple of unusual stats. Rox Shain had punts of 62,73, and 79 yards that season, with the latter still a City High record as of 2004. Dick Williams had the unusual distinction of returning a kickoff 96 yards but did not score, as he was tackled on the two-yard line.

One of the very best all-around athletes of all time at City High was produced in the 1940's. Gene Hettrick earned 12 letters in his City High career; four in basketball, three in football, three in baseball and two in track. That was the record until Matt Wooldrik earned 13 by the time he graduated in 2002. There will be more about Gene in the basketball section.

Jim Sangster recalls, "Until the 1948 season, football games were played at Shrader Field behind Longfellow School. The teams dressed in the lower locker room at City High, which was the varsity locker room at the time. The team boarded a Maher Bros. moving van and rode to Shrader Field standing up. They went on Fourth Avenue to Court Street to Oakland and then in the alley. Fans walking along Court Street to the game would cheer as the van passed. Cars parked around the field and horns sounded when the van appeared. After pre-game warm-up, the team retired to the Longfellow gym for last-minute instructions. Then they roared down the hill avoiding the steps, which were usually filled with late arriving fans. Shrader Field was a natural amphitheater and provided an excellent place to play. Since there was no TV at the time, going to City High games on Friday nights was a popular pastime, one that many U. of I. students attended. People in cars behind the north end zone would often make comments to players when the ball was close to that goal line. Every time a touchdown was scored the horns would honk again. In those days players did not go to the sidelines during timeouts and coaches did not come on the field. QBs called their own plays for the most part. After the game, the team jumped back into the van for a return to City High, singing and shouting after a win and being quiet on the rare times they lost. After dressing they usually went downtown to get something to eat, at the Princess Café in the early 40's and to Reich's Café starting in the mid 40's. The Princess Café and Reich's are long gone. Things are now different on Friday nights, but not necessarily better." Shrader Field is now used for soccer games.

*Bill Reichardt - 1947 All-State*

Richard Doran remembers the 1947 team, "…the most meaningful among the 'game memories' was Bill Reichardt's last game. He was not to be denied. Playing with a cast on his right ankle, he scored three times as we beat Decorah, 27-20. Every huddle, it was obvious that he was in pain, but all he said was 'give me the ball'…. you know I have some fond memories of my own personal high school achievements, both in football and in baseball, but none more memorable than Bill's "one-man gang" performance in his last high school game. His "All-State" selection was highlighted by a comment by Iowa Coach Eddie Anderson, who said 'he is one of the best that I have ever seen.' For me, he has always been <u>the best</u>", Doran remarked.

Another Bill Reichardt remembrance came from teammate Jim Sangster, "Bill was not too shy about his own abilities and he asked me, after a particularly good game by Bill, if there was a hyphen in All-State. The next game, after a not so outstanding game, I said to Bill that I know there's no hyphen in Honorable Mention."

## *1950's*

The first five years of the decade continued to produce championship football. Herb Cormack was gone but Frank Bates continued the tradition of excellence. The Little Hawks had undefeated Associated Press State Champion teams in 1950 and 1953. There were 16 Little Hawks named All-State in the 1950's. The 1950 through 1954 teams had a 36-6-3 record with two unbeaten State Championships and three MVC titles. The 1953 MVC title would be the last for City High until 1970. The 1950 squad became the first City High team to score 200 points since the 1917 team notched 229. That 1950 team had five selected to the All-State teams: Jim Freeman (E), Tom Kerf (T), Duane Davis (B), Jerry White (B), and Frank Frey (G). That team had its perfect season saved, in a game against St. Ambrose, when Mick Moore blocked an extra point and a field goal attempt in a 7-6 Little Hawk victory.

In 1953 the Little Hawks had what many people felt was the best team ever to represent City High until the Tim Dwight-led teams of the early 1990's, although the 1946 and 1960 teams could easily make the same claim.

In 1953 the State Champion Little Hawks tied the 1936 team's record of seven shutouts with the last six coming consecutively at the end of the season. Only two touchdowns were allowed (one on a blocked punt) as they outscored their opponents, 241-14. By scoring the third most points ever and allowing just two touchdowns, the Little Hawks showed great offense-defense balance. Quarterback Don Hedges had the outstanding stat of never throwing an interception the entire season. Frank Bates was chosen by the <u>Des Moines Register,</u> as the State Coach of the Year following that season. Chuck Sample (E), Buzz Nozek (FB), and Grant Grimm (T) were named All-State.

Following the 1950 season Tom Kerf, Duane Davis and Jim Freeman all were named first All-State. Freeman followed that up the next season by repeating on the All-State team and being named to the Scholastic Coach Magazine First All-America team. Freeman was certainly one of the top athletes of the 1950's as a three-year regular in football, leading scorer in basketball and State Champion in the shot put in track and field. More about Jim can be found in the basketball and track sections. In 2004 Jim was named to the IHSAA Football Hall of Fame.

Jim recalls his days at City High: "As I think back on all the good times at City High, I remember Frank Bates. For three years he called my house on Thursday nights to be sure I would be rested for Friday night's game. The most important thing to remember was that he was not only a coach to us but also a man with great values. He loved City High and what it stood for."

The 1957-58 school year saw two major changes in the MVC as the four Cedar Rapids public schools were consolidated into Washington and Jefferson and three Illinois schools Moline, East Moline and Rock Island joined the conference. This created a nine-school league. This also created some mismatches. City High had an enrollment of less than 1,000 and the Illinois schools were all over 2,000 students. The Illinois schools stayed in the MVC until the 1969 school year.

The end of the decade produced mixed results. The 1958 team had the first losing record (4-5) since 1944, but the 1959 team rebounded with an excellent 8-1 season in which they won eight straight after an opening game loss to Davenport. The team was second to Davenport in

*1950 - Coach Bates and Jerry White*

the MVC and finished third in the AP poll. The squad also produced four All-State players, Frosty Evashevski (QB), Phil Minnick (B), Butch Frantz (G), and Gary Freeman (T).

The season-ending game in 1959 saw the Little Hawks beat Rock Island in a game played in eight inches of snow in Rock Island.

Coach Bates, who coached in three different decades at City High, had a 60-25-5 record in the 1950's.

## 1960's

The 1960's saw a major change in the alignment and membership in the MVC conference and some unusual occurrences /outcomes for the football squads.

The 1960 season had an unusual twist. City High was awarded the Iowa State Championship but did not win the MVC title. Here's why: City High lost 28-26 to Rock Island in the opener. Then the Little Hawks won eight straight giving them the AP poll State Championship. Rock Island remained undefeated and won the MVC title.

Butch Frantz, Joel Jensen, Tony Welt and Phil Minnick all were named All-State. Welt scored seven touchdowns in a two-game stretch including a 95 yarder. Minnick went on to an eventual career with the Canadian professional league where he garnered an MVP Award.

The 1960's saw four major changes in the Mississippi Valley Conference. In 1960 Davenport High, with an enrollment well over 2,000, split and Davenport West opened and joined the MVC, bringing the membership to 10 teams. In 1968 a new high school opened in Cedar Rapids and the Kennedy Cougars joined the MVC. Iowa City West also opened that year, but did not join the MVC until 1970. In 1969 the MVC embarked on a major makeover. With 11 schools now in the league and scheduling difficult, the Illinois schools withdrew from the league and Bettendorf and Muscatine joined. Some rules differences between Iowa and Illinois Athletic Associations also contributed to the change.

In 1962 Don Rhoades accomplished a captaincy trifecta when he was chosen captain of the football, basketball and baseball teams. Don also later returned to be the head baseball coach at his alma mater in 1979.

The mid-1960s saw some good and bad stat lines. In 1963 Halfback Bob Falls had TD runs of 80 and 87 yards. In 1964 Russ Kennel had a near record 97-yard interception return for a TD and Tom Barbatti and Bob Martin were chosen for the first Iowa Coaches All-State game. The following year, 1965, the 87 points scored was the lowest team total since 1937.

Coach Frank Bates suffered a heart attack prior to the 1966 season and was replaced on an interim basis by long-time assistant Clyde Bean. Bean led the Little Hawks to a 5-4 season and was named the MVC Coach of the Year.

Frank Bates returned to coaching in 1967, then retired following that season, after 20 years as head football coach. His 20-year record stood at 112-63-5, with three State Champions (1950, 1953,1960), three MVC Championships (1950, 1952, 1953), and two unbeaten teams (1950, 1953). Frank Bates has also been named to the IHSAA Football Hall of Fame. His 112 wins stood as a record until 1996 when Coach Larry Brown surpassed that total. Clyde Bean was hired as the official replacement for Bates in 1968. In 1969 the City High football field was renamed the Frank Bates Field in honor of Coach Bates.

## West High Opens

With the opening of West High in the fall of 1968, City High's enrollment was cut in half to 730 students. With the Illinois schools still in the league and other larger schools well above 1,500 students, the 1968 squad suffered through the first winless season at City High since the flu-shortened season of 1918.

The last year of the 60's decade saw the first game ever between the cross-town rivals, City and West. The 1969 game was a classic, as a Bob Schultz-to-Steve Burkett pass with less than a minute remaining gave the Little Hawks a (26-21) come-from-behind win. The rivalry, which became known as the "Battle for the Boot," continues to be one of the most spirited rivalries in the state.

## How the "Boot" Began

The "Boot", the bronze football shoe trophy that is given to the winner of the regular season game between City High and West, became a reality in the spring of 1969. Its creator was Steve Holland, a West High junior that year, who had actually started his high school career at City High but living on the west side of town entered West when it opened at the beginning of the 1968-69 school year.

Steve first suggested an all-sports trophy but developing a formula proved too confusing so a football trophy was the outcome. The West student council was for it and soon the City High council also was on board. It was decided that a bronze football shoe would be the ideal symbol of football supremacy. The call went out to both schools to donate shoes. I'll let Steve take over from here:

"Late in the spring of 1969, I was sitting in the West High boys' locker room, surrounded by dozens of football shoes. One football shoe, to me, looked like another. I wanted to find one with character. Then I saw it. I came across an old lineman's shoe, one with a cleat torn out. I knew my search was over. It just so happened that Bob Kodros, then a West High football player was close by and told me that this was his shoe. I had fun laughing with Bob as to how this shoe would become a coveted item between the two schools. I remember Bob's laughter over the thoughts.

"When the first game between City High and West finally came on October 17, I was again granted another honor. Our student council asked if I would like to show the Boot to the crowd at halftime. I remember standing with Randy Dryer, an outstanding tennis player and council member at City High, on the Frank Bates Football field. I recall the thrill I felt as the crowd and players cheered.

*"We've got the Boot!"*

City High won that first game, 26-21. That's the first time I ever heard the shout 'We've got the Boot!' arise and fill the air. In the years that followed, through college, as a sportswriter for eight years for the "Iowa City Press-Citizen", and now as the chair of English at Muscatine Community College, I still look for the score of the Battle for the Boot each year. I love seeing the photographs of athletes hoisting the trophy high, no matter which school wins."

In 1980 the trophy case at City High was broken into and among the items stolen was the original "Boot". A similar high-topped football shoe replaced it. The players of those early years certainly feel that "Boot II" can't have the character of the original Bob Kodros shoe.

## 1970's

The 1970's started out with an explosion as the 1970 team won the MVC title. That was highlighted by one of the most exciting and dramatic wins in the100-plus-year history of City High football. The decade ended unfortunately with losing records in four of the final five years.

The magical 1970 season, following just two years after the first winless season since 1918, was indeed memorable. The MVC title was the first since 1953 and was won in dramatic fashion with a field goal after the game was thought to be over.

Everything seemed to go right for the Little Hawks that season. After winning the opener, the Little Hawks lost to Cedar Rapids Jefferson. Then City High ran off seven straight wins. Included was a come-from-behind 7-6 win at Clinton, with a late TD and great defensive performance. Also there was a fantastic win at home over Cedar Rapids Washington with a last minute score after an on-side kick recovery, and an untimed down field goal, <u>after</u> it was thought the game was over.

Details of that famous 1970 game would appear to be written by a Hollywood scriptwriter with a flair for the dramatic.

The game, played at City High, was for the MVC Championship. City High had to win the game outright and they were not favored. The game was also Dad's Night.

The game went back and forth. City High scored first, Bill Lucas on a one-yard run. Washington scored to tie. Ed Evans' seven-yard run put the Little Hawks back in front, 14-7. Washington scored on another pass, but Jeff Kautz blocked the PAT, 14-13. Evans again scores on a 57-yard run making it 21-13.

A third Warrior TD pass and a two-point conversion tied it, 21-21. In the fourth quarter each team has the ball twice before Washington scores with just 1:22 remaining. They now lead 28-21. On the kickoff, Jeff Dean takes a hand-off from Terry Keely on a reverse and returns to City High's 46 with 1:12 remaining.

John Piro completes two passes to Dean for three and 19 yards and Tom Kirkendall for five and the ball is at the Washington 16 with 0:46 on the clock. Dean runs an end around and gets out of bounds at the eight with 0:38 remaining. Keely runs for two and out of bounds. Piro then passes to Dean for the touchdown with the time 0:30, and the score 28-27.

A tie will not win the championship, so the Little Hawks must go for two. Keely's run is no good. The crowd groans then lets out with a roar to let the Little Hawks know they are proud of their effort.

With just 30 seconds left the only chance now is an on-side kick. It is executed perfectly and Kirkendall recovers. Piro passes to Dean for 19, who then runs out of bounds with 13 seconds left. An incomplete pass leaves just 0:06 remaining. Head Coach Clyde Bean, after conferring with backfield Coach John Raffensperger (who suggested a pass), decided to have Louie Villhauer attempt a 47-yard field goal.

The kick struck the right upright and bounced back, setting off a Washington celebration. But in the best Hollywood tradition, there was a flag on the play and the Warriors, in their zeal to block the kick, were offside. A game can't end on a defensive penalty so with the ball five yards closer and the clock at all zeros, Villhauer drilled it through the middle and the Little Hawks were MVC Champions, 30-28.

No one who was there can ever forget the excitement, and pure drama of that game and that moment. The team that was 0-9 two years earlier was now MVC Champs for the first time since 1953! (*Play-by-play details are courtesy of the Press-Citizen and reporter Bob Elliott.*)

All-State guard Dan McCarney remembers that game; "I will never forget the feeling I had as I watched the ball go though the uprights. I've spent 34 years as a division I player and coach in both the Big Ten and Big Twelve and had numerous conference and bowl championships, but that MVC Championship in 1970 ranks right up there with any of them."

Heroes were plentiful that season. Quarterback John Piro, often calling his own plays, engineered many vital scoring drives and his calm demeanor and leadership were crucial in the Clinton and C.R. Washington wins. A particularly outstanding statistic was his 124 passes with just one interception, that coming in the first game.

Louie Villhauer kicked the winning PAT at Clinton and, of course, the title-winning 42 yard field goal vs. C.R. Washington. "Heavyweight" Tom Lepic (110 lbs.) was perfect with long snaps all season to punters and field goal kickers. Max Villareal (115 lb.), another "heavyweight," led the team in tackles. Terry Keely (140 lb.) was the leading rusher. Steve Dean, Tom Kirkendall, Mike Gratz and Dan Zweiner, all in the 150-lb. range, made key plays all year. In the Clinton victory mentioned above, QB John Piro recalls the humorous end to that game involving long snapper Tom Lepic. "With about 13 seconds left in the game vs. Clinton, we scored a touchdown to tie it at 6-6. The all-important extra point kick by Louie Villhauer sailed true to make the score 7-6. On the play Tom Lepic made his snap to the holder, saw that the kick was good and proceeded to do a headstand. While standing on his head Tom pumped his legs in the air like riding a bicycle. This was caught on film and was run back and forth several times at the team's film session."

*Celebration following 1970 Championship*

Dan McCarney and Tom Jacks were the only starters over 190 lbs. and both were named to the All-State team. McCarney went on to stardom at Iowa as a player and coach and eventually became the head coach at Iowa State.

Twelve Little Hawks from that 1970 team were named All-MVC and Clyde Bean was named the MVC Coach of the Year. State playoffs were still two years away so the Little Hawks had to settle for third in the AP poll behind two unbeaten teams.

The 1972 team put together some impressive offensive stats and produced the All-State quarterback / wide receiver duo in Greg Cilek and Bill Schultz. Schultz became one of the top national recruits as he was named to the first-team Parade High School All-American team. Cilek passed for a then school record 1,352 yards in nine games, 751 of those to Schultz. Schultz went on to be a four-year starter at Iowa and Cilek was a starter at Dayton University.

The Little Hawks' 1973 MVC title was their last Championship until 1986. Clyde Bean's second MVC title in four years saw an 8-1 record with the fewest points allowed since the 1960 State Champions. Only two teams scored more than one touchdown against the City High defense. Doug Piro and Steve Groen were named All-State and nine were named to All-MVC teams.

The 1974 squad (6-3) had the last winning record until 1979. In 1977 Andy Piro became the fourth Piro brother to quarterback the Little Hawks. Clyde Bean retired at the end of the 1979 season after 12 years as head coach. He continued to teach and coach wrestling until his retirement in 1991.

Three Little Hawks of the 70's had NFL careers as players or coaches. Jay Hilgenberg (1976) had a 12-year career including seven Pro Bowls and a Super Bowl appearance with the Chicago Bears. His brother Joel (1979) was also selected to the Pro Bowl in his career with the New Orleans Saints. Carl Hargrave, MVP of the 1971 team, was a long-time assistant coach for the Minnesota Vikings.

## 1980's

The 1980's started slowly, but finished on a definite high note. Larry Brown started a 21-year career as head coach that put City High among the state's elite in high school football. One highlight was taking eight of 10 in the decade from West High.

In 1980 former Little Hawk Larry Brown succeeded Clyde Bean as head coach and became the first alumni to be named head football coach since H. C. Soucek in 1919. Coach Brown's first season was 3-6 and saw Norm Balke (DE) and Scott Froehle (DB) become the first of 56 players to be named All-State in Brown's 21-year tenure. Mark Grenko had a record setting 95-yard fumble recovery for a TD in 1980 also.

The 1981 team had the lowest point total since 1932. The first three teams of the 1980's were 8-19, but the Little Hawks rebounded from that three-year span with win totals of 7, 7, 8, and 7 before finishing the decade with seasons of 9-2 and 8-3 and three playoff appearances.

The 1983 squad started the 80's turnaround with a 7-2 record and some offensive fireworks. Quarterback Scott Flynn set single-game records for passes completed (25), passing yards (344), and single-season yards (1,522). He finished his career with a record 2,420 yards. Junior wide receiver Mark Lumpa, in the first of his two All-State years, set records for most catches in a game (12), yards in a season (917), and TD catches in one game (3). Senior tight end Tom Ward tied that record with three TD catches the same year. Linemen Jeff Beard and Mike Freeman were also named All-State.

In 1984 the Little Hawks had a second straight 7-2 record. Included in that season was a record scoring game vs. Iowa City West as City High retained the "Boot" with a 54-14 victory. This followed up the previous season's 48-14 win, giving the Little Hawks the biggest back-to-back point totals in the City High-West series.

Mark Lumpa, despite being double teamed, followed his '83 All-State season with a repeat in 1984 and became the second Little Hawk wide receiver to be named to the Parade All-American team. (Bill Schultz in 1972) Lumpa set a single-game receiving yards record (237), and a career record of 1,700 yards, 82 catches and 20 touchdowns. He was arguably the top athlete of the 80's as he also was named All-State in basketball and baseball. Lumpa went on to a fine career in baseball at Northern Iowa.

The second half of the 80's continued to have record-setting performances. The 1985 team was 8-1 and finished fourth in the AP poll, but still no playoff appearance as an unbeaten record was needed that year. Greg Brown set single-game (304) and single-season (1,181) rushing records in his All-State season. Orville Townsend had a record-setting kickoff return of 99 yards in the victory over West High and Larry Brown was named MVC Coach of the Year.

The 1986 season saw a three-way tie for the MVC crown and the first playoff appearance for the Little Hawks. The first playoff game ever was a 15-6 victory over Cedar Rapids Prairie. A second round loss to Linn Mar ended the first-ever venture into the playoffs. Quarterback Chris Hupfeld threw for a record 1,556 yards, 700 of those going to wide receiver Gerry Coleman, a total surpassed only by Lumpa. Brad Gehrke led the team in interceptions and tackles. A 20-13 victory over West High was the fifth in a row over the Trojans. Gehrke and Coleman were named All-State.

The year 1988 resulted in a 9-2 record, outright MVC title and second playoff appearance. The Little Hawks beat Burlington, 21-0, but lost to eventual State Champion Bettendorf in the second round. City High recorded five shutouts. Running back Brent Roth set a record with a 99-yard rushing touchdown and finished his two-year varsity career with a record 2,029 career rushing yards. Roth went on to a fine track career at Purdue as a hurdler. Roth and Corey Landeen (DT) were named All-State.

In the final year of the decade, the Little Hawks had an 8-3 record and a third appearance in the State playoffs. The playoff series was a duplicate of '88 as City High beat Burlington, but lost to Bettendorf. Defensive back Chad Krantz recorded a rare four-interception game, just one short of the City High record of five. Michael Roan (TE / FB) was first All-State, a three-year starter with Wisconsin and a five-year vet with Tennessee of the NFL. In the last six years of the decade the Little Hawks had a 49-19 record with two MVC titles and three playoff appearances.

## 1990's

The 1990's was a blizzard of offensive statistics, possibly unmatched in the history of Iowa high school football. The Larry Brown-coached teams of the decade had a 93-22 record, an average of 9.3 wins per year, five consecutive MVC titles, three state championships and one runner-up finish. The offensive records set between 1992 and 1996 could fill an entire chapter. The 50-point "mercy rule" added in 1992 kept the Little Hawks from even higher point totals. Forty-one players from this decade were named to All-State teams, with the 1993 team having a record of eight chosen, including five on the first team.

## *Tim Dwight Legacy*

No mention of City High football can ever be made without the recognition of Tim Dwight. Without question, Tim is the most outstanding football player ever at City High and arguably its greatest athlete. Tim burst on the City High football scene as a 15-year-old freshman, called up to the varsity for a playoff game. The first time he touched the ball he ran 80 yards for a touchdown and the Dwight legacy was born.

The 1990 team kicked off the decade with a rather modest 6-4 season and a first round playoff loss to Davenport Assumption. That game did launch the Tim Dwight era as the above-mentioned 80-yd. TD in a losing cause was the first carry of his varsity career.

In 1991, Dwight, now a sophomore and starting tailback, had the first of his three All-State years. Brion Hurley was named All-State kicker, the first of five straight kickers or punters named All-State for the Little Hawks.

The 1992 team was unbeaten MVC Champs, beat Davenport Central in the first round of the playoffs, then lost in a spectacular game to eventual State Champion Bettendorf, 31-28. Tim Dwight rushed for 1,299 yards and was named MVC Player of the Year and first team All-State. Five others-- Scott Jones (PK), Chris Hamdorf (QB), Jason House (LB), C. J. Thieleke (WR), and Andy Luett (C)-- were also All-State. Larry Brown was named MVC Coach of the Year.

Quarterback Chris Hamdorf had a record 2,018 yards passing and a five-touchdown game. He finished his career with 3,396 yards and 223 completions, both records. Hamdorf later became a

*1993 State Champs, 13-0. Best team ever?*

starting QB for Northwestern. Scott Jones had a record eight PAT's in one game and C. J. Thieleke tied Mark Lumpa's record of 12 catches in one game. Thieleke set a new single-season catch record of 53 and amassed 845 yards receiving.

In 1993 the Little Hawks fielded what most observers feel was the best City High team of all time. Even without Tim Dwight, this would have been a dominating team; with him, they were a spectacular scoring and defensive machine.

The team scored 563 points for a 43.3 average and gave up an average of only 7.8 points per game in a 13-0 State Championship season. In the four-playoff games they scored 35, 27, 25, and 42 points. Three games were ended by the 50-point mercy rule, including one at halftime. The six touchdowns in the 1993 title game established a final game record, along with 463 yards and Dwight's four touchdowns.

Dwight's stat line for the final year and career was incredible. Tim rushed for a record 2,113 yards, often playing only half the game. He scored 43 touchdowns and 264 points, scoring five touchdowns in two different games, once in just the first half. His career stats were; 4,148 yards rushing, 81 touchdowns, and 456 points scored. He also had a career record total of 11 passes intercepted. Teams refused to punt to him, often giving the Little Hawks excellent field position after out-of-bounds kicks. Tim was named State Player of the year again and the Midwest Gatorade Player of the Year along with being named to the Parade High School All-American team.

*Tim Dwight - Parade All-American - 81 TD's*

Dwight was far from a one-man team. Eight Little Hawks were named to the All-State teams including what appears to be a record five named to the first team. Quarterback Zach Grabinski threw for 1,456 yards. Matt Gabel was named All-State kicker as he punted for a 42-yard average and made 67 PAT including a record-tying eight in one game. Tackles Luke Donahue and Erik Nelson, both 6' 4", 235 lbs., were named All-State, as was (NT/FB) Corey Honore, (DT) Matt Lamb and (LB) Andy Johnson.

Junior backup tailback and starting defensive end Rob Thein was often spectacular in his own right and was among the leaders on the defense that allowed just 7.8 points per game. Coach Larry Brown was named the State Coach of the Year following the season.

Tim Dwight went on to be an All-American and record setter at Iowa, as a wide receiver and punt returner. His professional resume includes a Super Bowl appearance with the Atlanta Falcons and a continued career with the San Diego Chargers. His track career, equal if not better than his football career, will be chronicled in the track and field section.

In 1994 a repeat State Championship produced an 11-2 record. Oddly enough the regular season ended with two consecutive losses. Four wins in the playoffs brought home the State Championship. The final win was a 21-0 shutout of Linn-Mar to avenge a regular season loss. By winning the first seven games the Little Hawks put together a 20-game winning streak over two years. The team averaged 32.3 points per game.

Tailback Rob Thein had a spectacular season as he eclipsed the one-year-old Tim Dwight single- season rushing total with 2,243 yards and beat Greg Brown's single-game rushing total with a 313-yard game. Rob's 2,563 career yards were second only to Tim Dwight. He was named

Associated Press Player of the Year. Rob followed Dwight to Iowa and played four years with the Hawkeyes. Jeff Halter (C), Brian Mitchell (LB), Zach Grabinski (QB), and Todd Barnes (Punter) were also All-State.

Todd Barnes became the fourth consecutive City High kicker to be named to the All-State teams. For the third consecutive year a City High kicker--Shawn Conklin-- made eight PAT's in one game in a victory over Dubuque Hempstead.

Three team records were set: In a 42-24 victory over Cedar Rapids Regis, the Little Hawks rushed for 505 yards and had 580 total yards. For the season City High rushed for a record 3,638 yards. A loss to Linn-Mar snapped a 20-game win streak, and also ended a 27-game conference-winning streak.

A third consecutive MVC title came in 1995, but the State Championship eluded them in a 10-2 season. Both losses were to Iowa City West, 14-0 and 14-3. Todd Barnes repeated as All-State Punter and Luke Meredith (T), Ben Dombroski (DT) and Mike Richards (DB) were also All-State. Only three teams scored more than once against the Little Hawks defense as they gave up just 6.9 points per game.

The 1996 team closely resembled the 1993 team in many ways: A second 13-0 State Championship (third in last four years), 540 points (41.5), and seven on All-State teams. The last three playoff games saw City High put up 56, 38, and 45 point totals. The final game total of 45 vs. Ames was a new championship game total. The six touchdowns in the title game tied the 1993 Little Hawk record.

Another '93-'96 similarity was the tailback duo of Jesse Holland (2043 yards) and Jason Ringena (multiple track state champion like Dwight). Also outstanding was wide receiver Kahlil Hill, who set three pass receiving records: 54 receptions, 969 pass receiving yards, and 14 TD catches. Jesse Holland also set a single-game scoring record of 32 (5 TD's and a 2-point PAT) in a 61-14 win vs. Dubuque Senior. Quarterback Mitch Price, following the excellent City High quarterback tradition, passed for 1,388 yards in a balanced offensive attack. Holland finished his career with 2,544 rushing yards and Price had 2,391 passing yards. Not records, but excellent totals. The total yards mark of 5,130 yards was a team record.

The seven Little Hawks named All-State were Holland (TB), Hill (WR), Price (QB), Luke Meredith (DT), Alonzo Cunningham (T), Joey Myles (DL) and Mark Seaton (LB). Holland became the third Little Hawk to be named Associated Press Player of the Year.

The 1997 team saw the five-year MVC title streak broken, but the 9-4 team played its way into the State Championship game where it lost to Ankeny, 17-14. The team avenged a regular season loss to West with a 21-10 playoff victory and also had playoff wins over Davenport Assumption and Cedar Falls before falling to Ankeny. Zach Butler (C), Scott Gordon (LB), and Andy Stewart (T) were named All-State.

The 1998 season had a finish similar to 1995 as the Little Hawks had only two losses, but both came at the hands of West, twin shutouts 18-0 and 21-0. Games of 42, 37, 41, 49, 42 and 42 points showed the typical 90's offensive explosiveness. John Pantazis (DE) and Hugh John Barry (DB) were named to the All-State teams.

The last team of the decade posted a 7-3 record with two of the losses to West High again. The squad again averaged over 30 points a game with a high of 55 vs. Cedar Rapids Xavier. Junior Hakim Hill had an excellent 1,348 yards rushing; Steve Pfaller (WR) had 612 receiving yards to complement the running game. Pfaller (DB), Kory Hartwig (C), and Jamie Holland (DL) were named All-State.

Counting playoff games, the Little Hawks and West played 21 times in the 90's with City High winning 14 of the games. The Little Hawks played 25 playoff games in the 90's, winning 19 and losing just six.

## 2000's

The first year of the new century saw the Little Hawks post a 10-2 record. The season ended with a state semifinal loss to Bettendorf. Wins over C.R. Prairie and Cedar Falls preceded the Bettendorf loss. Hakim Hill rushed for 1,498 yards and finished his career with 2,846, which is second only to Tim Dwight in career yards. Hill, Chris Campbell(G) and Center Brian Ferentz were named All-State. Coach Larry Brown resigned after the season to devote full time to his Athletic Director duties. His career mark of 160-62 tops all other football coaches in total victories at City High.

Longtime assistant (19 years) Dan Sabers took over for Brown in 2001 with spectacular results. An MVC title and 12 straight wins put the Little Hawks in the state title game. Prairie, Cedar Falls and Bettendorf fell before a 35-15 defeat at the hands of West Des Moines Dowling ended the run.

Quarterback Connor Jostes had a record-breaking season. Records set by Jostes were season passing marks of 2,350 yards, 136 completions and 28 touchdown passes. He also set three kicking records: field goals in a game (3), season (8) and career (10). His career total passing yards of 2,457 ranked third all time.

Team marks set in 2001 were season passing yards (2,449), and most points and TD's in one game 61 and 9. Matt Wooldrik had 1,141 yards rushing and Calvin Davis (WR) had 53 catches, just one short of the record and 907 yards receiving (third all time). Warren McDuffie set a new tight end record with 616 yards receiving. Alex Ebinger had four interceptions in one game and tied Tim Dwight's career mark of 11. Jostes, Davis, Wooldrik, McDuffie and Angus MacKay (G) were named to the All-State teams. Jostes and Davis continued their careers in college.

*2001 team - State Runner-up (12-1)*

In 2002 a 4-5 record was the first losing record since 1987. As usual, there were some good passing- receiving statistics. Curtis Steyers threw for 1,173 yards. Wide receiver Caleb Recker had marks of 46 catches and 589 yards. Recker's 1,017 career yards placed him fifth all-time.

In 2003 the Little Hawks rebounded from a rare losing record with a 7-3 mark and a playoff berth. Unfortunately I.C. West avenged a regular season loss by beating City High in the first round. City High recorded four shutouts and only West managed more than one touchdown against the tough Little Hawk defense all season. Michael Sabers (DE) and Greg Altmaier (LB) were named to the All-State teams.

The year 2004 was Dan Saber's fourth season at the helm and he put a completely revamped offense on the field. An exciting no-huddle spread offense replaced the traditional tailback-centered offense of past years. The Little Hawks started out with four straight wins averaging 40 points a game.

Several days of rain preceded the annual "Battle for the Boot" with West High and this brought the high-powered offense to a crawl and a loss to West. This left the annual Boot rivalry at 24-12 in favor of City High. After a win against Linn-Mar and a loss to unbeaten C.R. Prairie, the Little Hawks rebounded with a 63-point game against East Waterloo and three more wins before losing to second-ranked Bettendorf in the State semi-finals. Included in the playoff wins was a revenge victory over Prairie and a defeat of unbeaten Cedar Falls.

Quarterback D.P. Eyman threw for 1,463 yards and 16 touchdowns and tailback Phil Kenney rushed for 1,206 yards in a well-balanced offense. Kenney scored 30 touchdowns. The Little Hawks won the Division title and Coach Sabers was selected MVC Coach of the Year. Other post-season honors went to Phil Kenney second team All-State defensive back and D.P. Eyman, second team All-State punter and third team quarterback.

The seventh game of the 2004 season against East Waterloo was a milestone as the Little Hawks played the 900th game in their history. As of the end of the 2004 season City High has played 904 games with an overall record of 565-304-35. The team has qualified for the State playoffs 16 times with three titles. They have a 27-12 playoff record.

Four Little Hawk coaches are in the IHSAA Football Hall of Fame: Herb Cormack, Frank Bates, Clyde Bean, and Larry Brown.

# All-State Football Recognition

Prior to 1914, when the <u>Des Moines Register</u> began picking All-State teams, a Mr. Clarkson picked the All-State teams. The following were named All-State between 1909 and 1914.

1909　Paul Hoerlein (HB)

1910　Guy Taylor (T) 1st, Robert Showers (C)1st, Charles Parsons 2nd, Stephen Swisher (QB) 2nd, Joe Munkoff (B) 3rd

1911　Joe Munkoff (HB, Captain) 1st, Carl Goetz

City High All State Football players as selected by the <u>Des Moines Register</u>. The <u>Des Moines Register</u> started picking all state football squads in 1914. There were as many as 7 teams picked at the beginning. There was just a one- class system until 1976 when smaller schools were represented by their own teams. Starting in 1974 separate offensive and defensive teams were picked. (Iowa Daily Press Association, now known as INA, also picks all state teams. Those will be listed separately only if they are different players than picked by the <u>Des Moines Register</u>.)

|  |  |
|---|---|
| 1915 | Hostetter (G) 2nd |
| 1917 | George Kloos (HB) 1st |
| 1918 | Robert Leinbaugh (T) 1st |
| 1919 | Seemuth (QB) 2nd |
| 1919 | Kendeika (T) IDPA 3rd |
| 1929 | Howard Moffit (QB) 2nd |
| 1933 | L. Fuhrmeister (B) IDPA 3rd |
| 1934 | Ballard (E) 4th |
| 1934 | John Elberts (G) IDPA 3rd |
| 1935 | "Ham" Snider (G) 1st |
| 1935 | Paul Ross (FB) 3rd |
| 1936 | Jens Norgaard (T) 1st |
| 1936 | Hora (B) IDPA 3rd |
| 1936 | Woody Maher (T) IDPA 3rd |
| 1937 | Eldon Patrizek (HB) 6th |
| 1937 | Jenkinson (C) IDPA 2nd |
| 1938 | Jack Hirt (T) 5th IDPA 2nd |
| 1938 | Wright (G) 5th |
| 1939 | Jack Hirt (T) 2nd |
| 1939 | Ted Lewis (FB) IDPA 1st |
| 1941 | Bill Bothell (E) 1st |
| 1941 | Joe Casey (FB) 2nd |
| 1942 | Bill Sangster (QB) 1st |
| 1942 | Joe Casey (FB) 1st |
| 1942 | Dave Danner (E) 2nd |
| 1942 | Dean Yanaush (T) 3rd IDPA 1st |
| 1942 | Halverson (G) 3rd |
| 1943 | Shay (FB) 4th |
| 1943 | Tom Hirt (G) 1st |
| 1943 | Dick Lee (T) 3rd |
| 1943 | Wayne Hopp (B) IDPA 3rd |
| 1944 | Tom Hirt (T) 2nd IDPA 1st |
| 1944 | Ruben Snider (G) 3rd |
| 1945 | Evan Smith (E) 3rd IDPA 1st |
| 1945 | Don Fryauf (G) 3rd |
| 1945 | Jim Sangster (QB) 4th IDPA 3rd |
| 1946 | Don Fryauf (E) 1st |
| 1946 | Jim Sangster (QB) 1st |
| 1946 | Jack Evans (G) 2nd |
| 1946 | Leo Zeithamel (T) 4th IDPA 3rd |
| 1947 | Bill Reichardt (E) 1st |
| 1948 | Francis Beasley (T) 2nd |
| 1948 | Gene Hettrick (E) 3rd IDPA 1st |
| 1949 | Bill Fenton (E) 2nd IDPA 1st |
| 1950 | Jim Freeman (E) 1st |
| 1950 | Tom Kerf (T) 1st |
| 1950 | Duane Davis (HB) 2nd |
| 1950 | Jerry White (HB) 3rd |
| 1950 | Frank Frey (G) 6th |
| 1951 | Jim Freeman (E)1st & Scholastic Coach All-American |
| 1952 | John Larew (T) 3rd |
| 1953 | Chuck Sample (E) 1st |
| 1953 | Fred "Buzz" Nozek (HB) 1st |
| 1953 | Grant Grimm (T) 3rd IDPA 2nd |
| 1954 | Jeff Langston (E) 2nd |
| 1956 | Jim Luper (E) 6th IDPA 3rd |
| 1957 | Bill Housel (FB) 5th |
| 1957 | Tony Houser (G) IDPA 3rd |
| 1958 | Jay Memler (C) IDPA 2nd |
| 1959 | Butch Frantz (G) 3rd |
| 1959 | Phil Minnick (HB) 2nd IDPA 1st |
| 1959 | "Frosty" Evashevski (QB) 3rd IDPA 2nd |
| 1960 | Butch Frantz (G)1st |
| 1960 | Phil Minnick (HB) 1st |
| 1960 | Joel Jensen (E) 3rd |
| 1960 | Tony Welt (HB) 4th |

| | | | | |
|---|---|---|---|---|
| 1961 | Dave Moss (G) 2$^{nd}$ | | 1993 | Luke Donahue (T) 1$^{st}$ |
| 1961 | Gary Snook (QB) 2$^{nd}$ | | 1993 | Erik Nelson (T) 1$^{st}$ |
| 1961 | Mike Cain (FB) 2$^{nd}$ | | 1993 | Corey Honore (DL) 1$^{st}$ |
| 1964 | Bob Martin (E) 1$^{st}$ | | 1993 | Matt Gabel (Punter) 1$^{st}$ |
| 1964 | Tom Barbatti (G) 2$^{nd}$ | | 1993 | Matt Lamb (T) 2$^{nd}$ |
| 1967 | Dave Jahnke (E) IDPA 5$^{th}$ | | 1993 | Andy Johnson (LB) 2$^{nd}$ |
| 1970 | Dan McCarney (G) 1$^{st}$ | | 1993 | Zach Grabinski (QB) 3$^{rd}$ |
| 1970 | Tom Jacks (T) 2$^{nd}$ | | 1994 | Jeff Halter (C) 1$^{st}$ |
| 1971 | Bill Schultz (E) IDPA 4$^{th}$ | | 1994 | Rob Thein (HB) 1$^{st}$ |
| 1972 | Bill Schultz (E) 1$^{st}$ & | | 1994 | Brian Mitchell (LB) 2$^{nd}$ INA 1$^{st}$ |
| | Parade All-American | | 1994 | Zach Grabinski (QB) 3$^{rd}$ |
| 1972 | Greg Cilek (QB) 2$^{nd}$ | | 1994 | Todd Barnes (Punter) 3$^{rd}$ |
| 1973 | Steve Groen (T) 3$^{rd}$ | | 1995 | Ben Dombroski (T) 1$^{st}$ |
| 1973 | Doug Piro (QB) 5$^{th}$ | | 1995 | Todd Barnes (Punter) 1$^{st}$ |
| 1974 | Dan Cilek (DB) 1$^{st}$ | | 1995 | Luke Meredith (T) 2$^{nd}$ |
| 1974 | Robbie Myers (G) IDPA 2$^{nd}$ | | 1995 | Mike Richards (DB) 2$^{nd}$ |
| 1974 | Jim Wilson (DE) 2$^{nd}$ | | 1996 | Kahlil Hill (E) 1$^{st}$ |
| 1976 | Doug Dunham (E) 1$^{st}$ | | 1996 | Luke Meredith (T) 1$^{st}$ |
| 1977 | Eric Klasson (DE) 1$^{st}$ | | 1996 | Jesse Holland (HB) 1$^{st}$ |
| 1980 | Norm Balke (DE) 1$^{st}$ | | 1996 | Alonzo Cunningham (T) 2$^{nd}$ |
| 1980 | Scott Froehle (DB) IDPA 3$^{rd}$ | | 1996 | Joey Myles (DL) 2$^{nd}$ |
| 1983 | Mike Freeman (C) 1$^{st}$ | | 1996 | Mark Seaton (LB) 2$^{nd}$ |
| 1983 | Mark Lumpa (E) 2$^{nd}$ | | 1996 | Mitch Price QB) 3$^{rd}$ |
| 1983 | Jeff Beard (DE) 1$^{st}$ | | 1997 | Zach Butler (C) 1$^{st}$ |
| 1984 | Mark Lumpa (E) 1$^{st}$ | | 1997 | Scott Gordon (LB) 1$^{st}$ |
| 1985 | Greg Brown (HB) 2$^{nd}$ | | 1997 | Andy Stewart (T) 3$^{rd}$ |
| 1986 | Brad Gehrke (DB) 1$^{st}$ | | 1998 | John Pantazis (DL) 1$^{st}$ |
| 1986 | Gerry Coleman (E) 2$^{nd}$ | | 1998 | Hugh John Barry (DB) 2$^{nd}$ |
| 1988 | Brent Roth (DB) 1$^{st}$ | | 1999 | Steve Pfaller (DB) 1$^{st}$ |
| 1988 | Corey Landeen (DL) 1$^{st}$ | | 1999 | Kory Hartwig (C)1$^{st}$ |
| 1989 | Michael Roan (DE) 1$^{st}$ | | 1999 | Jamie Holland (DL) 2$^{nd}$ |
| 1989 | Dave Spangler (DL) IDPA 2$^{nd}$ | | 2000 | Hakim Hill (HB) 1$^{st}$ |
| 1990 | Dave Schmucher (DB) 1$^{st}$ | | 2000 | Brian Ferentz (C) 1$^{st}$ |
| 1990 | Brian Atkins (DL) 2$^{nd}$ | | 2000 | Chris Campbell (G) 2$^{nd}$ |
| 1990 | Matt Gegenheimer (LB) INA 2$^{nd}$ | | 2001 | Calvin Davis (E) 1$^{st}$ |
| 1990 | Shane Moen (DL) 3$^{rd}$ INA 2$^{nd}$ | | 2001 | Angus McKay (G) 1$^{st}$ |
| 1991 | Brion Hurley (PK) 1$^{st}$ | | 2001 | Connor Jostes (QB) 1$^{st}$ |
| 1991 | Mark Mitchell (LB) INA 2$^{nd}$ | | 2001 | Warren McDuffie (DE) 1$^{st}$ |
| 1991 | Tim Dwight (HB) 3$^{rd}$ | | 2001 | Matt Wooldrik (DB) 2$^{nd}$ |
| 1992 | Tim Dwight (HB) 1$^{st}$ | | 2003 | Michael Sabers (DE) 1$^{st}$ |
| 1992 | C.J. Thieleke (E) 2$^{nd}$ | | 2003 | Greg Altmaier (LB) 2$^{nd}$ |
| 1992 | Chris Hamdorf (QB) 2$^{nd}$ INA 1$^{st}$ | | 2004 | Phil Kenney (DB) 2$^{nd}$ |
| 1992 | Scott Jones (K) INA 1$^{st}$ | | 2004 | D.P. Eyman (Punter) 2$^{nd}$ |
| 1992 | Jason House (DB) 2$^{nd}$ | | | INA (QB) 3$^{rd}$ |
| 1993 | Tim Dwight (HB) 1$^{st}$ & | | | |
| | Parade All-American | | | |

# Football

| Year | W - L | Coach | Captains | Misc. Information |
|------|-------|-------|----------|-------------------|
| 1907 | 4-3 | "Snapper" Spinden | Harry Berry | 1st year sanctioned by Sch. Bd., Player dies: Leo Strohmeyer |
| 1908 | 5-5-1 | "      " | John Morton | Shut out last 6 games |
| 1909 | 5-4-1 | A.H. Miller | Robert Grimm* Grant Keppler | Traveled by train to away games, *Grimm didn't return |
| 1910 | 6-1-1 | "      " | Gary Taylor | New uniforms ; $900 cleared on football this season,   5 made All-State |
| 1911 | 6-2 | "      " | Carl Goetz | All-State Teams - Goetz (T), Joe Munkhoff (HB),  Stephen Swisher (DB), Fritz Kinney (FB) |
| 1912 | 2-4-2 | "      " | Burns | 80-yd. KO Return - McGovern |
| 1913 | 5-2-2 | "      " | Arthur Hotz | Scored 106 pts. vs. Marshalltown |
| 1914 | 4-4 | McGinnis | James Harrison | Scored 66 pts. vs. W. Liberty |
| 1915 | 5-3-1 | Dr. Von Lackum | Leon Brigham | Hostetter All-State |
| 1916 | 7-1 | "      " | George Fiesler | George Kloos 95-yd. punt return TD vs. Fairfield,  Newton game snowed out. |
| 1917 | 8-0-1 | F.J. Voight | George Kloos | Kloos 100-yd. interception,  85-yd. punt return,  6 of 9 PAT,   State Champs |
| 1918 | 0-3 | "      " | Clifford Hirt Robert Leinbaugh | Nationwide flu closes school for 5 weeks. |
| 1919 | 7-3 | Henry Soucek | Ray Kaufman | Spring football starts 1919, Scored 69 pts. vs. West Liberty, Get 6 shutouts |
| 1920 | 5-3 | Walter Fiesler | George Koudelka | |
| 1921 | 3-4-1 | H. C. Soucek | Campbell Beals | Beals won 2 games with drop kicks |
| 1922 | 7-1 | "      " | Elvin Talton | 6 Shutouts |
| 1923 | 4-4 | "      " | Elmer Littig | Practice at Longfellow sch. & City Park.  Still play games at Iowa Field |
| 1924 | 5-2-1 | "      " | Edgar Slemmons | Started playing games at Shrader Field |
| 1925 | 3-3-1 | "      " | Bill Adrian Ken Judy | |
| 1926 | 5-2-1 | "      " | Ray Collins | |
| 1927 | 4-2-2 | Walter S. Knox | Everett Idema | |
| 1928 | 6-2-1 | "      " | Tim Fairchild | |
| 1929 | 6-1-3 | George Wells | Don Lucky | Howard Moffit All-State |

# Football

| 1930 | 4-4-1 | George Wells | Harrison Wright | Charles Crawford 3 TD with fumbles, Eldred Vestermark 5 interceptions in 1 game, 1st night game ever (at Clinton) |
|------|-------|--------------|-----------------|---|
| 1931 | 2-6-1 | "        " | Loren Isensee<br>Cleatus Stimmel | Night game at Fairfield<br>Shut out 7 times |
| 1932 | 1-9-1 | "        " | | Night game vs. U-High,<br>W. Waterloo wins 95-0, Shut out 9 times (11 games) |
| 1933 | 1-8 | "        " | | L. Fuhrmeister All-State |
| 1934 | 6-2-1 | "        " | | John Elberts 3rd All-State Guard |
| 1935 | 7-1 | Herb Cormack | Paul Rose | 4,500 at Homecoming game |
| 1936 | 8-0-1 | "        " | | MVC Champs - 7 shutouts, State Champs, 1st win over East DM in 22 yrs. |
| 1937 | 4-2-3 | "        " | | 3 tie games in a row |
| 1938 | 8-1 | "        " | Joe McGinnis<br>Ted McLaughlin | MVC Champs, Homecoming postponed twice, finally played 13 days later. |
| 1939 | 7-2 | "        " | Jack Hirt<br>Ted Lewis | Hirt and Lewis All-State |
| 1940 | 5-3 | "        " | | Ted Lewis (B), Bob Caywood (G), Bob White (G) picked for East-West Iowa All-Star game. |
| 1941 | 8-1 | "        " | Bill Bothell<br>Bob Crumley | Bothell and Joe Casey All-State |
| 1942 | 7-0-1 | "        " | Dean Yanaush | MVC Champs |
| 1943 | 7-2 | Wally Schwank | Wayne Hopp<br>Don Trumpp | Cormack enlists in Navy<br>Hopp and Shay All-State<br>Tom Hirt on 1st All-State |
| 1944 | 1-7-1 | "        " | Tom Hirt<br>John "Tug" Wilson | Tom Hirt 1st All-State again<br>Hirt & Rubin Snider get 4th letter, 1st ever Dad's Night held |
| 1945 | 7-1-1 | "        " | Bob Krall<br>Evan Smith<br>Lenard Strasburg | 1st win at Dav. in 24 years<br>Smith, Don Fryhauf, Jim Sangster All-State |
| 1946 | 9-0 | Herb Cormack | | Coach Cormack returns from the service, Coach of the Year, State Champs - 4 on All-State, MVC Champs, Cormack resigns - goes to ISU as assistant |
| 1947 | 6-3 | Frank Bates | Bill Reichardt<br>Virgil Troyer | Reichardt 1st All-State |

# Football

| 1948 | 7-2 | Frank Bates | Francis Beasley<br>John Fenton | Hettrick 1st All-State, Hettrick, Beasley, Rox Shain all 3rd letters. New field on City High Campus |
|------|-----|-------------|------------------|-----------------------------------|
| 1949 | 5-4 | "    " | | New Scoreboard donated by the Optimist Club |
| 1950 | 9-0 | "    " | | MVC & State Champs , 5 on All-State |
| 1951 | 6-2-1 | "    " | | Jim Freeman makes High School All-American Team |
| 1952 | 6-2-1 | "    " | John Larew | MVC Champs |
| 1953 | 9-0 | "    " | Fred Nosek | MVC & State Champs, 3 on All-State, 7 Shutouts, 1st City High team to win 2 MVC titles in a row |
| 1954 | 6-2-1 | "    " | Dave Mrak | Had first loss in 15 games |
| 1955 | 3-6 | "    " | | |
| 1956 | 4-4-1 | "    " | Paul Burgess<br>Jim Luper | Luper All-State |
| 1957 | 5-3-1 | "    " | Tony Houser | Houser and Bill Housel All-State |
| 1958 | 4-5 | "    " | Gene Rarick | Jay Memler All-State |
| 1959 | 8-1 | "    " | John Stevens | 4 on All-State team, Played in 8" of snow in Rock Island |
| 1960 | 8-1 | "    " | Butch Frantz<br>Phil Minnick | 2nd MVC,   State Champs Lost to Rock Island |
| 1961 | 6-2 | "    " | Dave Moss<br>Gary Snook | Skip Hohle - MVP, Moss, Snook, Mike Cain All-State |
| 1962 | 4-5 | "    " | Steve Moss<br>Don Rhoades | Don Rhoades - MVP |
| 1963 | 4-5 | "    " | Rod Kodros | Bob Falls MVP |
| 1964 | 6-3 | "    " | Mike Hunzinger | Dan Schapira - MVP |
| 1965 | 3-6 | "    " | John Kavanaugh | Mike Cilek - MVP |
| 1966 | 5-4 | *Clyde Bean | Terry Davis | *Bean takes place of Bates, who is ill. Terry Davis - MVP Bean MVC Coach of the Year |
| 1967 | 3-6 | Frank Bates | John Evashevski | Gary Smothers - MVP Bates retires after 21 years. |
| 1968 | 0-9 | Clyde Bean | Dave Brender<br>Bill Randall | First year of West High (only 700+ students at City High), Randall MVP |
| 1969 | 4-5 | "    " | Bob Schultz<br>Tom Roberts | Schultz MVP |
| 1970 | 8-1 | "    " | Mike Gratz<br>Dan McCarney<br>John Piro | MVC Champs,  Piro MVP McCarney 1st All State Bean MVC Coach of the Year |

# Football

| 1971 | 4-5 | Clyde Bean | Ed Evans<br>Carl Hargrave<br>Dave Kirkendall | Hargrave MVP |
|------|-----|-----------|---------|---------|
| 1972 | 5-4 | "    " | Greg Cilek<br>Terry Riley | Bill Schultz Pararde All-American,   Schultz MVP |
| 1973 | 8-1 | "    " | Dave Burke<br>Doug Piro | MVC Champs<br>Piro MVP and All-State |
| 1974 | 6-3 | "    " | Rick Griffin<br>Bob Sass<br>Jim Wilson | Sass MVP, Wilson, Dan Cilek, Robbie Myers All-State |
| 1975 | 4-5 | "    " | Paul Burgess<br>Kevin Davis | Doug Dean MVP |
| 1976 | 3-6 | "    " | Jay  Hilgenberg<br>Randy Miller | Miller MVP<br>Doug Dunham 1$^{st}$ All-State |
| 1977 | 3-6 | "    " | Kelly Evans<br>Andy Piro<br>Pete Wilson | Eric Klasson All-State |
| 1978 | 2-7 | "    " | Dave Chambers<br>Tom Greenwald<br>Jeff Kinney | |
| 1979 | 5-4 | "    " | Brian Thorne<br>Jeff White | Coach Bean retires after 12 years. |
| 1980 | 3-6 | Larry Brown | Scott Delsing<br>Scott Froehle<br>John White | Froehle and Norm Balke All-State |
| 1981 | 1-8 | "    " | Jeff Canfield<br>Craig Hagen<br>Brian Wellingham | Jay Chelf - Off. MVP<br>Scott Oakes - Def. MVP |
| 1982 | 4-5 | "    " | Jed Clark<br>Mike Pugh | MVP- offensive, Scott Flynn defensive, John Friedrich |
| 1983 | 7-2 | "    " | Dave Heyn<br>Steve Thorne | MVP - offensive, Jeff Beard defensive, Dave Heyn |
| 1984 | 7-2 | "    " | Larry Knock<br>J.D. White | MVP - offensive, Mark Lumpa, defensive, Knock, 54-14 vs. West, biggest margin ever,  7 of 9 opp. scored 14 pts. each |
| 1985 | 8-1 | "    " | Sean Anderson<br>Sean O'Brien | 2$^{nd}$ MVC  -  4$^{th}$ in AP poll, but no Playoff,   MVP-offensive, Greg Brown;  defensive, O'Brien, Greg Brown 2$^{nd}$ All State, 1,802 yds., 304 rushing vs. C.R. Prairie |

# Football

| 1986 | 7-3 | Larry Brown | Mark Fay<br>Brad Gehrke<br>Greg White | 3-way tie MVC title, 1st playoff appearance, beat Prairie 15-6, lost to Linn-Mar 42-14, MVP - offensive, Chris Hupfeld, defensive, Gehrke |
|------|-----|-------------|--------------------------------------|-------------------------------------------------------------------------------------------------------------------------------------------|
| 1987 | 3-6 | "        " | | |
| 1988 | 9-2 | "        " | Brent Roth<br>Tim O'Donnell | 1st MVC, Playoff - Beat Burlington, Lost to Bettendorf, MVP -offensive, Roth, def. Corey Landeen |
| 1989 | 8-3 | "        " | | Playoff - beat Burlington, lost to Bettendorf |
| 1990 | 6-4 | "        " | | Playoff - lost to Assumption |
| 1991 | 5-4 | "        " | | Brion Hurley 1st All-State |
| 1992 | 10-1 | "        " | | (Undefeated) MVC Champs, Playoff-lost to State Champ 31-28, Scott Jones 1st All-State kicker, Tim Dwight 1st All State, MVC player of the Year, Brown MVC Coach of the Year |
| 1993 | 13-0 | "        " | Luke Donohue<br>Tim Dwight | 1st MVC - State Champs - 5 on 1st team All-State - Dwight 43 TD's, also made Parade All-American, Brown State Coach of the Year |
| 1994 | 11-2 | "        " | Brian Mitchell<br>Rob Thein | MVC & State Champs (won 20 games in a row - 27 in MVC), MVP - off,, Thein - def., Jesse Fischer, 1st All State = Jeff Halter (C), Rob Thein (TB), Brian Mitchell (LB) - Thein 2,243 rushing yds. (new record), also 313 single- game rushing yds. |
| 1995 | 10-2 | "        " | Todd Barnes<br>Ben Meisner | MVC Champs and playoff team, MVP - offensive, Ben Dombroski, defensive, Barnes, 4 named to All-State |
| 1996 | 13-0 | "        " | Mitch Price<br>Mark Seaton | MVC & State Champs, MVP - offensive, Jesse Holland, defensive, Seaton, 7 named to All-State |

# Football

| 1997 | 9-4 | Larry Brown | Zach Butler<br>Scott Gordan | State runnerup (Ankeny 17-14),<br>MVP - off., Gordan -def., Butler |
|------|-----|-------------|------------------------------|----------------------------------|
| 1998 | 9-2 | "       " | Nick Linder<br>John Pantazis | MVC (8-1), playoff team,<br> MVP -offensive Linder<br>defensive Pantazis, Lost to West<br>twice 18-0 & 21-0 |
| 1999 | 7-3 | "       " | Kory Hartwig<br>Steve Pfaller | MVP -offensive, Hartwig<br>defensive, Pat Campbell<br>Lost to West in 1$^{st}$ round playoff |
| 2000 | 10-2 | "       " | Chris Campbell<br>Brian Ferentz | MVP - offensive, Hakim Hill<br>defensive, Pat Campbell<br>Hill = 2,846 career rushing yds.,<br>Lost in semifinals to Bettendorf,<br>Brown retires after 21 yrs. |
| 2001 | 12-1 | Dan Sabers | Connor Jostes<br>Angus MacKay<br>Matt Rhoades<br>Matt Wooldrik | MVC Champs, State runner-up,<br>MVP - Jostes<br>5 make All-State teams |
| 2002 | 4-5 | "       " | Jared Gadson<br>John Morrison<br>Caleb Recker<br>Curt Steyers | First losing record since 1987 |
| 2003 | 7-3 | "       " | Greg Altmaier<br>Zach Buxton<br>Ryan Kennedy<br>Scott Knight<br>Mike Sabers | Lost Playoff, 1$^{st}$ round, to West,<br>Ryan Kennedy = 1,885 yds.<br>passing, 3$^{rd}$ best All-time. Ryan<br>Grenko made Top 10 in 3<br>receiving categories. |
| 2004 | 9-3 | "       " | D.P. Eyman<br>Sean Hosseni<br>Alex Smith | 1$^{st}$ MVC, 16$^{th}$ trip to playoffs,<br>beat Prairie and Cedar Falls, lost<br>to Bettendorf, the State<br>Champions, Eyman and Phil<br>Kenney 2$^{nd}$ All-State<br>Sabers MVC Coach of the Year |

# Men's Cross Country 1922-2004

Yearbook records indicate that City High participated in the University of Iowa Cross Country meet in the fall of 1922, which was the equivalent of the State Meet at the time. The State of Iowa did not hold its first official State Meet until 1930, but the IHSAA lists State Champions from 1922 until 1929 and list the Little Hawks as winning the State title in 1923. The State also sponsored a State Mile Team race in the fall up through at least 1968. H. C. Soucek was the coach of the first three Little Hawk teams.

*1923 State Cross Country Champs*

In the 1922 University of Iowa meet, sophomore Wallace Elliott finished third and two others competed. In 1923 the Little Hawks had an outstanding team showing at the University of Iowa meet as Wallace Elliott was second, Frank Stutzman third, Lloyd Riley fifth, and James Elliott sixth. This was the above-mentioned State title team; 16 points was an outstanding team total. City High was fourth in the U. of I. meet in 1924 and had a dual meet victory over U-High.

From 1925-1937 very sporadic results were found in yearbooks or newspaper archives. Several dual and triangular meets were indicated, mostly with U-High and area schools. In 1938 under Coach Francis Merten the team finished 12th out of 21 teams in the State Meet.

From 1939-45 there were no teams. Throughout the first three decades of City High Cross Country teams, it was indicated that there was not a full-time coach and that the coaches were also coaching football at the same time. This often meant that one of the athletes was in charge of the team much of the time. A prime example of this was Jack Davis in 1946 and 1947. Davis was City High's first official State Cross Country Champion, winning the IHSAA race in 1946 in 10:32.7. Jack also finished first in the state-sponsored Mile Team race that fall. The 1947 yearbook said, "Jack Davis helped coach the team as Coach Howard Moffit is busy with football." The 1948 team finished second in the MVC and State Mile Team race.

From 1949 through 1954 there again was no official City High team. From 1955-57 "Chic" Forwald did the coaching while also serving as line coach for the Little Hawks football team.

Those teams finished third, sixth and sixth in the MVC Mile Team race and the 1957 Cross Country team finished fifth in the State mile team race and 10th in the State cross country competition.

In 1958 City High hired its first paid, full-time coach for cross country as Mac Gore started a four-year term as coach. That 1958 team finished third in the State cross country meet and second in the State Mile Team race. That was the best State finish for the Little Hawks until the 1991 team won the State Championship. In 1959 Dick Corso finished as State runner-up.

In 1962 Coach Forwald left football coaching and returned to Cross Country, this time on a full-time basis. Forwald coached the next nine seasons for a total of 12 at the helm of the Little Hawks fall program. The yearbook from 1962-70 again had only sporadic results printed with just three years reported. In 1967 City High had the top MVC finish (5th MVC, 10th state in cross country and 8th MVC, 12th State in Mile Team).

## *Randy Jackson Wins State*

Following the 1970 season Coach Forwald retired from all duties and was succeeded by Orrie Rew, who was head coach for the next 10 years. Coach Rew's teams finished in the top 10 at State four times. He coached some excellent individuals, the best of which was Randy Jackson, who

*Randy Jackson - 1975 State Champion*

was probably the top distance runner in Little Hawk history. Randy was the State cross country champion in 1975 and went on to finish third at the National Junior Olympic Championship meet in Houston, Texas, later that year. His time at the 2-mile distance at the State was the third best in history before the distance was increased. Randy was also outstanding in spring track and was the 1980 NCAA Champion in the steeplechase for the University of Wisconsin.

In 1978, Matt Trimble finished second at the State Meet and the team had its highest MVC finish (third) until 1984.

In 1982 Bev Boddicker, a former All-American runner at the University of Iowa, became the first woman to coach a man's team at City High. The team had an 8-4 dual record and was fifth in the MVC.

The year 1983 started a new and exciting era in City High cross country. "Bud" Williams, a long-time junior high coach in the district, took over the combined men's and women's programs. Over the next 14 years as head coach, Williams turned the Little Hawks into a state power with five men's titles and six women's titles along with numerous MVC titles.

Coach Williams' second team (1984) captured the first MVC cross country title ever for City High with the 1985 team capturing the first District title ever. These would be the first of many (8 MVC, 7 District) titles for the Little Hawks under Williams' guidance.

The last four years of the 80's saw no MVC or District titles, but 1990 was a break-through year with a District Championship and third place in the State Meet. MVC and District wins came in 1991 followed by the first men's Cross Country State Team Championship ever for City High and Coach of the Year honors for Bud Williams.

The 1991-94 period saw four MVC, District and State titles for the Little Hawks as they dominated the state scene. They only lost three meets in that stretch. The 45 points scored in 1993 is the third best all-time at the State meet.

The state winning streak ended in 1995 with a third place finish, but the Little Hawks reached

five consecutive wins in the MVC and Districts. In 1996 the Little Hawks returned to the throne by winning the State after being upset in the District Meet. The MVC streak reached six as Coach Williams retired after 14 years at the helm. He left with eight MVC titles, seven District titles, and five State Championships and a lasting legacy of success in cross country.

*1991 Men and Women's State Champions*

Steve Maresh succeeded Williams, but stayed just one season before taking a position in Wisconsin. His 1997 team ran the MVC streak to seven, won the District and finished second in the State Meet.

The next head coach served as an assistant for both Williams and Maresh. Jayme Skay, a very successful junior high coach, stepped up to the head position. Skay continued the outstanding winning ways of the program with six District titles and four MVC wins along with three-second place finishes. His first team --1998-- was second at State and followed this up with State Championships in both 1999 and 2000. Skay was named State Coach of the Year in 1999. In a great show of depth, the 1999 team won the title despite not having anyone finish in the top 10.

*2000 Cross Country State Champions*

Two fourth-place finishes in 2001 and 2002 and a State runner-up in 2003 further established the Little Hawks as one of the top programs in the state. Skay was named Regional Coach of the Year in 1998, 2000, 2001, 2002, and 2003 to go along with six MVC Coaching Awards.

In 2004, City High won both the MVC and District meets and finished third at the State meet. Gabe Munoz-Fitch had the highest place (5th). Jayme Skay was named MVC Coach of the Year for the sixth time in his seven-year career as head coach.

The fact that City High has seven State Team titles in its history and only two individual winners (neither from State Champion teams) indicates outstanding team depth and excellent coaching.

In the 70 years (with some interruptions) since the first team in 1922, the Little Hawks have won 13 MVC crowns, 14 District titles, and seven State Championships. They have qualified for the State meet 18 times in history. All of these came in 1984 or later. Jack Davis (1946) and Randy Jackson (1975) were individual winners for the Little Hawks. Wallace Elliott (1923), Dick Corso (1960), and Matt Trimble (1978) were State runners-up.

In the last 15 years, the Little Hawks have never finished lower than fourth place at the State meet.

# Men's Cross Country

| Year | W - L | Coach | Captains | Misc. Information |
|------|-------|-------|----------|-------------------|
| 1922 | | H. C. Soucek | | Soph. Wallace Elliott runs in U.of I. CC meet (State Meet of the times), finishes 3$^{rd}$ (2 others also ran) |
| 1923 | | " " | Wallace Elliott | <u>Not sanctioned by the State</u>, but state lists City High as team champion. U of I Meet -Elliott 2$^{nd}$, Frank Stutzman 3$^{rd}$, Lloyd Riley 5$^{th}$, James Elliott 6$^{th}$ |
| 1924 | | " " | | 4$^{th}$ Iowa CC Invitational Beat U-High 9-15 |
| 1925 | | Carl Campbell | Paul White | |
| 1926 | | " " | | |
| 1927 | | " " | Charles Dalton | |
| 1928 | | Mr. Harrington | | Lost to U-High, beat Kalona |
| 1929 | | | | |
| 1930 | | | | First year CC State meet is sanctioned by the State Athletic Association |
| 1931 | | | | 2$^{nd}$ in triangular with Muscatine and U-High |
| 1932 | | | | |
| 1933 | | | | 4 meets plus State Meet |
| 1934 | | NO TEAM | | |
| 1935 | | " " | | |
| 1936 | | " " | | |
| 1937 | | | | Lost to U-High |
| 1938 | | Francis Merten | | State = 12$^{th}$ of 21 teams |
| | | | | |
| | | | | |
| 1946 | | Howard Moffit | | Jack Davis 1$^{st}$ in Mile Team Race and State Champion in CC |
| 1947 | | " " | Jack Davis | Davis helps coach because Moffit helps with football. Davis is State champion. |
| 1948 | | " " | | Mile Team - 2$^{nd}$ in MVC & State |
| 1949 | NO | TEAM UNTIL | 1955 | |
| 1955 | | "Chic" Forwald | | Mile Team 3$^{rd}$ MVC Forwald also coached football |
| 1956 | | " " | | Mile Team - 6$^{th}$ MVC, 6$^{th}$ State |
| 1957 | | " " | | CC Team- 5$^{th}$ State Mile Team - 6$^{th}$ MVC, 10$^{th}$ State |

# Men's Cross Country

| Year | Record | Coach | Assistant/Other | Notes |
|------|--------|-------|-----------------|-------|
| 1958 | | Mac Gore | Norm Maske | First paid full-time coach<br>CC Team- 4$^{th}$ MVC, 3$^{rd}$ State<br>Mile Team - 3$^{rd}$ MVC, 2$^{nd}$ State |
| 1959 | | " " | | Dick Corso is State runner-up |
| 1960 | | " " | | |
| 1961 | | Mac Gore | | |
| 1962 | | Chic Forwald | | |
| 1963 | | " " | | Mile Team - 10$^{th}$ MVC |
| 1964 | | " " | Roger Mildenstein | |
| 1965 | | " " | Ed Elliott<br>Pat Holland | Mile Team - 7$^{th}$ MVC<br>CC Team- 8$^{th}$ MVC |
| 1966 | | " " | | |
| 1967 | | " " | Al Flores | CC Team 5$^{th}$ MVC, 10$^{th}$ State,<br>Mile Team - 8$^{th}$ MVC, 12$^{th}$ State |
| 1968 | | " " | John Wilson | Wilson - MVP |
| 1969 | | " " | Jim Knoedel | Knoedel - MVP |
| 1970 | | " " | | |
| 1971 | 4-3 | Orrie Rew | | 7$^{th}$ MVC, 9$^{th}$ State |
| 1972 | | " " | Dick Evans | |
| 1973 | 12-4 | " " | | 5$^{th}$ MVC, 9$^{th}$ State |
| 1974 | 10-5 | " " | | 6$^{th}$ MVC, 10$^{th}$ State |
| 1975 | 8-4 | " " | Randy Jackson<br>Kevin Michel | 5$^{th}$ MVC, 7$^{th}$ State,   Randy<br>Jackson  State Champ & MVP |
| 1976 | | " " | | 10$^{th}$ MVC, 10$^{th}$ District |
| 1977 | | " " | | |
| 1978 | 6-3 | " " | Matt Trimble | 3$^{rd}$ MVC, 7$^{th}$ District,  Matt<br>Trimble  2$^{nd}$ State & MVP |
| 1979 | 3-3 | " " | Steve Rummelhart | 8$^{th}$ MVC, 13$^{th}$ District |
| 1980 | 2-3 | " " | | 7$^{th}$ MVC, 11$^{th}$ District |
| 1981 | | John Clark | Greg Unsicker | 3$^{rd}$ MVC, 8$^{th}$ District,  MVP -<br>Unsicker |
| 1982 | 8-4 | Bev Boddicker | Gary Brack<br>Dave Munson | First woman to coach boys' sport,<br>5$^{th}$ MVC, 11$^{th}$ District ,  MVP -<br>Brack |
| 1983 | 7-3 | "Bud" Williams | Dave Munson | 5$^{th}$ MVC, 5$^{th}$ District |
| 1984 | 7-3 | " " | Steve Choice<br>Ivan Lorkovic | 1$^{st}$ MVC, 2$^{nd}$ District, 4$^{th}$ State,<br>Steve Choice MVP<br>Williams MVC Coach of the Year |
| 1985 | 7-4 | " " | Mark Dawson | 1$^{st}$ MVC, 1$^{st}$ District, 4$^{th}$ State,<br>Steve Choice is 7$^{th}$ at State and<br>MVP,  Williams MVC Coach of<br>the Year |

# Men's Cross Country

| 1986 | 5-4 | Bud Williams | Joe Ruth | 3$^{rd}$ MVC, 2$^{nd}$ District, 6$^{th}$ State, MVP - Glen Lomenick and 9$^{th}$ at State |
|------|-----|--------------|----------|------|
| 1987 | 1-7 | "    " | Glen Lomenick | 6$^{th}$ MVC, 9$^{th}$ District, MVP Lomenick |
| 1988 | 3-7 | "    " | Brad Dawson | 6$^{th}$ MVC, 7$^{th}$ District, MVP Dawson |
| 1989 | 2-9 | "    " | Carl Seidler | 5$^{th}$ MVC, 4$^{th}$ District, MVP Seidler |
| 1990 | 5-5 | "    " | Pete Simons | 1$^{st}$ MVC, 1$^{st}$ District, 3$^{rd}$ State, MVP Simons, Williams MVC Coach of the Year. |
| 1991 | 12-0 | "    " | Josh Briggs Dave Novotny | 1$^{st}$ MVC, 1$^{st}$ District, 1$^{st}$ State, Novotny 5$^{th}$ at State, Frank 9$^{th}$ at State, MVP Novotny and Erik Frank, Williams MVC Coach of the Year |
| 1992 | 10-1 | "    " | Erik Frank | 1$^{st}$ MVC, 1$^{st}$ Super (first one held), 1$^{st}$ District, repeat 1$^{st}$ State, Frank is 4$^{th}$ at State and MVP, Williams MVC Coach of the Year |
| 1993 | 10-2 | "    " | Steve Kurth | 1$^{st}$ MVC, 2$^{nd}$ Super 1$^{st}$ District, 1$^{st}$ State (3$^{rd}$ in a row), 3 in top 10 at State, MVP Kurth, Williams - MVC Coach of the Year |
| 1994 | 12-0 | "    " | Sam Argall | 1$^{st}$ MVC, 1$^{st}$ District, 1$^{st}$ State (4$^{th}$ in a row), Ross Conklin is 8$^{th}$ at State, MVP and MVC Athlete of the Year, Williams MVC Coach of the Year |
| 1995 | 10-2 | "    " | Jesse Ammerman | 1$^{st}$ MVC, 1$^{st}$ Super, 1$^{st}$ District, 3$^{rd}$ State Ross Conklin, 8$^{th}$ at State and repeats as MVP and MVC Athlete of the Year, Williams MVC Coach of the Year |
| 1996 | 10-2 | "    " | Mark McPherson | 1$^{st}$ MVC, 1$^{st}$ Super, 2$^{nd}$ District, 1$^{st}$ State, McPherson is 6$^{th}$ at State, MVP are McPherson & Soloman Richards, Coach Williams MVC and State Coach of the Year and retires after 14 years |
| 1997 | 12-0 | Steve Maresh | John Hensley | 1$^{st}$ MVC (7$^{th}$ in a row), 1$^{st}$ Super, 1$^{st}$ District, 1$^{st}$ State, MVP - Brent Behrens |

# Men's Cross Country

| 1998 | 8-4 | Jayme Skay | John Farlinger<br>Jacob Smith | 2$^{nd}$ MVC, 1$^{st}$ Super, 1$^{st}$ District, 2$^{nd}$ State . MVP - Bob Moreno, Skay is MVC and Regional Coach of the Year |
|------|-----|------------|-------------------------------|-------------------------------------------------------------------------------------------------------------------------------|
| 1999 | 11-1 | "         " | Quincy Ely-Cate<br>Paul Kresowik<br>Eric Mittman<br>Bob Moreno | 2$^{nd}$ MVC, 1$^{st}$ Super, 1$^{st}$ District, 1$^{st}$ State (no one in top 10), MVP - Moreno,  Skay is MVC and State Coach of the Year. |
| 2000 | 12-0 | "         " | Quincy Ely-Cate<br>Jon Lamb<br>Bo Rydze<br>Pat Snyder | 1$^{st}$ MVC, 1$^{st}$ Super, 1$^{st}$ District Undefeated State Champs, Jeremy Mims 6$^{th}$ at State and MVP, Skay is MVC and Regional Coach of the Year |
| 2001 | 10-2 | "         " | Mark Kresowik<br>Jon Lamb<br>Pat Snyder<br>John Williams | 1$^{st}$ MVC, 1$^{st}$ Super, 1$^{st}$ District, 4$^{th}$ State,  Kresowik is 6$^{th}$ at State and MVP,  Skay is Regional Coach of the Year |
| 2002 | 8-4 | "         " | Luke Bross<br>Jon Humston<br>Jon Lamb<br>Dirk Marple<br>Chris Shultz | 1$^{st}$ MVC, 1$^{st}$ Super (8 in a row),1$^{st}$ District, 4$^{th}$ State,  MVP - Lamb Skay is MVC and Regional Coach of the Year |
| 2003 | 11-1 | "         " | Dan Groepper<br>Dirk Marple<br>Mike Mittman<br>Chris Pretorius | 1$^{st}$ MVC, 1$^{st}$ Super, 1$^{st}$ District, 2$^{nd}$ State, Elite All-State - Colin Swaney, MVP - Groepper & Marple,  MVC Athlete Of the Year. - Groepper,  Skay is MVC and Regional Coach of the Year |
| 2004 | 9-3 | "         " | David McKay<br>Jacob Mason-Marshall<br>Gabe Munoz-Fitch<br>Travis Robertson | 1$^{st}$ MVC,  2$^{nd}$ Super, 1$^{st}$ District, 3$^{rd}$ State, City High has finished in the top 4 at State for 15 straight years. Munoz-Fitch is 5$^{th}$ at State, Skay is MVC Coach of the Year |

# Women's Cross Country 1979-2004

Women's cross country had its start in the fall of 1979. Orrie Rew, long-time coach at City High in several sports, was the first coach. Orrie was already the coach for the men's cross country and women's track so it was a natural fit when the program was organized. Coach Rew retired from coaching after the 1980 season and was followed by John Clark, Bev Boddicker and finally Bud Williams in 1983.

In the first season of 1979 Jodi Hershberger became the initial place winner from City High by finishing fifth in the State Meet. The Little Hawks finished sixth in the MVC and eighth in the District that inaugural season.

*First women's Cross Country team, 1979*

## 1980's

The 1982 team, coached by Bev Boddicker, was the first to place at State finishing eighth after a third place finish in the MVC. MVP Diane Pessagno was the highest finisher. The following season (1983) "Bud" Williams started his 14-year run as head coach with an MVC third place finish and seventh at the District. Helene Wieting finished ninth at State that season.

The 1988 team claimed the first City High MVC title and a seventh place State finish. That team set the stage for a tremendous run for women's cross country. For the next nine seasons the Little Hawks dominated with nine MVC crowns, seven District wins and six State titles, including five consecutive from 1989 through 1993.

The first state title came in 1989. Michelle Nason was MVP and Bud Williams was named MVC and State Coach of the Year. In 1990 Williams repeated as Coach of the Year and Cara Wolf (6th), Courtney Usher (7th), Stephanie McAndrew (8th) and Missy Novotney (9th) all finished in the top 10 at the State meet. The following season Novotney, Usher, and Anya McMurray were top 10 as the Little Hawks won their third title in a row.

## 1990's

The year 1992 saw a fourth straight title, four in the top 10 again (Usher, McMurray, Wolf and McAndrew) and a fourth straight State Coaching honor for Williams. The 1993 season was more of the same, a fifth straight State win and Coach of the Year for Williams. Keely Barnett finished third at the State and Jenny Mulder was fifth. Barnett was chosen MVC Cross Country Athlete of the Year, her first of three such honors.

*1995 - Women's State Cross Country Champions*

In 1994 the State streak was stopped but the MVC streak reached seven. Barnett was State runner-up and MVC Athlete of the Year. Bethany Young finished sixth at the State meet. City High returned to the top in the State in 1995 and Keely Barnett capped off her career with an individual State Championship, the first ever for a Little Hawk.

In 1996 the Little Hawks had their first losing season (5-7) since 1988, but did win the MVC for the ninth straight year and were third at the State. Lindsay Wetzel was MVC Athlete of the Year. Following the 1996 season, Coach Williams retired after 14 seasons. His resume included six State titles, seven District wins, and nine MVC crowns. The MVC wins came in consecutive seasons 1988-96. Coach Williams was named to the Iowa Track Coaches Hall of Fame in 1995. A Bud Williams' Scholarship is awarded each year to a member of the men's and women's cross country team.

Steve Sherwood succeeded Williams and coached one season (1997) and was in turn succeeded by former assistant coach Tom Mittman, who has remained to the present time. The year 1997 was also the beginning of the Michelle Lilienthal era, a three-year career that saw Lilienthal emerge as one of the top female distance runners in the State of Iowa in both cross country and spring track. Bethany Young won the 1997 State title with sophomore Lilienthal 10th. The team finished second at the District and State meets, but won a 10th consecutive MVC title.

*1999 - Women's State Cross Country Champions*

Lilienthal was a three-time team MVP and in 1998 became City High's third women's individual Cross Country State Champion in Tom Mittman's first year at the helm. The 1999 team returned the State title to City High after a three-year absence despite a rare second place finish in the MVC. Michelle repeated her State championship in 1999 and went on to a fine career at the University of Wisconsin. Lilienthal finished 10th, first and first at State in her last three years at City High. (More about her exploits in the women's track section.)

***2000's***

In 2000 and 2001 the Little Hawks were winners of both the MVC and District, but came in second at State both years. The MVC title in 2000 started a new string that carried through 2004. In 2000 freshman Nelle Trefz was sixth at the State meet and the team was second. In 2001 Jennie Funk, a transfer from West Des Moines Valley, was second at the State meet as the Little Hawks again finished second as a team.

The following two seasons 2002 and 2003 saw City High in its familiar role of MVC, District and State Champions. In 2002 the Little Hawks won the MVC, District and State as Nelle Trefz finished fourth and Jennie Funk fifth at State. In 2003 an undefeated season followed as Trefz was second and Funk third, closing out their careers with a repeat State title for the Little Hawks. The State titles brought the overall total to nine, all in the last 15 years. Jennie Funk and Nelle Trefz were both team MVP's and high State placers and had stellar spring track careers, which will be noted in the Track and Field chapter.

In the 2004 season, with an almost entirely new squad, the Little Hawks had a 9-3 record, winning the MVC and District titles and finishing second at the State meet. Coach Mittman was chosen MVC and Regional Coach of the Year.

*2003 - Women's State Cross Country Champions*

City High has had 26 seasons of women's cross country (1979-2004). In these seasons there have been six coaches who helped produce nine State titles, 13 District wins and 15 MVC titles. There have been four individual state winners with Michelle Lilienthal the only repeat winner. The program has been one of the dominant women's cross country programs in the state since the late 1980's. Since 1997 the team has never finished lower than second at the State meet.

37

# Women's Cross Country

| Year | W - L | Coach | Captains | Misc. Information |
|------|-------|-------|----------|-------------------|
| 1979 | 1-3 | Orrie Rew | | First year for sport - 6th MVC 8th District, Jodie Hershberger 5th at State, First State place winner from City High |
| 1980 | 0-4 | "     " | | 8th MVC |
| 1981 | | John Clark | Kathy Huss | 7th MVC |
| 1982 | 10-1 | Bev Boddicker | Kathy Huss | 3rd MVC, 4th Dist. , 8th State, MVP - Diane Pessagno |
| 1983 | 4-5 | Bud Williams | Denise Organ | 3rd MVC, 7th District, Helene Wieting 9th at State |
| 1984 | 4-5 | "     " | Kristen Gisolfi | 2nd MVC, 7th District, MVP Helene Wieting |
| 1985 | 5-7 | "     " | Pam Fischer | 3rd MVC, 3rd Dist., 7th State, MVP - Helene Wieting |
| 1986 | 2-7 | "     " | Helene Wieting | 5th MVC, 8th District, MVP - Wieting |
| 1987 | 3-6 | "     " | Jeanne Sherburne | 3rd MVC, 6th District, MVP Sharie Brooker |
| 1988 | 5-6 | "     " | Chris Lovell | 1st MVC, 3rd Dist., 7th State, MVP Michelle Nason, Williams MVC Coach of the Year |
| 1989 | 8-3 | "     " | Hillary Paul | 1st MVC, 1st District, 1st State Championship Team ever, MVP Michelle Nason, Williams MVC and State Coach of the Year |
| 1990 | 9-1 | "     " | Pam Kriege | 1st MVC, 1st District, Repeat 1st State, 4 in top 10 at State, MVP Cara Wolf, Williams repeats as Coach of the Year |
| 1991 | 11-1 | "     " | Anya McMurray | 1st MVC, 1st District, 1st State (3rd in a row), 3 in top 10 at State, MVP Missy Novotny and Stephanie McAndrew, Williams repeats as Coach of the Year |
| 1992 | 10-1 | "     " | Stephanie McAndrew | 1st MVC, 1st Super (first Super Meet), 1st District, 1st State (4th in a row), 4 in top 10 at State, MVP Cara Wolf, Williams repeats as Coach of the Year |
| 1993 | 9-3 | "     " | Courtney Usher | 1st MVC, 2nd Super, 1st District, 1st State (5th in a row), Keely Barnett MVP and MVC Athlete of the Year, Williams - C. O. Y. |

# Women's Cross Country

| 1994 | 11-1 | Bud Williams | Kim Harding<br>Lisa Thomae | 1$^{st}$ MVC, 1$^{st}$ District, 2nd State, Keely Barnett State runner-up, and also MVP and MVC Athlete of the Year, Williams MVC Coach of the Year |
|------|------|--------------|-----------|---------|
| 1995 | 11-1 | "      " | Katie Sidwell | 1$^{st}$ MVC, 1$^{st}$ Super, 1$^{st}$ District, 1$^{st}$ State, Keely Barnett MVP and State Champion, Williams named to State CC Hall of Fame |
| 1996 | 5-7 | "      " | Jenny Mulder | 1$^{st}$ MVC, 2nd Super, 2nd District, 3rd State, MVP - Lindsay Wetsel Coach Williams retires after 14 years. |
| 1997 | 8-4 | Steve Sherwood | Alison Nair | 1$^{st}$ MVC, 3$^{rd}$ Super, 2$^{nd}$ District, 2$^{nd}$ State, MVP Michelle Lilienthal, Bethany Young - State Champion |
| 1998 | 6-4 | Tom Mittman | Anne Heefner<br>Kaye Sparks | 2$^{nd}$ MVC, 2$^{nd}$ Super, 2$^{nd}$ District, 2$^{nd}$ State, Michelle Lilienthal MVP & State Champ |
| 1999 | 11-1 | "      " | Michelle Lilienthal<br>Melissa McGivern<br>Hillary Mills | 2$^{nd}$ MVC, 1$^{st}$ Super, 1$^{st}$ District, 1$^{st}$ State, Michelle Lilienthal State Champ and MVP |
| 2000 | 11-1 | "      " | Laurie Hickman<br>Karen Johnson<br>Abby Krueger | 1$^{st}$ MVC, 1$^{st}$ Super, 1$^{st}$ District, 2$^{nd}$ State, Nelle Trefz is 6$^{th}$ at State MVP - Johnson |
| 2001 | 9-3 | "      " | Julie Bender<br>Rachel Gannon<br>Megan Huisenga<br>Erilynn Russo | 1$^{st}$ MVC, 1$^{st}$ Super, 1$^{st}$ District, 2nd State, Jennie Funk , 2$^{nd}$ at State and MVP |
| 2002 | 9-3 | "      " | Carolyn Brigham<br>Kara Evans<br>Katelynn Kerstetter<br>Monica Mims | 1$^{st}$ MVC, 1$^{st}$ District, 1$^{st}$ State, Nelle Trefz, 2$^{nd}$ at State and MVP Jennie Funk, 5$^{th}$ at State |
| 2003 | 12-0 | "      " | Willa Cmiel<br>Rachel Manuel | 1$^{st}$ MVC, 1$^{st}$ District, 1$^{st}$ State, Nelle Trefz, 2$^{nd}$ at State, Jennie Funk 3$^{rd}$ at State, MVP - Funk & Trefz |
| 2004 | 9-3 | "      " | Maggie Leyendecker<br>Katie Lumpa<br>Becky Russo<br>Paige Towers | 1$^{st}$ MVC, 2$^{nd}$ Super, 1$^{st}$ District, 2$^{nd}$ State<br>Samantha Sidwell - MVP |

# Men's Golf 1939-2004

*Author's note: Because of spring yearbook publishing deadlines, it is difficult to get fully accurate information on spring sports for many of the years. Men's golf was moved to the fall season in 1974.*

## 1939-1959

The first organized men's golf team was introduced in the spring of 1939 with Francis Merten, well known basketball coach, as the head coach. Merten coached through the 1944 season, following which he entered the military.

In that first season of 1939, the team was fourth in the MVC and Dean Reasley was fourth individually. The following season the team was fifth and Reasley also fifth. No team was fielded in 1941, but in the next three seasons the Little Hawks were MVC champs.

The 1942 and 1943 MVC champs had Gene Matthews (first) and Bill Sangster (second) both years. The next two seasons after Coach Merten left for the military, the team was coached by "committee" so to speak as Iver Opstad, Fred Jones, and Herb Cormack were all listed in the yearbook as coaching. Harry Dean was second in the MVC in 1945, but no information was listed for 1946.

In 1947 Jack Orr was hired to head up the golf program and began a 21-year career as the head coach. That first team was MVC champs for the fourth time in the eight years of the program. They finished seventh in the State meet.

From 1948 through 1956 results were difficult to obtain. District and some MVC finishes were noted during that time period. The years 1951 and 1952 had third- place MVC finishes and in 1952 John Comer was co-medalist. The 1954 squad was District champs and finished third in the State for the highest finish of this period. In 1955 John Leichty was co-medalist of the District runner-up Little Hawks.

In 1958, the team was second at the MVC and junior John Peterson was medalist. Peterson went on to finish second in the State meet. The following year the team was second at the District and third at the State championship. Peterson followed up his second in 1958 with a third-place finish in '59.

## 1960's

In 1960 with Coach Orr in his 14th season and Frosty and Jim Evashevski leading the way, City High won its first District team crown since 1954. Frosty Evashevski went on to finish second at the State meet.

The 1962 squad won the MVC championship, its first conference title since at least 1947. The 1964 team followed that up with another MVC title and unbeaten dual season. Mike Hanrahan, Wayne Karson and Gary McIntosh were the leaders.

In 1966 the Little Hawks finished second at the District meet and sixth at the State. Chris Larson was MVC medalist. The 1967 season was Coach Orr's 21st and final season as head of the golf program. The little Hawks sent him out with a bang as they won the MVC title and finished second at the State meet. Senior Joe Liechty was the captain and leader.

Coach Orr closed out his 21-year career with four MVC titles, seven top-three District finishes and three top-three State team finishes.

Dick Miller was named to succeed Jack Orr for the 1968 season. That squad, led by John Evashevski, won the MVC title and placed sixth at the State meet. In 1969 Steve Vorhies was State runner-up.

*1967 - Coach Jack Orr's 21st and last team*

## 1970's

Dick Miller stayed just one more season and was replaced by Dick Sundblad, who coached the 1970 team to a second place MVC finish before also leaving after one season.

In 1971 Ken Klein began a five-year stint as the head coach. Starting in 1974 the Little Hawks had both a fall and spring season, often with different coaches for each season. The fall season was started by the State Athletic Association to alleviate the crowded conditions at golf courses. City High continued to have teams both seasons from 1974 through 1978. Starting in 1978 through 1986 the City High yearbook reported only a spring team. In the fall of 1986 the program moved to the fall full time.

If you feel confused with all this, you are not alone. The author taught and coached at City High during this period and he's still a little confused.

Ken Klein resigned after the 1974 season and for the next four seasons, four different coaches headed up the program. Starting in the spring of 1977 Larry Knipfer became the coach and except for one season (1989), he coached the Little Hawk golfers until 1994 for a total of 18 seasons.

## 1980's

The 1980, '81, and '84 teams all had just one-loss seasons with the 1982 team having the highest MVC finish (third). In 1984 the squad finished third at MVC and sixth at State.

In the fall of 1986, still being coached by Larry Knipfer, the season was moved full time to the fall. The 1988 team, after finishing third in the District, became the first City High team to qualify for the Fall State meet, finishing sixth.

In 1989 Dave McLaughlin replaced Knipfer for one season. The Little Hawks had an 11-3 record in duals and finished third in the MVC; they also qualified for the State meet where they were runner-up.

## 1990's and 2000's

Coach Knipfer returned the next season (1990) and led the Little Hawks to fourth in the State as Greg Shank became City High's first, and as of 2004, only individual State Champion.

In 1991 City High won its only MVC title of the 1990's. The Little Hawks also earned a District title as well and were fifth at the State meet. Knipfer coached through the 1994 season and left after 18 years at the helm.

*1991 - MVC and District Champs*

Don Brown, who also had been both men's and women's basketball coach and coached the fall golf team in 1977, succeeded Knipfer and remained for the next eight seasons. Coach Brown's 1995 team was second in the MVC, sixth in the Super meet and fifth in the District. None of Brown's teams finished below third in the MVC Divisional standings.

The best District finish was second by the 1997 team, which was led by two-time MVP Sean Dervrich. Consecutive top three MVC finishes in 1998 (second), 1999 (second), 2000 (third), and 2001 (third) were led by David Hayek, Ned Carter, Jon Doern, and Butch Searls, respectively. In 2000 Ned Carter and Jill Frantz were the medalists at the Co-ed State tournament. These preceded an MVC Championship team in 2002. Ned Pirotte and Trey Skaugstad were the leaders of the championship squad.

In 2003, City High graduate Jerry Hora became the new coach after Don Brown's retirement. The team finished seventh in the MVC and Bryan Boal was the MVP.

In 2004 the team tied for fifth in the MVC and was 12th in both the Super and the District meet. Freshman Matt Gatens was the MVP. Hora, who also coaches the women's team in the spring, remains at the head of both programs at this writing.

# Men's Golf

| Year | W - L | Coach | Captains | Misc. Information |
|------|-------|-------|----------|------------------|
| 1939 | | Francis Merten | | First time as a sport, 4th MVC, Dean Reasley 4th Individual |
| 1940 | | "      " | | 5th MVC, Dean Reasley 5th Individual |
| 1941 | | NO TEAM | | |
| 1942 | 3-2 | Francis Merten | | 3rd year of Golf - 2nd MVC, Gene Matthews 1st MVC (75), Bill Sangster 2nd (79) |
| 1943 | | "      " | | 1st MVC, Matthews repeats 1st MVC and Sangster 2nd |
| 1944 | | "      " | | 1st MVC |
| 1945 | | Iver Opsted | | 2nd MVC - Coach Merten gone to Armed Forces, Harry Dean 2nd in MVC |
| 1946 | 5-0 | Herb Cormack Fred Jones Iver Opsted | | |
| 1947 | | Jack Orr | | 1st MVC, 7th State - one of the best teams in the state. |
| 1948 | | "      " | | 6th District |
| 1949 | | "      " | | 3rd District |
| 1950 | | "      " | | 6th MVC |
| 1951 | | "      " | | 3rd MVC, 4th District |
| 1952 | | "      " | | 3rd MVC, 4th District , John Comer was MVC co-medalist |
| 1953 | | "      " | | 2nd MVC, 3rd District |
| 1954 | | "      " | | 1st District, 3rd State |
| 1955 | | "      " | John Liechty John Wicks | 2nd District, Liechty was co-medalist (71) |
| 1956 | | "      " | Jim Galiher Jim Luper | 6th MVC, 7th District |
| 1957 | | "      " | | 5th MVC |
| 1958 | 2-1 | "      " | Bob Galiher John Peterson | 2nd MVC, Peterson medalist Peterson State runner-up |
| 1959 | 1-2 | "      " | John Peterson | 1st in Iowa City Invitational, 2nd District, 3rd State, Peterson 3rd at State |
| 1960 | 1-0-1 | "      " | Frosty & Jim Evashevski | 1st District, Frosty Evashevski 2nd at State |
| 1961 | | "      " | | 6th MVC, 6th District |
| 1962 | | "      " | | 1st MVC, 6th State |
| 1963 | | "      " | Mike Langston | Won Iowa City and Clinton Invitationals. |

# Men's Golf

| Year | Record | Coach | Players | Notes |
|---|---|---|---|---|
| 1964 | 4-0-1 | Jack Orr | Mike Hanrahan<br>Wayne Karson<br>Guy McIntosh | 1st MVC<br>Undefeated dual season |
| 1965 | 1-1 | " " | Mike Dickerson<br>Mike Roberts | 8th MVC |
| 1966 | | " " | Steve Barthalow<br>Mike Judiesch | 2nd District, 6th State, Chris Larson MVC Medalist |
| 1967 | | " " | Joe Liechty | 1st MVC, 2nd State, last year for Coach Orr-21 yrs. |
| 1968 | | Dick Miller | John Evashevski | 1st MVC, 6th State |
| 1969 | | " " | Steve Vorhies | Vorhies 2nd at State |
| 1970 | 5-1-2 | Dick Sundblad | Tom Roberts | 2nd MVC |
| 1971 | 3-6 | Ken Klein | Dan Zwiener | 5th MVC |
| 1972 | 5-5 | " " | Louie Villhauer | 4th MVC |
| 1973 | | " " | Kevin Villhauer | |
| 1974 | | " " | | 1st Sectionals<br>Beat West 3 times |
| *F1974 | 0-7 | " " | | *Golf also in the fall now |
| S1975 | 4-0-1 | " " | Brad Hansen | 10th MVC, 4th Sectionals |
| F1975 | | | | |
| S1976 | 3-3 | Steve Willey | John Murphy | 6th Sectionals |
| F1976 | | John Raffensperger | Dean McCormick<br>Elliott Smith | 5th MVC |
| S1977 | 5-1 | Larry Knipfer | | 7th MVC |
| F1977 | 2-5 | Don Brown | Barry Hansen<br>Dave Rubright | |
| *S1978 | 5-2 | Larry Knipfer | | *Apparently golf returned to only a spring sport. |
| S1979 | 3-3-1 | " " | | 7th Sectionals<br>Beat West in Districts |
| S1980 | | " " | | Late snows kept them from holding several early meets. |
| S1981 | 10-1 | " " | | 5th MVC,<br>MVP - Allen Goode |
| S1982 | 9-2 | " " | | 3rd MVC |
| S1983 | 8-7 | " " | | 3rd MVC, 3rd Sectionals |
| S1984 | 13-1 | " " | | 3rd MVC, MVP - Scott Flynn |
| S1985 | 7-5 | " " | | 3rd MVC, 3rd Sectionals<br>5th District |
| S1986 | 7-3 | " " | | 5th MVC, 5th Sectionals<br>MVP - Terry O'Brien |
| *F1986 | 6-6-1 | " " | | *MVC Golf moved to fall sport,<br>5th MVC, 9th District, MVP Jeff Johnson |

# Men's Golf

| Year | Record | Coach | Captains | Notes |
|---|---|---|---|---|
| F1987 | 7-8-1 | Larry Knipfer | | 4th MVC, 3rd District, |
| F1988 | 11-7 | " " | | 4th MVC, 3rd District , 6th State First team to qualify for fall State Meet |
| F1989 | 12-5-1 | Dave McLaughlin | | 3rd MVC, 2nd State |
| F1990 | 7-3-1 | Larry Knipfer | | 3rd MVC, 3rd District, 4th State, Greg Shank individual State Champ |
| F1991 | 10-3-1 | " " | | 1st MVC, 1st District, 5th State, snow delayed State meet, Knipfer MVC Coach of the Year |
| F1992 | | " " | | 3rd District, 8th State, 5th year in a row team qualified for State |
| F1993 | 6-12 | " " | | 4th District |
| *F1994 | 4-9-1 | " " | Tiger Rotenburger | **\*IHSAA moved all 4A Golf to fall sport,** 10th District, MVP - Rotenburger |
| F1995 | | Don Brown | Carl Hensley | 2nd MVC, 6th Super, Jarret Martin tied school record for low score at District meet, MVP-Hensley |
| F1996 | | " " | Sean Dervrich Greg Kirkman | 3rd MVC, 9th Super, 5th District, MVP - Dervrich |
| F1997 | | " " | Sean Dervrich David Hayek | 3rd MVC, 2nd Super, 2nd District, Qualified for State meet. MVP - Dervrich |
| F1998 | | " " | Chris Doern David Hayek | 2nd MVC, 4th Super, 5th District, Hayek was 7th Indiv. at State MVP - Hayek |
| F1999 | | " " | Ned Carter Tim Zeithamel | 2nd MVC, 3rd Super, 5th District, Ziethamel qualified for State MVP - Carter |
| F2000 | | " " | Cody Coffin Jon Doern | 3rd MVC, 3rd Super, 5th District, MVP - Doern, Ned Carter and Jill Frantz second at co-ed State |
| F2001 | 4-8 | " " | Zach Hammes Butch Searls | 3rd MVC, 9th Super, 5th District, MVP - Searls |
| F2002 | | " " | Ned Pirotte Trey Skaugstad | 1st MVC, 8th District, Super rained out, MVP - Pirotte |
| F2003 | | Jerry Hora | Bryan Boal Ryan Funk | 7th MVC, MVP - Boal |
| F2004 | | " " | | 7th MVC, 12th District |

# Women's Swimming 1968-2004

Swimming was the second officially sanctioned sport for women at City High. In the 1968-69 school year, a group representing the Iowa City Swim Club much like Mona Schallau in tennis, petitioned the Iowa City School Board to enter a team of City High girls in the District swim meet. The group, made up mostly of ninth graders from Central Junior High, won both the District and State Championships.

This 1968 team became the first City High women's team to win a State Championship. Freshman Marcia Mauseth won both the 50 and 100 freestyle events to become the second female (after Mona Schallau) to win an individual state title. Denny Roberson of the Iowa City Swim Club was the coach.

The following year (1969), Ralph Kyrder was hired as the official coach of the Little Hawk swim team and started a 10-year stint as both women's and men's coach. This second City High team returned to State where they tied for second with West Des Moines Valley.

The 1970's had mixed results due to having to use the Iowa City Recreation Center pool and practicing at odd times when that pool was available. In 1978 Krista Peterson was a State Champion in the 50 freestyle and the team was second in the District and ninth in the State.

## 1980's

In 1980 the team had its best State showing since the second year of the program, finishing in eighth place. This followed a fourth in the MVC and a third in the District meet. Erica Wockenfuss won the 100 freestyle title. This was the fourth individual title won by a City High female. Wockenfuss was later named to the Women's Swimming Hall of Fame.

## 1980 State Champion

### Erica Wockenfuss
100-yd. Freestyle / 53.75

Coach Paul Eaton's
City High Team
Finished 8th in
State with 96 points.

*Erica Wockenfuss - 1980 State Champion*

In 1981 the Little Hawks, under the guidance of their third coach in three years, Ian Bullock, had an even better season as they took third at the MVC, second at the District, and fourth at the State meet.

1982 saw the fourth coach in four years as Sue Chadima took over. Chadima was the first female coach after five men had headed the program. She had a nine-year term as head coach. In 1983 Coach Chadima, who coached both men's and women's teams, became the second female at City High to coach a men's team.

## 1990's

Derrick Abromeit was named coach in 1991 and had a seven-year stint as head coach. He coached both women and men until the position was split in 1996. Derrick continued as women's coach through the 1997 season.

Amy Kaduce became the first City High Diving State Champion in 1992 with Lindsay Clemons finishing third.

In 1997 the programs for City High and West shared the same coach and practiced together, but they maintained separate teams. In 1999 the City High team picked up its first MVC title. Kristy Hirokawa and Molly Gable were outstanding. The team had an 11th place finish at State.

46

Becky Miller became the second Little Hawk to win the diving title when she won in 1999. The Little Hawks won the MVC tourney after finishing fifth in the regular season. Keith Branstetter headed the program from 1998 through 2002.

## 2000's

In 2001 the team again was MVC champs. Katie Funk and Robin Karkowski shared the MVP award. The team's sixth place finish was its highest finish at State since 1981. The next season (2002) had another top 10 finish (ninth) with Kristin Lee as MVP. Coach Branstetter resigned following the 2002 season and was succeeded by Monica Orton.

Veronica Rydze finished second in the State diving in both her freshman and sophomore years (2003 and 2004).

*2001 MVC Champs - 6th at State*

The women's swimming program has had nine coaches in the 37-year (1968-2004) history of the sport. In the five-year span from 1978 to 1982 there were five: Ralph Kryder, John Fitzpatrick, Paul Eaton, Ian Bullock, and Sue Chadima. Since 1982 there have been only four head coaches as the program has stabilized somewhat. Women's swimming has the honor of being the first Little Hawk women's program to win a State team title (1968).

# Women's Swimming

| Year | W - L | Coach | Captain | Misc. Information |
|------|-------|-------|---------|-------------------|
| 1968 | | Denny Roberson | | Team organized just for State Meet. Won State! Marcia Mauseth (9th grader) won 50 & 100 freestyle |
| 1969 | | Ralph Kryder | Sharon Miller | 2nd District, 2nd State (tie) |
| 1970 | 3-2 | " " | Sharon Miller | 10th State - Anne Full was State Champ |
| 1971 | 9-1 | " " | Danette Riley | 5th District, 16th State |
| 1972 | 4-6 | " " | Debbie Stamp | |
| 1973 | 6-5 | " " | Sara Eicher Jenny Seydel | 4th District, 11th State |
| 1974 | 4-9 | " " | Julie Conklin Trudy Hammer | 7th MVC, 5th District |
| 1975 | 2-9 | " " | | 9th MVC, 8th District |
| 1976 | | " " | Mary Frederick Cindy Stell Angie Ward | Sue Buxton MVP |
| 1977 | | " " | Suzanne Kennedy Deb Ries | |
| 1978 | 11-2 | " " | Krista Peterson | 3rd MVC, 2nd District, 9th State, Krista Peterson, 1st State -50 freestyle |
| 1979 | 6-6 | John Fitzpatrick | Lori Pattinson | 6th MVC, 4th District, 14th State |
| 1980 | 4-2 duals | Paul Eaton | Jackie Dutton Lynn Pattinson | 4th MVC, 3rd District, 8th State, Champion Erica Wockenfuss, 100 freestyle |
| 1981 | 2-3 | Ian Bullock | Patty Dautremont Patrice Noel Erica Wockenfuss | 3rd MVC, 2nd District, 4th State, Wockenfuss MVP |
| 1982 | 3-4 | Sue Chadima | Joan Geraghty Sheral Oliver | MVP - Kristen Vanderhoef |
| 1983 | 2-6 | " " | | 8th MVC, 7th District, 14th State |
| 1984 | 3-4 | " " | Jenny Newell Kristen Wockenfuss | 8th MVC, 7th District MVP - Newell |
| 1985 | 3-4 | " " | Rachel Van Gilder | 8th MVC, 5th District MVP - Karen Wieting |
| 1986 | 2-4 | " " | Alyson Jepsen Kristy Schnetzler Rachel Van Gilder | 6th MVC, MVP - Karen Wieting |
| 1987 | 2-5 | " " | | 8th MVC, 6th District |

# Women's Swimming

| Year | Record | Coach | Captains | Notes |
|---|---|---|---|---|
| 1988 | 2-5 | Sue Chadima Chelf | | 8th MVC, 6th District |
| 1989 | 2-6 | "      "      " | | 6th MVC, 5th District |
| 1990 | 1-6 | "      "      " | | 7th MVC, 6th District |
| 1991 | 0-8 | Derrick Abromeit | | 7th MVC, |
| 1992 | 2-6 | "      " | | 11th MVC, 7th District Amy Kaduce 1st State - Diving, Lindsay Clemons 3rd State -Diving |
| 1993 | 2-6 | "      " | | 11th MVC, 6th District |
| 1994 | 0-8 | "      " | Sandra Smalley Kristina Konnath Tatum Vittetoe | 11th MVC, 7th District MVP - Smalley |
| 1995 | 1-7 | "      " | Mandy Benge Sandra Smalley Heather White | 10th MVC, 9th District MVP - Smalley |
| 1996 | 3-5 | "      " | Katie Divelbiss Nina Lohman Ellen Stimmel | 11th MVC, 6th District MVP - Divelbiss |
| 1997 | 4-6 | "      " | Ellen Stimmel Micah Swesey | Now combined program with West 10th MVC, 5th District |
| 1998 | 3-3 | Keith Branstetter | Ellen Stimmel Micah Swesey | 8th MVC, 3rd District, MVP Hannah Rapson & Stimmel |
| 1999 | 21-2-4 | "      " | Molly Gable Jenny Harper Kristy Hirokawa Alison Thomas | 5th MVC,  won MVC Tourney, 11th State MVP - Hirokawa,  Becky Miller - State diving champ |
| 2000 | 4-5 | "      " | Bridget Casey Molly Gable Robin Karkowski | 7th MVC, 4th District MVP - Molly Gable |
| 2001 | 11-1 | "      " | Christine Bursch Katie Funk Robin Karkowski Kristen Lee | 1st MVC, 2nd Super, 3rd District, 6th State MVP - Funk & Karkowski |
| 2002 | 5-3 | "      " | Kristin Lee | 5th MVC, 4th District, 9th State, MVP - Lee |
| 2003 | | Monica Orton | Heather Gray Paige Knebel | MVP - Gray,  Veronica Rydze 2nd State Diving |
| 2004 | | "      " | Sarah Berg Kayla Casavant Elysia Dolder | 11th MVC,  Veronica Rydze 1st District Diving and 2nd at State |

# Volleyball 1971-2004

Volleyball was one of three sports introduced for women in the 1971-72 school year, gymnastics and golf being the others. Kay Pundt was the volleyball coach in that first-ever season. The schedule was an abbreviated one with just seven contests, mostly against smaller schools. Just five MVC schools had volleyball at that time.

The first season of volleyball had a 2-5 record. One of the wins was over cross town rival West who also added volleyball that year. Kay Pundt was the coach the first four seasons and the team struggled against more experienced teams. The team had 2-5, 3-3, 5-8 and 2-7 records but was showing improvement, especially in tournaments.

*First Volleyball team to qualify for State, 1975*

In 1975 under new coach Carol Havens the Little Hawks had just a 1-5 dual record but did well in tournaments, especially the last two before the District. In the District, City High had a 7-1 record and advanced to the State Tournament for the first time in school history. The Little Hawks had a 1-5 mark in the State Tourney.

The next season saw a District title and second straight appearance in the State Tourney. A fifth place finish at State highlighted the season. Carol Havens was again the coach and MVP Tracy Taylor would return 10 years later to be head coach of the Little Hawks.

In 1978 Connie Kensinger started an eight-year term as head coach. This would be the longest volleyball coaching tenure at City High. Dual meet records were not outstanding, but some of the top female athletes ever at City High were part of those teams. Lisa Nicola, Michele Conlon, Michele Gehrke and Liesl Kolp were all MVP's during the 1980's.

## 1980's and 1990's

Starting in 1981 City High and West began playing for a traveling trophy known as 'The Spike'. The teams had played each other since 1971, but these were not a part of the trophy competition. As of the 2004 season 'The Spike' series stands at 13-11 in favor of City High.

Connie Kensinger was voted MVC volleyball coach of the year in 1984. The Little Hawks lost in the Regionals that season to North Scott. Michele Gehrke was voted team MVP for the second straight season.

Coach Kensinger resigned following the 1985 season and was succeeded by 1976 captain and MVP Tracy Taylor. That started a seven-year period where the Little Hawks had five different

*1993 MVC Champions (34-6-4)*

coaches: Taylor, Christy Wiederhold , Kelly Scott, Deb Juehring and Greg Vraspier.

    Greg Vraspier took over in 1992 and had four very successful seasons as head coach, recording season win totals of 22, 34, 33 and 18. The 1993 team won three tournament titles along with 34 wins and was MVC Divisional winner. The 1993 team snapped Wahlert's 100+ winning streak against Iowa teams. The 1994 team followed up with 33 wins and Molly Shurr was MVC Player of the Year.

    Bond Shymansky took the reins in 1996, and in 1997 had a 37-8 mark and second place in the MVC. The Little Hawks qualified for the State tournament in 1997 for the first time in 21 years and only the third time in school history. They lost in the semifinals to Johnston. Teesa Price was voted MVC Player of the Year. Price (2nd), Stacy Moss(3rd) and Kelli Chestnut (3rd) were named All-State. Shymansky left following the 1997 season to take a college coaching position.

    Former assistant Diane Delozier took over in 1998 and began a great four-year stint as volleyball coach. Coach Delozier's first team put together a record setting 44-1-1 record and the

*1998 State Champions (44-1-1)*

first State Championship for City High volleyball. The Little Hawks' only loss came in the MVC Tourney. City High defeated Oskaloosa , Davenport North and Waverly in winning the State title. Setter Stacy Moss was voted team MVP for the second straight season and Kelli Chestnut was MVC Volleyball Player of the year and Elite All-State. She was also named State Player of the Year. Moss (2nd), Teesa Price (2nd), and Tanya Hammes (3rd) were named to All-State teams. Moss, Chestnut, Price and Hammes went on to outstanding college careers.

The following season (1999) the Little Hawks again qualified for the State Tourney after finishing third in the very tough MVC. City High lost to Davenport North at State. Kelli Chestnut was named to the first All-State team. Jessie Hodge was named to third team All-State.

## 2000's

In 2000, City High christened the new century by making it to State for the third straight season. The Little Hawks ended the season by losing to Dubuque Hempstead at State and finished with a 28-10-2 record. Lindsay Quigley was named third All-State and Megan Kennedy made the fifth team All-State.

Coach Delozier resigned after the 2001 season with three state appearances in four years and one State Championship. Craig Pitcher succeeded her. Coach Pitcher's second squad (2003) posted a 36-7 record and a State Tournament appearance. The team lost in the semifinals to State Champion Dubuque Hempstead. Junior Mari Royster-Crockett (1st), Megan Gatens (2nd), and freshman Brynja Rodgers (3rd) were named to All-State teams.

The 2004 team earned a repeat trip to the State tournament (the teams' eighth all-time). Coach Pitcher was named MVC and State Coach of the Year and sophomore Brynja Rodgers was named MVC Athlete of the Year. The team made it to the championship match where they were defeated 3-1 by top-ranked Ankeny. The Little Hawks finished with a 38-6 record, the second most wins in City High history. Sophomores Katie Kennedy and Brynja Rodgers were named to the 4A All-Tournament team. Rodgers and Kennedy were named All-State. Rodgers made the Elite All-State team. Liz Ingram was named to the second team and Allison Smith to the third team.

In the 34-year (1971-2004) existence of women's volleyball, City High had 11 different coaches, with only one with more than four seasons as coach. The team has made eight appearances in the State tournament with one State title (1998) and one runner-up finish (2004).

*2004 - State Runner-up*

# Volleyball

| Year | W - L | Coach | Captains | Misc. Information |
|------|-------|-------|----------|------------------|
| 1971 | 2-5 | Kay Pundt | | First year for this sport |
| 1972 | 3-3 | "      " | | |
| 1973 | 5-8 | "      " | Julie Kron | |
| 1974 | 2-7 | "      " | Sue Miller | |
| 1975 | 1-5 duals | Carol Havens | Janet Shaffer | Qualified first time for State Tournament |
| 1976 | 7-5 | "      " | Ann Poepsel Tracy Taylor | 1st Dist., 5th State (2nd straight year for State Tournament), Taylor MVP |
| 1977 | 4-9 | "      " | Deb Sagen Jackie Wright | |
| 1978 | 3-12 | Connie Kensinger | | |
| 1979 | 1-8 | "      " | | |
| 1980 | 3-8 | "      " | | 8th MVC |
| 1981 | 6-16 | "      " | Kellie Alberts Lisa Nicola | Nicola MVP |
| 1982 | 9-16-6 | "      " | Michele Conlon Beth Lainson | MVP - Conlon |
| 1983 | 6-19-1 | "      " | Michele Gehrke | MVP - Gehrke |
| 1984 | 5-5 duals | "      " | Amy Hagen Katy Roan | MVP -Michele Gehrke Kensinger - MVC Coach of the Year |
| 1985 | 10-15-2 | "      " | Liesl Kolp | MVP - Kolp |
| 1986 | 5-20-2 | Tracy Taylor | Dawn Alvarez Amy Burke Lisa Hintze Sara Kennedy | MVP - Hintze |
| 1987 | 7-6-1 | "      " | | |
| 1988 | 6-21-2 | Christy Wiederhold | | |
| 1989 | 5-10 | Kelly Scott | | 7th MVC |
| 1990 | 15-16-3 | Deb Juehring | | |
| 1991 | 15-13-6 | "      " | | |
| 1992 | 22-11-5 | Greg Vraspier | Carrie Houghton Sandra Woolson | 3rd MVC, 12th Ranked |
| 1993 | 34-6-4 | "      " | Tara Fumerton Rachel Hurley | 1st MVC, 1st Sectionals |
| 1994 | 33-5-5 | "      " | Kathie Kempf Molly Shurr Jessica Thieleke | 1st MVC, 5th ranked into Tourney Molly Shurr - MVC Player of the Year, MVP = The Team |
| 1995 | 18-5-5 | "      " | MacKenzie Bell Jessica House Sarah Hurley | 3rd MVC MVP - House |

# Volleyball

| 1996 | 18-14-4 | Bond Shymansky | Jill Blake<br>Kristen Haugen<br>Abbie Rohret | MVP - Haugen |
|------|---------|----------------|--------------------------------------------|--------------|
| 1997 | 37-8-0 | "          " | Amber Dykstra<br>Stacy Moss | 2nd MVC,  State qualifier lost in semi-finals,  Moss, Teesa Price & Kelli Chestnut All-State, MVP - Moss,  MVC Athlete of the Year - Price |
| 1998 | 44-1-1 | Diane Delozier | All the Seniors | 1st MVC and  State Champs Lost 1 game in MVC Tourney, Kelli Chestnut MVC & State Athlete of the Year and Elite All-State,  Price , Moss, Tanya Hammes All-State,  MVP - Stacy Moss |
| 1999 | 21-15-5 | "          " | Cassie Corbett<br>Jessie Hodge | 3rd MVC, qualified for State, lost in first round,  MVP - Allison Crosby,  Hodge - 3rd All-State |
| 2000 | 28-10-2 | "          " | Kelsie Linder<br>Megan Mueller | Qualified for State,  Lost to Dub. Hempstead,  Lindsay Quigley (3rd) & Megan Kennedy (5th) All-State,   MVP - Mueller |
| 2001 | 13-17-3 | "          " | Emily Hodge<br>Kari Kutcher<br>Mandy Wyss | 3rd MVC<br>MVP - Hodge |
| 2002 | 19-10 | Craig Pitcher | Jessica Elliott<br>Kimberly Welter | MVP - Elliott |
| 2003 | 36-7 | "       " | Megan Gatens<br>Emily Triplett | 3rd State,  lost in semi-finals to Dubuque Hempstead,  Mari Royster-Crockett (1st) & Brynja Rodgers (3rd) All-State,  Gatens was 2nd All-State and also MVP |
| 2004 | 38-6 | "       " | Carrie Wagner<br>Megan Wyss | 1st MVC,  2nd MVC tourney, 2nd State (8th trip to State tournament) lost to Ankeny in Finals,  Brynja Rodgers team & MVC Athlete of the Year  & Elite All-State,  Kennedy (1st), Liz Ingram (2nd), Allison Smith were All-State,   Coach Pitcher named MVC & State Coach of the Year |

# Men's Basketball 1906-2004

The history of City High basketball can never be discussed without mentioning the famous 1946 State Championship team. This team, before the age of the three-point goal, was able to score three baskets in the last 55 seconds to come-from-behind and beat LeMars for the first Basketball State title ever for the Little Hawks.

City High won just one more State title in its history (1989), but has had four runner-up finishes and several other appearances at State.

## *The Early Years   Pre-1920's*

The first official school-sponsored team was in the 1906 season, but no win/loss record was found. In the 1906-07 season the team, under the direction of A.F. Siepert, had a 0-4 season. The 1907 Red and White stated that "The first game played with another team on the new gym floor was with West Liberty on February 1, 1907 with West Liberty winning 38-16." The Red and White also stated that the "School Board made improvements in the gym. The court was extended ten feet and was covered with a new floor." The previous year (1906) heat was added to the dressing rooms, which I'm sure was appreciated by the athletes.

*Gym in the old high school*

The 1907-08 team was captained by Earl Sangster, whose brother, sons, grandchildren and great grandchildren, all played for and graduated from City High. Earl was also an outstanding baseball player. Mr. Sangster returned to coach baseball at City High in 1945 and the City High baseball field is named after him.

From 1906 through 1914 only one winning season was recorded. That was 1910, with a 6-2 record. In that nine-year period there were six different coaches and one year (1911) where no coach was hired. It was that year the City High team had its first All-State player, Grant Keppler. Keppler set a then single-game record in 1910 with 13 field goals and 27 points.

The 1908 <u>Red and White</u> had an interesting quote regarding the loss to Davenport. "Undoubtedly we would have won the game had it not been for the decisions of the Davenport officials. Our boys outplayed the Davenport five, but could not overcome this sixth man." In another instance involving a 26-12 defeat at West Liberty, the <u>Red and White</u> stated, "We started the scoring, but were soon discouraged by the shady decisions of the West Liberty official."

In a 1913 loss to Columbus Junction the <u>Red and White</u> stated, "The Iowa City forwards could not get shots at the basket on account of being unable to stand on the slippery floor that was used as a dance floor and was waxed." That same year the Little Hawks played in their new gym. In 1914 Martin McGovern tied Keppler's record of 13 field goals and 27 points.

Overtime rules at the time called for a sudden-death period. The Little Hawks, in a rare game against an out-of-state foe, played Lincoln, Nebraska, at City High in 1915 and won 16-14, after a seven-minute sudden-death period. Lincoln was the Nebraska State Champion. City High lost to the eventual Iowa State Champ, Ottumwa, in the Sectional Tourney.

In 1917 and 1918 City High, under the leadership of Coach Henry Soucek, put together one of the best two-year records ever, going 32-5 and finishing State runner-up both years to Mt. Pleasant. In 1917 the Little Hawks won their first 11 games, then six in the tournament before losing in the championship game, 28-22, to Mt. Pleasant. The final record of 17-2 would be the highest number of wins until the 1941 team won 18. Otis Darner was chosen captain of the All-State team and George Fiesler and Harold Konvalinka were also named to the team.

In early rounds of the Sectional and District tournaments it was common to play two games in one day. City High did this both in 1917 and 1918 in reaching the State Tourney. The 1918 team lost again to Mt. Pleasant in the Championship game (17-16) and finished with a 15-3 record. Otis Darner repeated as All-State. Frank Shimek also was named All-State. Darner set the City High scoring record with 202 points.

## 1920's

Coach Soucek returned from serving in WWI for the 1920 season and led City High to an 11-1 record, the only loss being to Battle Creek in the Sectional Tourney.

The 1921 team just missed making the State Tournament, losing to Davenport, 15-11, in the District final. Buck McQuire was named All-State and led in scoring with 157 points.

The 1923 team played an end-of-the-season game against Tilden Tech High School of Chicago and lost, 32-21. The Little Hawks lost in the District (25-20) to Iowa City U-High.

In 1925 the Little Hawks had an undefeated regular season (11-0), but lost to Wilton Junction in the tournament to finish with an outstanding 13-1 season. The final four years of the 20's saw only a 29-32 record. Coach Soucek left after the 1927 season with an 11-year record of 113-54 and two State runner up trophies.

The year 1928 was the first for the MVC Basketball Conference. Davenport won the title in 1928 and City High finished 1-7 in MVC games. Sophomore Howard Moffit was named All-MVC that first year and repeated in 1929 along with being named to the second All-State team. Ralph Erbe was also named All-State second team.

## 1930's

George Wells started a six-year run as basketball coach in 1930. Coach Wells also coached football, track and tennis during his City High coaching tenure. His first squad in 1930 had a 14-6 record, including five wins in the tournament, before losing to West Waterloo. Howard Moffit was again named to All-MVC and All-State teams. Howard returned to City High to coach basketball, track and cross country between 1946 and 1953. He also served as City High's first Athletic Director.

In 1931 the Little Hawks finished the regular season with a 7-6 record, but had a nice run in the tournament, winning five straight including a victory over Keokuk, which was 24-0 at the time. The Little Hawks dropped their next game to Muscatine to finish 12-7 and miss the State Tournament.

The 1932 team had the misfortune to have three starters graduate at mid-year. Mid-year graduates were common up through the 1940's. New rules for 1933 saw the mid-court 10-second line violation become a rule and numbers to be worn on both the front and back of the jersey.

In 1935 Francis Merten began a nine-year stint as head coach. Like many other coaches of the time Coach Merten coached multiple sports at City High. In seven of the nine years at the helm, Coach Merten had double-figure win seasons including a then record 18 in 1941 and a new record 19 in 1942.

Ken Moss, who played in 1934, '35, and '36, remembered a game played at Vinton where "Paul McCune had his basketball pants scorched when he was pushed up against the heating stove in the corner of the gym." Included in the 1936 team's 16 victories were wins over Austin, Minnesota, and Maplewood High School of St. Louis. Three of the five losses were to Davenport, including a 27-23 defeat in the District. Jerry Pooler was named second team All-State. A major rule change occurred after the 1937 season when the center jump following each basket was eliminated.

The last two years of the 30's decade saw City High record 15-8 and 16-5 seasons. Russ Hirt was named All-State in both of those seasons and led the MVC in scoring in 1939. In 1939 City High played the first game ever in the new high school building, a 23-21 victory over Williamsburg.

## 1940's

The 1940's was an outstanding decade for City High Basketball. Included were the first-ever MVC Championship (1941), three more MVC titles ('45, '47, '49), the first-ever State Championship (1946), and a record setting 20-2 season in 1949. In eight of the 10 seasons the Little Hawks had the MVC's leading scorer.

### First-Ever MVC Championship

In 1941 the Little Hawks, led by All-State forward Ray Sullivan, won a then-record 18 games and became the first City High team to win an MVC title. Francis Merten, who also was a successful track and cross country coach, was the head coach from 1940 to 1944.

Sullivan was the MVC leading scorer and was named to the first All-State team. His 309 points was a City High record that stood until Gene Hettrick surpassed that total in 1949. City High beat Iowa City St. Patrick's in the tourney in the first meeting ever between the Iowa City schools. Fairfield ended the Little Hawks' season in the sub-state game.

In 1942 City High broke the one-year-old record for wins with 19 and advanced to the sub-state final where they lost to eventual State Champion Ottumwa in overtime, 30-28. City High was hampered by the fact that All-Stater Ray Sullivan was a mid-year graduate and missed the last 11 games. Junior Dave Danner picked up the slack by leading the MVC in scoring and was named first All-State. A statistical highlight was outscoring Cedar Rapids Wilson 21-1 in the first quarter. The Little Hawks finished third in the MVC.

In 1943 Danner repeated both as MVC leading scorer and first team All-State. Danner, who had a 30-point night against Wilson High School, went on to a three-year starting career at the University of Iowa, where he also earned All-Big Ten honors. In 1944 Coach Merten left after a nine-year coaching tenure.

In 1945 Wally Schwank, who was also head football coach, had a one-year term before moving to the college ranks as a football coach. Coach Schwank led the Little Hawks to a 14-4 record and their second-ever MVC title. Junior Bob Freeman and senior Jim Van Deusen finished 1-2 in MVC scoring. City High played Oskaloosa in the Iowa Fieldhouse as a prelim to the Iowa-Illinois game that year.

*First ever MVC Basketball Champs, 1941*

The year 1946 was a magical season for City High basketball. Not because the record was the greatest (18-7), but because of the way the season ended. That end came in the finals of the State Tournament before a capacity crowd at the Iowa Fieldhouse with a miraculous come-from-behind victory over LeMars.

## First-Ever State Title

This was the first-ever State Basketball title and one of only two the Little Hawks have ever won, the other coming 43 years later in 1989. The Little Hawks finished third in the MVC and finished the regular season with a 10-7 mark. They lost six of seven during one stretch and then reeled off 13 straight wins to finish as State Champions of Iowa. This was Coach Gil Wilson's first season as City High basketball coach. Bob Freeman, the star of the championship game, led the MVC in scoring again and was named first team All-State. Guard Harry Dean was named to the third All-State squad.

In the championship game LeMars held a 40-35 lead with less 60 seconds to play. There were no three-point goals at that time so City High needed three possessions to try and overcome the deficit. With steals and missed LeMars shots, Bob Freeman made three baskets in that last minute and the Little Hawks pulled it off before a soldout Iowa Fieldhouse. All State guard Harry Dean sealed it with a steal and tie-up after Freeman's last basket.

Leading up to the final game City High beat Lansing (39-30), Harlan (53-32), and then had to knock off giant killer Danbury (with only 11 boys in their high school) who had upset the state's number one team, Clinton. The Little Hawks won that game, 25-24, to set up the final against LeMars. Only the Iowa City fans were cheering for the Little Hawks since the remaining fans in the Fieldhouse were for the underdogs, Danbury and LeMars.

Of that dramatic season, Freeman said of Coach Gil Wilson, "Gil worked hard to teach us his system. He was very patient. He was quiet. Gil's goal was to teach, coach, and improve performance. As a result of his efforts, our performance did improve.

"During the halftime of the 13th game of the season, Coach Wilson made a statement that I will never forget. 'The next game you lose will be in the state championship game.' Remember our team had only won five games. He believed in us more than we believed in ourselves.

"We won that 13th game, and we won the next four regular season games. Gil took every opportunity to tell us that we were good, and that the next game we would lose would be the Iowa State high school basketball championship game. With each victory, the seed that Gil planted grew deeper roots. We started to believe.

"Gil was a great coach and a psychologist. When we arrived at the University of Iowa fieldhouse for the title game we dressed in almost complete silence. Gil cut our floor warmup short and motioned the team to return to the dressing room. He gathered us around him and then talked to us about winning the game. We really did not need the motivation part of his talk. Every player on the team was confident we could win and that we were going to do everything possible to bring City High its first basketball state championship trophy.

"Before we left the dressing room to play the game, Coach Gil had us do some special exercises that he guaranteed would take away all tightness and anxiety. He then gave us some odd colored cubes to take that he claimed would help us to relax. We found out later that they were dextrose sugar. A coach and a psychologist…you bet!

"The championship game was a classic. City High won the game by one point. The game is a classic, because our team scored six points in the last minute of the game to overcome a five-point deficit. The rules of the game in 1946 allowed teams to stall and retain possession of the ball rather than shoot free throws after a team member was fouled. A five- point lead with a minute to play was almost a lock on a win. I believe the only people in the Fieldhouse that thought we could win the championship were the members of the City High team and its coach. We did it…we were the very first City High team to win a state basketball championship." [Bob modestly did not mention that he scored all three of those baskets.]

Harry Dean, a junior starter on this team, remembers how a game-night superstition figured into the championship. "We drove to the Fieldhouse in cars. On the way I said I needed some gum so my dad stopped at Racines. I ran in and grabbed three packs of gum and since everyone knew me I said, "I'll be back later to pay for these." We won that first game so every game after that I did the same thing and the guy at the counter said he was expecting me each time."

*1946 - State Basketball Champions*

Bob Freeman continues, "The Monday after the game, there was a pep rally, the trophy was presented and school was dismissed for the day. There was a parade in downtown Iowa City, and team members were given honorary positions in the city for one day. I was honorary mayor of Iowa City for one day.

*Coach Gil Wilson, 78-19 career record*

"We won the state championship because of our Coach Gil Wilson. It was his motivation, skill in coaching and teaching, his skills and talents that made it possible. Without him and his leadership, we would have been an unremarkable average team. He believed in us more than we believed in ourselves."

The following season (1947) the Little Hawks won the MVC with an undefeated 16-0 record and won at Davenport for the first time in 25 years. Sophomore Gene Hettrick, who had been brought up to the varsity the previous year as a freshman, led the MVC in scoring. The Little Hawks beat Davenport twice during the season, but lost to them in the tournament, 41-32, to finish with an 18-4 record. Jim Sangster was named third All-State. In an unusual schedule situation, City High had an overnight road trip where they played at Ottumwa and Centerville before returning home.

Harry Dean, who had been a starter on the State Champion team in 1946, recalled: "After our win at State Coach Wilson promised us new uniforms and white shiny warm-ups. The post-war recession was on however, and all we got were white t-shirts with a red IC stenciled on them."

The 1948 squad finished third in the MVC and in a late season game snapped Davenport's 30-game winning streak. Unfortunately the Blue Devils won the rubber match in the tournament again. Gene Hettrick repeated as MVC scoring champ and set a conference record. Hettrick was named first team All-State. The Little Hawks again played a preliminary game to a Hawkeye game in the Fieldhouse.

The last team of the decade (1949) is often considered one of the best to ever represent City High. The team recorded a record 20-2 season, winning the first 15 games of the season. The regular season ended 18-1 with two victories over perennial state power Davenport.

The Little Hawks had a 13-0 MVC title season as Gene Hettrick won the scoring title for the third time, breaking his own MVC record with 279 points, averaging 21.9 per game. His total season scoring shattered Ray Sullivan's 1941 City High school record. Hettrick repeated as first team All-State and Whitey Diehl was named to the sixth team. Hettrick earned his fourth varsity letter (to go with three in football). Gene went on to play for the Hawkeyes.

Unfortunately, for the second time in three years the Little Hawks, despite beating Davenport twice in the regular season, lost to the Blue Devils in the District final before a soldout

*Gene Hettrick, three time MVC Scoring Champ*

crowd at the Fieldhouse. The game had been scheduled to be played at Muscatine, but officials moved the game to Iowa City to accommodate the crowd. With over 15,000 in attendance, it was also reported to be the largest crowd ever to attend a non-state championship game anywhere in the country at that time.

The following quote from All-Stater Whitey Diehl indicates the ability of that 1949 squad. "Also our Little Hawks scrimmaged Indiana University at the Fieldhouse prior to our Davenport game and more than held our own. After the scrimmage, three of us were offered scholarships by the Indiana coach (McCracken, I believe)." (This scrimmage would of course be a NCAA violation today.)

Following the 1949 season Coach Wilson resigned to take a position at Cornell College. He left with a spectacular four-year career record of 78-19 (79%), with a 40-9 MVC mark. Included were winning streaks of 13 (1946) and 15 (1949), two MVC titles and one State Championship.

# 1950's

In 1950 Howard Moffit succeeded Gil Wilson and had a four-year term as head coach. A new rule in the 50's saw an increase in the number of fouls allowed each player, from four to five. That season the Little Hawks again had the MVC's leading scorer in Bill Fenton. He had the honors with a 16.6 average. The team had a 13-6 record to kick off the 50's and Fenton was third All-State. The 1951 squad beat Cedar Rapids Franklin by 55 points, 83-28, which may have been the largest victory margin ever. They also played Ft. Madison in a preliminary game at the Iowa Fieldhouse.

In 1952 Jim Freeman, who was one of City High's best all-time overall athletes, was the leading scorer and had four games with more than 25 points. The team lost to Clinton in the District tournament for the third consecutive season.

The 1953 squad at 8-13 had the first losing season at City High since 1944. The season ended with the fourth consecutive tournament loss to Clinton. Coach Moffit left to take a job at the university. Former Hawkeye Bob Schulz was the new coach for 1954 and coached just one year.

## Holmstrom: 15-year Career as Head Coach

In 1955 Bill Holmstrom, highly successful coach at Clarence, Iowa, began a 15-year career as head coach of the Little Hawks. His first squad proved to be one of his best, compiling a 16-8 record and finishing runner-up in the State Tournament.

The obvious leader of the squad was 6' 7" center Bill Scott. Scott shattered the school scoring record with 531 points (22.1 average). He capped off his season with a spectacular State Tournament where he was named MVP of the tourney and set six new state tournament records. Included in the records were most points, field goals, and free throws in the tournament and most points in the final game (26) and most free throws in one game (16). He was also named first All-State center.

Scott was not a one-man team. Jeff Langston was named to the fifth All-State team and Dave Bradbury was named to the All-State Tournament team. Jim Kelley made 13 free throws in one game and in an overtime victory over Davenport scored all 12 Little Hawk points.

The 1956 team had a rare losing record (6-14) as all starters from the 1955 State runner-up team graduated. Jim Luper led the team in scoring. This was the last season with four schools in Cedar Rapids. Wilson, Franklin, McKinley and Roosevelt were combined to form Jefferson and Washington.

In 1957 not only were Washington and Jefferson new to the MVC, but three Illinois schools, Rock Island, Moline, and East Moline joined the MVC to create a nine-team league. This squad had a 12-11 record and upset a U-High squad in the tourney that was led by flashy guard John Raffensperger.

The 1958 squad (14-9) won three games in the tournament before losing to Davenport, 41-40, in the sub-state at the Fieldhouse. The team hit 29 of 32 free throws against Clinton including 16 in a row by Al Scott. Pat Phillips was named to the fourth All-State team.

The last year of the decade saw the Little Hawks beat archrival Davenport two times in the regular season, but again losing to them in the tournament. Guard Ed Watt was named first All-State and had a 35-point night against Jefferson. Watt went on to a fine major league baseball career, mostly with the Baltimore Orioles.

## *1960's*

The decade of the 60's was the first to finish below the .500 mark with a 10-year record of105-107. In 1960 another change occurred as Davenport High with close to 3,000 students split and Central and West high schools were formed. That made the MVC a 10-team conference. The league retained this format until 1967-68 when C.R. Kennedy joined to create an 11-team league.

The 1960-62 teams finished 33-33. The l961 team lost in overtime to C.R. Washington in the District final. Third team All-State guard Gary Snook, who had a 19.2 average and topped the 30-point mark twice, led the 1962 team.

The 1964 and 1965 teams had identical 13-8 marks. In 1964 Donn Haugan led the MVC in scoring and John Gough made 12 of 13 field goal attempts versus Clinton. The following year Mike Wymore was named second All-State guard and the Little Hawks beat Williamsburg in two overtimes in the District, but lost to MVC rival Jefferson in the next game.

The 1966 and 1967 teams had a combined record of 16-25 and lost to Iowa City Regina both years in the tournament. In 1967, forward Steve Cilek was named third All-State and had a 14-rebound game. Center Al Jones had a 15-rebound game and scored 31 points versus Muscatine in the opening District game. The team made 36 of 47 free throws in that game.

The 1968 (14-7) team looked to be one of the area's best, but a football injury kept forward Steve Piro out of much of the early season. Guards Tim Koch and John Heitshusen and center Ward Stubbs led the team early. Koch had games of 25, 27, and 28 points. Heitshusen had a 28-point game and Stubbs had two 15-rebound games. Just as Steve Piro was set to return to this lineup, Tim Koch developed an illness that would sideline him for the rest of the season. His 17.8 average and leadership would be missed. Piro was outstanding the rest of the season with several 20-point games including 28-and 30-point performances.

The Little Hawks had three big wins to lead off the District, winning by 15,13, and 32. In the sub-state final the team lost a heartbreaking 57-55 game to Ottumwa. Steve Piro had 30 of the 55 points in that game. Press-Citizen newspaper reporter Bob Elliott described it as the best individual performance he had ever covered in a high school game. Piro was named third All-State despite playing less than half a season. The team set a school scoring mark in an 87-64 early season win over Marion.

The final team of the 60's was also Coach Bill Holmstrom's 15th and final season at City High, as he resigned to take the Athletic Director post at Clinton. This squad with just one starter returning from the 1968 team struggled to a 6-12 regular season finish. The team came together to win four straight tournament games to qualify for the State tournament.

City High beat first-year school Iowa City West three times including a 56-33 tournament win. The Little Hawks followed that up with wins over Regina (68-62), Keokuk (83-61), and Oskaloosa (59-53) to reach Des Moines. A 70-61 loss to Carroll Kuemper in the first round ended the season with a final record of 10-13. Guard Kevin O'Rourke was named to the fifth All-State team. Coach Holmstrom left as the winningest coach in City High history with 167 wins.

The Quad City schools dropped out of the MVC after the 1968 season and Bettendorf, Muscatine, and newly formed Dubuque Hempstead (1969) joined. Iowa City West High joined the league the following year (1970).

# 1970's

The 1970's era started off with a new coach as City High sophomore coach Ron Schnack succeeded long-time coach Bill Holmstrom. Schnack's first team had a 13-6 record and for the second year in a row defeated Iowa City West three times. Kevin Kroeger was the leading scorer and was third in MVC scoring. He had a 31-point game against C.R. Jefferson.

The 1971 team split with West after running the winning streak to seven straight. Forward Mark Welsh was named fourth All-State. The 1972 team also split regular season games with West, but won the rubber game in the District. The season ended with a sub-state loss to Burlington.

## Clay Hargrave Era

The mid-point of the 1973 season began the "Clay Hargrave Era" at City High as the sophomore transfer from Regina became eligible in January. He led the Little Hawks to the state tournament. The Little Hawks won four tourney games to qualify for the State, but a 63-56 loss to MVC rival Kennedy at State ended their hopes.

In 1974 City High had a 14-4 regular season record, including two losses to West. In the District, the Little Hawks avenged a regular season loss to C.R. Washington, then upset number one ranked and unbeaten Iowa City West before losing to Davenport West in the sub-state final.

Clay Hargrave had 70 blocked shots during the season including a record nine in one game and the junior was named first All-State. The team broke the single-game scoring mark in a 94-73

*Clay Hargrave, two time All-State*

victory over Dubuque Hempstead. Point guard Doug Piro set a school record with 132 assists. Piro felt the upset of number one ranked West was one of his biggest thrills in high school.

The 1975 team equaled the school record of 1949 with a 20-2 record. This included a 17-1 regular season and nine and 11-game winning streaks. Clay Hargrave was obviously the leader, but the senior-dominated team had great balance and athletic ability.

The MVC championship snapped a 26-year drought. The 1949 team had been the last to record an MVC championship. Several team records were set: most points in one game (99 vs. South Tama), 70.8 scoring average and 48% team field goal shooting. Individual records included 43 points and 20 field goals by Clay Hargrave vs. Muscatine.

The Little Hawks 20 wins included three over West High and tournament blowouts by scores of 76-40 (Muscatine), 61-51 (West), and 80-44 Ft. Madison in the sub-state final. In the State Tournament game versus Ames, three first half fouls (including two in the first five minutes) on Clay Hargrave seriously altered the game plan. With the Little Hawks scoring 22 points under their average, they lost to Ames, 54-48, to end their dream season at 20-2.

Clay Hargrave repeated as first-team All-State and finished his career with a record 1,050 points and 785 rebounds in just two-and-a-half seasons. He went on to play for the Hawkeyes where at 6'4" he led the Big Ten in rebounds one season.

Coach Ron Schnack resigned following the season to enter law school. He left with a six-year record of 88-39 and one MVC championship.

A very interesting sidelight to the 1975 season was the fact that the City High gym, built in 1939, was found to have serious structural defects and was officially condemned. That meant no practices or games could be played until repairs were made.

The team practiced when and where they could, Southeast Junior

High, Regina, Halsey gym (U.of I.), Iowa Fieldhouse, North gym and West High gym. Games were played at West and the Iowa Fieldhouse. Despite those problems the team kept its focus and had an MVC championship season.

City High assistant Ken Klein was named the new head coach following the 1975 season and he held the position for two seasons. City High lost twice to West in 1976, but won the tournament game. In 1977 Andy Knoedel was named MVP and became the third Knoedel brother to be named MVP or captain in three different sports at City High.

In 1978 Don Brown, sophomore coach, was promoted to replace Ken Klein who resigned. Don began an eight-year term as head coach. The 1978 team beat West twice in regular season, but lost an overtime thriller in the District.

## 1980's

The 1980's started with losing records in three of the first four seasons, but the 1981 team (16-4) captured the co-championship of the MVC. With twin towers 6' 8" D. J. Carstensen and 6' 5" Norm Balke in the front line and guards Mark Brown and Mike Bogs, the Little Hawks had a 16-3 regular season mark. A District opening upset by C.R. Prairie (44-42) marred the season and left the overall record at a very good 16-4.

D. J. Carstensen was the MVC scoring champ (19.9) and was named to the second All-State team. Point guard Mark Brown was named first All-MVC.

This unfortunately was the highlight of the 80's, until the State Champion team of 1989, as the next few teams suffered through records of 5-15, 1-19 and 12-10. The 1983 squad that finished 1-19 had a 17-game losing streak.

The 1985 squad (14-8) beat West High twice and went to the sub-state final before losing to C.R. Washington. One highlight of that season for sure was the play of guard Mark Lumpa, who was named third All-State. Lumpa was also named to All-State teams in football and baseball at City High. Coach Brown resigned following the 1985 season, his eighth year as head coach with one MVC title.

The City High administration again stayed within the "family" as current sophomore coach Tim Linder was named to succeed Don Brown. Tim began an 11-year term as head coach in 1986 with a 12-10 record and a fourth-place MVC finish. That team beat West three times and lost to Burlington in the sub-state.

The next two seasons were 11-9 and 12-8 including four wins over West High, running the streak to 10 consecutive victories over the crosstown rival.

## Second State Title

The last year of the 80's had a spectacular finish after an up-and-down 11-8 regular season and a fifth place MVC finish. With four and sometimes five juniors in the starting lineup, the Little Hawks, after losing the final regular season game, put together a six-game streak through the tournament to win their second State Championship in history by beating Davenport North, 66-55.

Brian Kueter a 6' 7" junior center led the way and was named State Tourney MVP and broke Clay Hargrave's shot block record with 117 for the season. Junior Michael Roan, a 6'4" forward, also was named All-Tournament and had 14 rebounds in the quarterfinal win over East Waterloo. Roan went on to become an All-American tight end at Wisconsin and played for the Tennessee Titans in the NFL.

Byron Young and Shad Flynn, two more juniors, played vital roles. Young's two free throws with 13 seconds left clinched the semifinal victory over Marshalltown. Flynn's leadership at point guard was vital both in the tournament and during the regular season. Flynn's comment summed up the attitude of the team, "I didn't want to leave the court after the game. I didn't want the feeling to end."

64

*1989 - State Champions (2nd State title)*

## 1990's

With four starters returning, 1990 looked very promising indeed for the Little Hawks.

The 1990's started where the 80's left off. The 1989 season ended with a State Championship and four starters returning. With a preseason number one ranking, the Little Hawks were unbeatable early in the season. They won their first 12 games, which ran the winning streak to 18 games, before losing to MVC rival Dubuque Senior. A one-point loss to non-conference foe Davenport West, three games later, was the final loss before the State Championship game.

Five times the Little Hawks scored over 90 points with a school record 105 points in a victory over North Scott. The senior-dominated team finished the regular season 17-2 and were MVC Champs. Prairie, Muscatine and Burlington fell in the District and sub-state, qualifying City High for the State.

The first-round state tournament game was more of the same as City High had an easy 81-57 victory over West Des Moines Valley. The semi-final game was closer, but Ankeny fell, 72-68. This set up a championship game against East Waterloo and a rematch of the 1989 first-round state tournament game.

The final was one of the top all-time state tournament games. East prevailed in overtime by an 89-84 score. This was the highest scoring game in State Tournament history. The defeat left City High with a 22-3 record, which is an all-time record for wins at City High.

Michael Roan and Byron Young were named to the first All-State team following the season. Two wins over West brought the winning streak over the Trojans to 15 in a row.

The 1991 team with 6' 8" Scott Kueter and 6' 5" David Kruse leading the way had a 16-5 mark and two more wins over West running the streak to 17.

In 1992 the Little Hawks returned to the state tournament for the third time in four years. The 18-5 record included two more wins over West and the streak was now 19 in a row.

Fairfield, Prairie and Ft. Madison were dispatched to get the Little Hawks to Des Moines where they met for the third time the East Waterloo Trojans. East pulled out the first round game despite a state tournament record, eight three-point baskets by Jason House. House was named to the All-Tournament team and went on to a fine career with the Hawkeye football squad.

David Kruse was named first All-State forward. He played college basketball at Mankato State and professionally in Europe for several years.

In 1993 the Little Hawks had their first losing record (8-13) since 1983 and started a five-year streak of losing records. The 19-game streak against West was snapped as West won twice, but City High did defeat West in District play.

Following the 1996 season Coach Tim Linder resigned after 11 years and a 140-99 career mark. This is the third most career coaching wins behind the 167 of Bill Holmstrom and the 144 of Francis Merten.

Dave Tremmel, coach at Washington, Iowa, was named the new head coach and remained just two years before taking a coaching job in Newton. Grant Hilton made the third All-State team in 1998, Tremmel's second year. Iowa City West began turning the tables on City High in 1995 and by the end of the 90's had won 14 in a row to off set the earlier 19 won by the Little Hawks.

In 1999 new Coach Denny Thiessen, formally of C.R. Prairie, took the head job and had a first-year record of 8-13. The team did establish new single-game (13) and season (155) totals for three-point baskets.

## 2000's

The year 2000, in Thiessen's second season, saw improvement (10-11) and with four sophomores promoted to the varsity squad the future looked good. The following year with four juniors starting, the team had an outstanding 19-6 record and a berth in the State Tournament.

That 2001 squad had a 16-4 regular season record and finally snapped the string of 17 straight losses to West with three victories including a District Tournament win. In the State tourney the Little Hawks beat Pleasant Valley in the first round, but lost to Urbandale in the semi-finals. In the consolation game MVC rival Wahlert defeated City High for the second time to put the final record at 19-6, the most wins since the record-setting 1990 team won 22. Guard Calvin Davis was named to the second All-State team.

In a shocking event, less that 10 days following the team's fourth-place finish at State, head coach Denny Thiessen, 55, died suddenly. Coach Thiessen was a very popular and respected coach and counselor in his three years at City High. He was known to be a very demanding, but fair coach who would be missed by all who knew him.

With four starters returning from the 2001 State Tournament squad, the season began with high expectations. Curt Johansen of Missouri was named to succeed Denny Thiessen. Despite two regular season losses to West, the Little Hawks won the divisional title with a 14-7 regular season record. A second-round district win over C.R. Prairie set up a sub-state matchup with West High at the Five Seasons Center in Cedar Rapids. Unfortunately the outcome was the same as West won for the third time, 65-48, ending the Little Hawks' season at 15-8.

Calvin Davis was again named All-State. This followed up an All-State football season and prior to winning two individual state titles in track. More about his track exploits in that section. Matt Wooldrik was named captain, the second of an unmatched total of four captaincies he achieved (football, basketball, track and baseball).

Unfortunately the Little Hawks had 4-16 and 9-13 marks in 2003 and 2004. This left City High with just three winning records in the last 12 years (1998, 2001, 2002).

The City High-West rivalry stands 48-42 in favor of the Little Hawks as of the end of the 2004 season. City High had a 19-game winning streak in the rivalry (1985-92) and West followed shortly after with a 17-game streak between 1994 and 2000.

In the 98-year history of "official" City High basketball (1907-2004), there have been twenty-three head coaches with Bill Holmstrom (15 yrs.), Henry Soucek (11 yrs.) and Tim Linder (11 yrs.) having the longest tenures. The Little Hawks posted 1,059 victories over that span.

City High is represented in the IHSAA Basketball Hall of Fame by two coaches, Bill Holmstrom and Denny Thiessen, and four players; Dave Danner (1943), Bob Freeman (1946), Gene Hettrick (1949), and Clay Hargrave (1975).

# All-State Basketball Recognition

City High All-State Basketball players as selected by the <u>Des Moines Register</u>. <u>The Des Moines Register</u> started picking All-State basketball squads in 1921. There was just a one-class system until 1976 when smaller schools were represented by their own teams.

(Iowa Daily Press Association, now known as INA, also picks All-State teams. Those will be listed separately only if they are different players than picked by <u>the Des Moines Register</u>.)

| | | | | |
|---|---|---|---|---|
| 1929 | Ralph Erbe (C) 2nd | | 1959 | Jim Hughes (C) 7th |
| 1929 | Howard Moffit (F) 2nd | | 1962 | Gary Snook (G) 3rd IDPA 2nd |
| 1930 | Howard Moffit (F) 2nd | | 1964 | Donn Haugen (C) 2nd |
| 1936 | Jerry Pooler (G) 4th IDPA 2nd | | 1965 | Mike Wymore (G) 2nd |
| 1938 | Russ Hirt (F) 2nd | | 1967 | Steve Cilek (F) 3rd |
| 1939 | Russ Hirt (F) 2nd IDPA 1st | | 1968 | Steve Piro (F) 4th IDPA 3rd |
| 1939 | Devine (F) 5th | | 1969 | Kevin O'Rourke (G) 5th IDPA 2nd |
| 1941 | Ray Sullivan (F) 2nd IDPA 1st | | 1970 | Kevin Kroeger (F)  IDPA 4th |
| 1942 | Dave Danner (F) 2nd IDPA 1st | | 1971 | Mark Welsh (F) 4th |
| 1943 | Dave Danner (F) 2nd IDPA 1st | | 1973 | Jim Hobart (F) IDPA 5th |
| 1945 | Bob Freeman (F) 3rd | | 1974 | Clay Hargrave (F) 1st |
| 1946 | Bob Freeman (F) 1st | | 1975 | Clay Hargrave (F) 1st |
| 1946 | Harry Dean (G) 3rd | | 1981 | D.J. Carstensen (F) 3rd IDPA 2nd |
| 1947 | Jim Sangster (G) 6th IDPA 3rd | | 1985 | Mark Lumpa (G) INA 3rd |
| 1948 | Gene Hettrick (F) 2nd IDPA 1st | | 1990 | Michael Roan (F) 1st |
| 1949 | Gene Hettrick (F) 1st | | 1990 | Brian Kueter (C) INA 2nd |
| 1949 | Whitey Diehl (F) 6th | | 1990 | Byron Young (G) 2nd |
| 1950 | Bill Fenton (F) 2nd IDPA 1st | | 1992 | David Kruse (C) 2nd INA 1st |
| 1955 | Bill Scott (C) 1st | | 1998 | Grant Hilton (G) 3rd |
| 1955 | Jeff Langston (F) 5th | | 2001 | Calvin Davis (G) 2nd |
| 1958 | Pat Phillips (G) 4th | | 2002 | Calvin Davis (G) 3rd |
| 1959 | Ed Watt (G) 1st | | | |

# Men's Basketball

| Year | W - L | Coach | Captains | Misc. Information |
|------|-------|-------|----------|-------------------|
| 1906 | | | | |
| 1907 | 0-4 | A. F. Siepert | Marshall | |
| 1908 | 4-4 | Jewell | Earl Sangster Arlo Wilson | |
| 1909 | 1-9 | " | Frank Mezik | |
| 1910 | 6-2 | Burr Brown | George O'Brian | Grant Keppler 13 FG / 27 pts. |
| 1911 | 3-2 | (No Coach hired) | Grant Keppler | Keppler on All-State |
| 1912 | 3-5 | Parsons | Ackerman | |
| 1913 | 1-3 | Henry Hudson | | 8 games scheduled |
| 1914 | 1-8 | Beck | Martin McGovern | Mc Govern = 13 FG / 27 pts. New Gym |
| 1915 | 7-7 | " | James Harrison | Played Lincoln, Neb. and won in 7 min., sudden-death OT |
| 1916 | 10-5 | Henry Soucek | Henry Prentiss | |
| 1917 | 17-2 | "       " | Otis Darner | 2nd in State, Darner is All-State along with Fiesler and Konvalinka Won 11 in a row, 6 more in State, State runner-up |
| 1918 | 15-3 | "       " | Otis Darner | Darner 2nd time All-State, At State again and 2 made All-Tour-nament team, State runner-up |
| 1919 | 9-4 | A. P. Twogood | Lyle Brigham | Coach Soucek in WWI |
| 1920 | 11-1 | Henry Soucek | Leo Seemuth | Only loss was in Tournament Won 11 in a row. |
| 1921 | 12-4 | "       " | Joe Figg | Won first 4 games in Tourney, then lost to Davenport, Buck McQuire - Leading scorer with 157 pts. and All-Tournament |
| 1922 | 8-8 | "       " | Clarence Hay | |
| 1923 | 9-6 | "       " | Campbell Beals | Played Tilden of Chicago Lost to U-High in tourney |
| 1924 | 5-6 | "       " | Bill Wallen | Lost to Davenport in tourney |
| 1925 | 13-1 | "       " | Dick Boyles | Undefeated regular season - only loss is in tourney, 2 on All-Tourney team, Won 11 in a row |
| 1926 | 5-8 | "       " | Bob Prentiss | |
| 1927 | 8-6 | "       " | Tracey Shelley | |
| 1928 | 6-9 | Walter Knox | Don Brown | First year for MVC in Basketball |
| 1929 | 10-9 | "       " | Ralph Erbe | Howard Moffit All MVC and All-State teams |
| 1930 | 14-6 | George Wells | Howard Moffit | Moffit All-MVC and All State |
| 1931 | 12-7 | "       " | Eldred Vestermark | Beat Keokuk in Tourney, when Keokuk was 24-0! |

# Men's Basketball

| Year | Record | Coach | Captain(s) | Notes |
|------|--------|-------|-----------|-------|
| 1932 | 6-10 | George Wells | Cleatus Stimmel | 3 starters graduate at midyear |
| 1933 | 9-8 | " " | | |
| 1934 | 13-8 | " " | | |
| 1935 | 10-11 | " " | | |
| 1936 | 16-5 | Frances Merten | Alvin Miller | Played Austin, Minn. & Maplewood H.S. of St. Louis, Won both! Pooler 2nd All State |
| 1937 | 11-8 | " " | | Played Streator, Ill. (lost), Center Jump eliminated after this season |
| 1938 | 15-8 | " " | Wayne Putnam | Played Streator, Ill. again and won, Russ Hirt on All-State |
| 1939 | 16-5 | " " | Russ Hirt | Russ Hirt All-State again |
| 1940 | 9-10 | " " | | |
| 1941 | 18-4 | " " | Ray Sullivan | Sullivan 1st All-State, MVC Champs - first ever! |
| 1942 | 19-6 | " " | John Thompson | 3rd MVC, Dave Danner 1st All-State - leads MVC in scoring Outscored C.R. Wilson 20-1 in 1st quarter |
| 1943 | 15-7 | " " | Dave Danner | 3rd MVC, Danner 1st All-State again, leads MVC in scoring. Played Solon and Sharon Center the same night |
| 1944 | 6-10 | " " | Gene Matthes | |
| 1945 | 14-4 | Wally Schwank | Jim Van Deusen | 1st MVC, Bob Freeman, Jim VanDeusen 1-2 in MVC scoring, Freeman 3rd All-State |
| 1946 | 18-7 | Gil Wilson | Bob Freeman Jim Van Deusen | 3rd MVC, State Champs - 13 straight wins, Freeman 1st All-State, leads MVC in scoring again, Harry Dean 3rd All-State, |
| 1947 | 18-4 | " " | Dick Drake Jim Sangster | 1st MVC (11-0) 1st win at Dav. In 25 yrs., Overnight road trip to Ottumwa & Centerville. Sangster 3rd All-State, Hettrick (just a soph) leads MVC in scoring |
| 1948 | 17-6 | " " | Bob Beals Gene Hettrick | 3rd MVC, Beat Davenport again. Hetrick leads MVC again, 1st All-State, Sets record 237 in 12 games (19.8 ave.) |
| 1949 | 20-2 | " " | Bob Diehl Gene Hettrick | 1st MVC 13-0, 18-1 regular season, including 15 straight wins, Hettrick breaks MVC scoring record (279) Repeats 1st All-State |

# Men's Basketball

| 1950 | 13-6 | Howard Moffit | Bill Fenton | Fenton leads MVC, 183 in 11 games, 6th straight year City High player leads MVC |
|------|------|---------------|-------------|--------------------------------------------|
| 1951 | 11-8 | "      " | Gene Brawner Duane Davis | Defeated C.R. Franklin by 55 pts. (83-28) |
| 1952 | 11-8 | "      " | John White | Jim Freeman is leading scorer, has 4 games of over 25 points |
| 1953 | 8-13 | "      " | | Lost to Clinton in tournament for the 4th straight year. |
| 1954 | *11-5 | Bob Schulz | | *Tourney not included |
| 1955 | 16-8 | Bill Holmstrom | Jeff Langston | 2nd in State, Bill Scott, 1st All-State, sets 6 State Tourney Records, Langston 5th All- State |
| 1956 | 6-14 | "      " | Jim Luper | Luper is leading scorer (208) |
| 1957 | 12-11 | "      " | | Les Nicola = 14 FT, Illinois schools join MVC, C.R. Washington and Jefferson formed |
| 1958 | 14-8 | "      " | Pat Phillips | Team hits 29 of 32 FT vs. Clinton Al Scott had 16 in a row, Phillips 4th All-State |
| 1959 | 14-7 | "      " | Ed Watt | Watt 1st All-State, Jim Hughes 7th All-State |
| 1960 | *9-9 | "      " | Frosty Evashevski | *tournaments not included MVP - Evashevski |
| 1961 | 13-10 | "      " | Clark Jones | Lost to C.R. Washinton in OT at Fieldhouse, District Final |
| 1962 | 10-13 | "      " | | Gary Snook 442 pts. (19.2), 194 rebounds, scored 30 twice |
| 1963 | 6-13 | "      " | Don Rhoades | Beat Cosgrove & U-High in District, but lost to Regina |
| 1964 | 13-8 | "      " | John Gough | Donn Haugen leads MVC in scoring (344 pts.) Gough 12 of 13 FG vs. Clinton, Gough MVP |
| 1965 | 13-8 | "      " | Mike Wymore | Wymore 2nd All-State , Beat Williamsburg in 2 OT at Fieldhouse (District) |
| 1966 | 6-14 | "      " | Dick Rembolt | Lost to Regina in tourney, Rembolt MVP |
| 1967 | 10-11 | "      " | Jerry Frantz | Steve Cilek 3rd All-State, 14 rebounds. Al Jones 15 rebounds & 14 FT, Team hits 36 of 47 FT vs. Muscatine in District, Lost to Regina in District |

# Men's Basketball

| Year | Record | Coach | Players | Notes |
|------|--------|-------|---------|-------|
| 1968 | 14-7 | Bill Holmstrom | Tim Koch<br>Steve Piro | Piro 3rd All-State, Ward Stubbs 15 reb. Koch over 25 pts. 3 times |
| 1969 | 10-13 | " " | Kevin O'Rourke<br>Ward Stubbs | State Tournament, lose to Carroll Kuemper, Holmstrom leaves for Clinton AD job. |
| 1970 | 13-6 | Ron Schnack | Kevin Kroeger | Droeger 4th All-State |
| 1971 | *12-6 | " " | Tom Jacks<br>Mark Welsh | 2nd MVC, Welsh 4th All-State<br>*tournaments not included |
| 1972 | 13-8 | " " | Jim Fransen | C.R.Washington scores 98, C.R. Jefferson scores 92 against City High, MVP - Fransen, Lost in sub-state to Burlington |
| 1973 | 14-11 | " " | Jim Blank | Lose to C.R. Kennedy in State Tourney, soph. transfer Clay Hargrave becomes eligible at mid-year (start of Hargrave era) |
| 1974 | 16-5 | " " | Doug Piro | Lost to Dav. West in Sub-State, Score 94 pts. vs. Hempstead. Hargrave All-State -70 blocked shots, 9 in one game and MVP |
| 1975 | 20-2 | " " | Clay Hargrave | 1st MVC, State Tourney-lost to Ames. Hargrave 1st All-State, 43 pts. vs. Musc. (20 FG), team scoring record 99 pts. vs. South Tama, Hargrave's Career = 1,050 points and 785 rebounds, MVP - Hargrave |
| 1976 | 10-11 | Ken Klein | Dan Cummins | |
| 1977 | 3-16 | " " | Andy Knoedel<br>Elliott Smith | MVP - Andy Knoedel |
| 1978 | 10-9 | Don Brown | Jerry Johnson | Lost to I.C. West in OT in District |
| 1979 | 7-11 | " " | Dave Chambers | Regina scores 98 |
| 1980 | 8-11 | " " | Andy Frantz<br>Bryant Robinson | |
| 1981 | 16-4 | " " | | MVC co-Champs<br>D.J. Carstensen 2nd All-State |
| 1982 | 5-15 | " " | Todd Black<br>Steve Frantz | MVP - Todd Black |
| 1983 | 1-19 | " " | Brad Peterson | Scott Flynn MVP |
| 1984 | 12-10 | " " | Scott Flynn<br>Tim Smith | 4th MVC, Lose to State Champs 43-40 in sub-state Final, MVP - Paul Zweiner |
| 1985 | 14-8 | " " | | MVP - Jeff Schnack |
| 1986 | 12-10 | Tim Linder | | MVP - Scott Hansen |

# Men's Basketball

| Year | Record | Coach | Captains | Notes |
|------|--------|-------|----------|-------|
| 1987 | 11-9 | Tim Linder | | |
| 1988 | 12-8 | " " | | Eric Washpun 1st team MVC |
| 1989 | 17-8 | " " | | State Champs - defeated East Waterloo, Marshalltown, Davenport North, Second State title ever |
| 1990 | 22-3 | " " | | 1st MVC, State runner-up, Byron Young and Michael Roan 1st team All-State, Scored 105 points vs. North Scott |
| 1991 | 16-5 | " " | | MVC (10-4) |
| 1992 | 18-5 | " " | | Jason House - Record 8 -3 pt. goals, in 1 game during State Tournament, David Kruse 1[st]All-State, Lost to East Waterloo, 19-game winning streak vs. I.C. West |
| 1993 | 8-13 | " " | | Lost to Ottumwa in 2nd round at District, Lost to I.C. West twice, beat them in District |
| 1994 | 9-12 | " " | | Lost to Davenport West in District |
| 1995 | 5-15 | " " | Scott Lantz Bill Wildman | MVP - Adam Loria Lost to Muscatine in District |
| 1996 | 10-11 | " " | Adam Loria Sharif Youesef | MVC (9-7) |
| 1997 | 8-12 | Dave Tremmel | Rob Fumerton Kevin Suchomel | MVP - Fumerton and Grant Hilton, Beat Burlington, Lost to I.C. West in District |
| 1998 | 11-10 | " " | Grant Hilton Leroy Watley | MVP - Leroy Watley Grant Hilton 3rd All-State |
| 1999 | 8-13 | Denny Thiessen | Josh Hobart Jon Houghton Nick Linder | MVC (4-12) MVP - Josh Hobart |
| 2000 | 10-11 | " " | Brian Claussen Matt Reinhold | 4th MVC, MVP - Lawrence Hill, Record # of 3 pts. made in 1 game |
| 2001 | 19-6 | " " | Quincy Ely-Cate Nick Pirotte | 4th in State Tourney, MVP - Calvin Davis and 2nd All-State |
| 2002 | 15-8 | Curt Johansen | Calvin Davis Matt Wooldrik | 1st MVC, MVP - Lawrence Hill, Calvin Davis 3rd All-State, lost to I.C. West in District |
| 2003 | 4-16 | " " | Ian Ely-Cate Scott Houghton | MVP - Caleb Recker |
| 2004 | 9-13 | " " | Ryan Kennedy Michael Sabers | MVP - Ryan Kennedy 7th Division, lost to C.R. Kennedy in first round of District |

# Women's Basketball 1974-2004

Women's basketball was the next to last sport added for women at City High with the first game being played in the 1973-74 school year.

Basketball in Iowa for women was a very unique sport as it was played in the six-on-six style with three guards at one end of the floor and three forwards at the other end . Only the forwards could shoot and only two dribbles were allowed each time a player touched the ball. Iowa was one of the last states to use this type of game.

*First women's Basketball team, 1973-74*

Women's basketball was limited to the small towns of Iowa and no big cities like Des Moines, Waterloo or the MVC cities had teams. Finally after much pressure large schools all over the state added women's basketball.

The inaugural squad at City High was coached by Kay Pundt, a physical education teacher at City High and former basketball player. The first game ever played was a 62-42 victory over Cedar Rapids Kennedy, which likewise was playing its first game ever. The team actually won its first three games and finished with a 5-8 record. Included were two regular season wins over West High, although West High was victorious in the first tournament game ever played by both schools.

In 1975 Dianne Havens, who as Dianne Frieden was a Hall of Fame basketball player in Iowa high school ranks, succeeded Kay Pundt. Coach Havens remained two seasons. The 1975 team won six games and junior Ruth Hibbelar scored a record 50 points in one game. That total still stands as a City High record. The Little Hawks beat West twice. In 1976 with a 13-8 record the team advanced out of the sectionals for the first time, but lost to Vinton. A sectional win over West was a highlight.

In 1977, Ken Putney, who had assisted Dianne Havens, became the new head coach and started a seven-year term as the head coach.

At each level of tournament play, one player from each team was selected by their team to take part in a free throw contest. The winner at each level went on to the next tournament even if their team did not advance. Tracy Taylor, of the 1977 team, won both the Sectional and District Championship to advance to the Regional.

Taylor was the leading scorer with 452 points and guard Kristi Kinney led the defense with 85 rebounds on Coach Putney's first team. Pam Niermann (377 points) and Shelly Freeman (125 rebounds) set records in 1978.

*1979 team - Scoring and Rebounding records*

In 1979 Pam Niermann established a new high in scoring with 688 points (29.9). That mark still stands today. Shelly Freeman led the defense with a new record, 152 rebounds, and Lynn Ries also broke the old record with 134 rebounds. The 1977 squad made it to Districts again and finished with a 15-8 mark. Chris Skelly had the honor of being chosen captain both in 1978 and 1979.

## 1980's

In 1980 Shelly Smith led with 356 points and sophomore Lisa Nicola scored 165. Kami Frantz led the defense with 107 rebounds. Carla Williams and Janet Skog were also top players.

The 1981 Little Hawks won a record 16 games with just five losses and finished second in the MVC. The team led the MVC in defense. Lisa Nicola led the scoring with 499 points (23.7) and Kami Frantz was named fourth team All-State and Area Player of the Year.

The 1982 squad followed up with a 15-win season and several records. An all-time team scoring record was set when they scored 100 points against Dubuque Wahlert. They earlier set the mark with 88 against West. They advanced to the Regional Tournament for the first time and lost to perennial power Mediapolis. Lisa Nicola scored 603 points (28.7) and set the City High career scoring mark with a three-year total of 1,267. Two more victories over West brought the streak to five.

The 1983 squad was Sectional Champs in Coach Putney's final season. They lost to Marshalltown in the Regional. Michele Conlon recalls, "Our basketball coach Ken Putney yelling at me during the game to go to state in Marshalltown, "Quit shooting the 3's!" It was the inaugural year for the 3-point shot and I had already shot a few air balls just that night (from WAY too far out…but I was open.) Late in the game we were way down and desperate. So, I launched a couple more 3-point shots. They went in! The other team called a time out. Coach Putney came over to me and begged, "Keep shooting the 3's, keep shooting the 3's!" We lost the game but have some fun laughs about my horrible shooting judgment."

Connie Hargrave, Michele Conlon, Beth Lainson and Marti Miller were the leaders. Ken Putney finished his career with 75 wins, the most of any coach in the six-player game at City High. Michele Conlon shared another memory: "Coach Putney pulled us into the locker room during basketball practice. He chewed us out for lack of effort. On the first play back on the court my teammate,

Connie Hargrave, dribbled the ball, <u>spun</u> it on her finger and threw it behind her back to a teammate. I can still hear the gasps by the team. And, I can still see the smile on Coach Putney's face."

Another of Michele's memories was "Watching teammate Beth Lainson pull a plastic race car, tethered by fishing line, behind one of the yellow buses on our way to a basketball game in Dubuque. The little car rode smoothly on the highway until the bus driver saw it, pulled over and everyone got in trouble."

In 1984 the last year of six-on-six basketball the Little Hawks suffered through their worst season. Kevin Klein took over for Ken Putney and with all starters from the previous season gone, had City High's only winless season at 0-19.

## *Five-on-Five era begins*

The five-on-five era began in 1985 with an opening victory and an overall season record of 6-14. Included were two victories over West in the first five-player games between the two schools. The season ended with a first-round tournament loss to MVC rival C.R. Washington, also in their first year of five-on-five.

The 1986 season saw the Little Hawks win 13 games, which would be the most until 1990. They did beat West three times, including a 44-41 overtime victory in the tournament. The 1987 season was Kevin Klein's fourth and final season as head coach.

The last three seasons of the 80's had losing records including a 1-20 season, which was the most losses ever for City High. The only win of the year came in the first round of the tournament when they beat West Branch. The next game, which was the third loss of the year to West, ended their season. Don Brown, former men's coach, took over the program in 1988 and coached the next four seasons.

## *1990's*

A brief turnaround took place in 1990 as the team won a then record 17 games which was the best win total until it was matched in 1999. Michelle Nason was named first All-State and selected as Miss Iowa Basketball as the top women's player in the State. She remains the only City High basketball player to be given this honor.

Don Brown's last year was 1991. Assistant coach and Hall of Fame player Tina Koepnick took over the program in 1992. Tina coached three seasons. Her 1993 team beat West three times and won three tournament games before losing in the Regionals to top-rated Solon.

In Coach Koepnick's final season, the Little Hawks split with West during the season, then won the tourney match up by winning the District Championship. A Regional loss to Muscatine ended their season.

In 1995 Brent Brown was named to succeed Tina Koepnick. As Don's son, they became the first father-son combination to ever be head coaches at City High. Brent's first two seasons were 4-15 and 7-13, but they rebounded to a 13-8 mark in 1997 and the first-ever MVC title for the Little Hawks in women's basketball. They lost to West in the tourney after splitting in the regular season.

The 14 wins the next season (1998) were the most since the 17 wins recorded in 1990. The Little Hawks finished third in the MVC and lost to West Des Moines Dowling in the sub-state final. Brent Brown resigned following this season, his fourth.

In 1999 Bill McTaggart, an Iowa City native who was coaching in Texas, was named the new coach. Coach McTaggart is still the head coach at this writing and will tie Ken Putney for the longest term as head coach with his seventh in the 2004-05 season.

Coach McTaggart's first team tied the record for most wins in a season, 17-4. His team won the first nine games of the season and went on to finish second in the MVC with a 13-3 conference mark. Tanya Hammes was named first All-State forward. Three wins over West, including one in the tourney, made it five in a row over West to end the decade. A loss to CR Xavier in the District final ended the season.

## 2000's

The early years of the new century proved to be outstanding. In 2000 a new record for wins was established with a 19-4 record and an MVC Championship. The team also set a record for most points in a season. Junior Kelsie Linder set a new school record for assists with 100. Jill Frantz and Shannon St. John shared the MVP honors.

*First ever State Tournament team, 2001*

The win record lasted just one season as the 2001 team won 22 games and sent the Little Hawks to their first-ever State Tournament. The team won the first 13 games of the season to establish another mark. Jill Frantz won her second MVP award. West Des Moines Dowling ended the best-ever season for City High in the first round of the State Tourney. Two victories over West ran the streak to 10 in a row.

In 2002 with most of the 2001 State Tourney team gone, the Little Hawks had a 10-13 season, but beat West three times to run the consecutive victory streak to 13. Stacey Duarte was MVP.

The 2003 team with many young players posted a 13-9 mark. Jamie Frantz, Megan Gatens, Monica Mims and MVP Jameia Bush were the team leaders. The streak against West moved to 15.

In 2004 a 19-5 record brought the Little Hawks an MVC title and a berth in the State Tournament for the second time ever. The team had another great start as they won their first 10 games before a minor mid-season slump saw three straight losses including one to West that stopped the City High streak at 16 straight over West.

After one more loss, City High reeled off eight straight wins to qualify for the State Tournament. A loss to Des Moines Hoover at State ended the run. Jameia Bush and Calie Sobaski were named to the second All-State team. Coach McTaggart was named MVC and Southeast Iowa Coach of the Year. The game that put the Little Hawks into the State Tourney was the one-hundredth victory of Bill McTaggart's career at City High.

*2003 team - 15-game winning streak vs. West*

# Women's Basketball

| Year | W - L | Coach | Captains | Misc Information |
|------|-------|-------|----------|------------------|
| 1974 | 5-8 | Kay Pundt | | 1st year for this sport |
| 1975 | 6-10 | Dianne Havens | | Ruth Hibbeler scores 50 points. |
| 1976 | 13-8 | " " | LuAnn Baker<br>Ruth Hibbeler | 3rd MVC, 1st time in Districts<br>Ruth Hibbeler MVP |
| 1977 | 4-15 | Ken Putney | Debbie Frank<br>Tracy Taylor | Taylor was Sectional and District FT Champ. Taylor scored 452 points, Kristi Kinney had 85 Rebounds |
| 1978 | 10-9 | " " | Mary Ahern<br>Chris Skelly<br>Jackie Wright | Pam Niermann scored 377 points, Michelle Freeman had 125 rebounds |
| 1979 | 15-8 | " " | Lynn Ries<br>Chris Skelly | Made it to Districts again. Pam Niermann scored 688 points, Freeman had 152 and Ries 134 rebounds |
| 1980 | 6-15 | " " | Janet Skog<br>Carla Williams | Shelley Smith scored 356 points and Lisa Nicola had 165, Kami Frantz had 107 rebounds |
| 1981 | 16-5 | " " | Kate Daniher<br>Kami Frantz<br>Lisa Nicola | 2nd MVC, team leads MVC in defense, Nicola scored 499 points, Frantz was 4th All-State and Area Player of the Year |
| 1982 | 15-6 | " " | Lisa Nicola<br>Colleen Powell | 1st MVC, 1st Sect., Powell 2nd team MVC, Nicola scored 603 pts., 3rd in MVC scoring, sets career record: 1,267 points. Team scored 100 points vs. Wahlert. |
| 1983 | 9-13 | " " | Beth Lainson<br>Marti Miller | MVC (3-11), Sectional Champs, Connie Hargrave and Lainson All-MVC |
| 1984 | 0-19 | Kevin Klein | Amy Smothers<br>Jenny Lee<br>Susan Pietrzyk | Pietrzyk MVP,<br>last year of 6-on-6. |
| 1985 | 6-14 | " " | Lara Paris | 1st year 5-on-5 basketball won opening game, MVP - Lara Paris |
| 1986 | 13-11 | " " | Gayle Oakes<br>Lara Paris<br>Greta Sokoloff | MVC (7-8), MVP - Sara Kennedy |
| 1987 | 6-13 | " " | | MVC (2-10) |

# Women's Basketball

| Year | Record | Coach | Players | Notes |
|---|---|---|---|---|
| 1988 | 1-20 | Don Brown | | MVC (0-14), lost 19 straight |
| 1989 | 8-12 | " " | | MVC (4-10) |
| 1990 | 17-5 | Don Brown | | Michelle Nason 1st All-State and Miss Iowa Basketball |
| 1991 | 6-14 | " " | | MVC (4-10) |
| 1992 | 5-15 | Tina Koepnick | | MVC (2-12) |
| 1993 | 12-11 | " " | | Beat I.C. West three times |
| 1994 | 12-9 | " " | Angela Goepferd Kathie Kempf | MVC ( 9-7), District Champs MVP - Marie Haag |
| 1995 | 4-15 | Brent Brown | | |
| 1996 | 7-13 | " " | Julie Baker Jessica House | MVC (6-10), MVP - Jessica House |
| 1997 | 13-8 | " " | Jill Blake Kelly Triplett | MVC Champs - First ever! MVP Tanya Hammes |
| 1998 | 14-8 | " " | Kami Berry Emmy Cilek Kari Nace | 3rd MVC (9-7)  lost to Dowling in Sub State Final (Dowling won State), MVP - Tanya Hammes |
| 1999 | 17-4 | Bill McTaggart | Kami Berry Emmy Cilek Tanya Hammes | 2nd MVC (13-3), started season 9-0,  Tanya Hammes MVP and 1st All-State |
| 2000 | 19-4 | " " | Sara Brummond Nicole Gatens Kristen George Shannon St. John | 1st MVC, most wins in a season, MVP - Jill Frantz and Shannon St. John |
| 2001 | 22-3 | " " | Jill Frantz Kelsie Linder | 1st MVC, most wins, won first 13 games, first time at State Tournament, MVP - Jill Frantz |
| 2002 | 10-13 | " " | Stacey Duarte Monica Mims | 4th MVC, MVP - Stacey Duarte |
| 2003 | 13-9 | " " | Jamie Frantz Megan Gatens Monica Mims | MVP - Jameia Bush |
| 2004 | 19-5 | " " | Jamie Frantz Katie Krei Calie Sobaski | 1st MVC, won first 10 games, State Qualifier (lost 1st round), Jameia Bush MVP, 1st Team MVC and 2nd Team State, Sobaski 1st MVC, 2nd team State, McTaggert MVC & SE District Coach of the Year. |

# Men's Swimming 1921-2004

## The Early Years

Swimming was introduced as a sport for City High in 1921. H. C. Soucek, coach of most of the sports teams at the time, was the coach. There was a pool at the high school where the team practiced. The only meet information found was participation in the U. of Iowa meet, considered to be the state championship of the time. The squad finished second to West Des Moines. The team finished second in the relay (Boyles, Lambert, Littig, Gilpin). Gilpin and McCollister got thirds and Littig got a fourth.

*Original pool in old high school, 1924*

I found only a smattering of results for 1922-24 with a fifth place at the U. of Iowa meet in 1922 and a dual meet victory over University High in 1924. Apparently swimming was dropped as a sport after 1924, as no information was listed in any yearbooks until 1951.

Irving Weber, noted Iowa City historian and All-American swimmer for the Hawkeyes, was a City High graduate in 1918 and he was mentioned as helping coach the teams in the early 1920's.

## 1950's

In 1951, Chic Forwald, a 1925 City High graduate who had been a member of the 1923 and 1924 swim teams and was now a member of the faculty, sponsored a team. He arranged for Duane Draves, the captain of the University of Iowa swim team, to be the coach of this revival of City High swimming.

The 1951 team consisted of eight members. The team entered the state meet and scored three points. The team worked out in the old armory pool on the U. of Iowa campus (across the street from where Hubbard park is now located). An interesting note was that because this was a male-only building, the boys swam in the nude.

The following season, 1952, there was no team. Bob Reed, a member of the 1951 squad and who would have been on the 1952 squad, recalled, "we didn't have a team that next year". Reed went on to become an All-American swimmer for the Hawkeyes.

In 1953, under the direction of Arnold Fransen, the team was revived. Fransen coached through the 1956 season where again the team was disbanded until its revival permanently in 1965.

The 1953 and 1954 teams entered only the state meet, where they finished fifth both years. Individual placers were not noted. In 1955 and 1956, dual meet records of 1-3 and 0-3 were mentioned in the yearbooks. From 1957 to 1964 there were no teams.

# 1960's

During the 1965 season, under the coaching of Dennis Vokalek, the Little Hawks had a 1-7 season and a 13th place finish in the State meet. Workouts were held at the Iowa City Recreation pool. Vokalek's 1966 squad was fourth in the District meet and had an excellent sixth-place showing at the State meet. Bill Van Epps was the leader of that squad. Vokalek left after the 1967 season to take a coaching position out of state.

The next three seasons saw three different coaches. Swimmers Steve Full, Ted Ostrem, Jon Phillips and diver Jerry Full led those teams.

# 1970's

In 1970 Ralph Kryder was hired and began a ten-year career as head coach of both the men's and women's swim programs.

Low numbers and lack of a stable practice facility and practice times, handicapped the 1970's. West High, which opened in 1969 and which also had no pool, practiced with City High and the same coach handled both programs, although the teams were separated at meets.

From 1970 through 1974 the team finished no higher than sixth at the District meet. In 1971 Terry Riley finished second in the State 100-yard breaststroke for the highest individual finish in history to that point. The 1975 team had the highest district finish, fourth, since the 1966 squad, which also finished fourth. Bill Buxton and Tracy Stamp led that team.

The 1976 team did one better as they finished third in the District, fifth in the MVC and 12th at State, all high points for the program. Chuck Klasson, Steve Noel and Bruce Ogeson were the leaders. In 1977 the team repeated its third place District finish with John Chambers and Mike Noel the leaders.

Little Hawk MVP swimmers are now honored with the John Chambers award in honor of the late John Chambers.

In 1978 Dirk Wilkening finished runner-up in the State Diving competition. Jim Heininger, Paul Kienzle and Steve Stein led the teams in 1978 and '79 respectively. The year 1979 was also the 10th and last year for Ralph Kryder as coach of City High swimming.

# 1980's

In 1980 John Fitzpatrick was named the coach to replace Ralph Kryder. John coached just one season, as did the next two coaches. In 1983 Sue Chadima became the fifth coach in five seasons of the Little Hawk swim team. She also became the second woman ever to be named head coach of a men's sport at City High. She coached for 10 seasons to match the longevity of Ralph Kryder.

The Little Hawks did not place higher than fifth in the District the first eight years of the 1980's. John Clancy ('81), Chris Nielsen ('82), Tim Zaiser ('83), Mike Geraghty ('84), Scott Kisker ('85), and Kurt Vanderhoef ('86) were listed as MVP's in that time span.

The 1989 team recorded the highest District finish (fourth) since 1977 and had an 11th place State finish.

# 1990's

In 1990 the Little Hawks had the first of two straight undefeated dual meet records, 7-0 both years. This team started a three-year streak of finishing second in the MVC and District. The 1990 and 1991 teams both finished third at State with Jose Hildago winning the State Diving title in both years.

The 1992 team lost a dual meet for the first time in three years, finishing with a 7-1 record. This team was also the 10th and final season for Coach Chadima.

Doug Helm was named to succeed Sue Chadima in 1993. He remained just one year. That squad had finishes of third (MVC), second (District) and third (State). Derrick Abromeit took over

*1991 team - 3rd in State, unbeaten regular season*

in 1994 and stayed two seasons. His first team matched the previous season finishes in the MVC, District and State.

For the first time in City High men's swimming competition, the Little Hawks won a State swimming event. The 400 freestyle relay team of John Herr, Kamden Draper, Jacob Everhart and Victor Sosa won the State title in 1994.

Diving was discontinued as an event following the 1994 season.

The year 1995, which was Abromeit's second and final season as head coach, also saw the first individual event winner in City High history. Matt Hamer won the 100 breaststroke title and led the Little Hawks to fifth in the MVC, fourth in the District and 12th at State. As of this writing this was the last event won at the State for the Little Hawks. Matt Hamer returned to be a head coach in 2005.

Phil Luebke was named the head coach in 1996 and remained the head coach for five seasons. The 1997 season was the last season that City High remained solely under the banner of City High. That team was fourth in both the MVC and District.

The following season (1998), due to declining numbers, the programs of City High and West combined into one team to be known as Iowa City. Third place finishes in both the MVC and District highlighted that season. Nathan Kron and Chris Andino were the leaders.

JOHN HERR   MARIO SOSA
JACOB EVERHART   KAMDEN DRAPER
STATE CHAMPIONS
400 METER FREE RELAY
SWIMMING
1994

*1994 - State 400 Freestyle Relay Champions*

82

# 2000's

Zach White and Adam Yack led the combined team to third place MVC and District finishes and a seventh place at the State meet in 2000.

There was another new coach in 2001, Bogdan Deac, who remained just one season. Rob Meiezniowski was hired in 2002 and that team won the first MVC title in City High history. The team had a second place District finish. Scott Stimmel, Matt Shepard, and Brandon Fiagle were the leaders.

Meiezniowski stayed through the 2004 season. The 2004 team finished third in Districts. Peter Cilek was the captain of this team. Matt Hamer, a 1995 City High graduate and former State Champion, was named to succeed Meieznoiwski for the 2005 season.

In the 49-year history (1921-2004) of the City High men's swimming program there have been 16 different coaches, eight of whom stayed just one season, and almost as many locations where the team has had to practice. The team has won four State events in its history, two diving titles (1990 and 1991), one relay (1994), and one individual event (1995).

*2004 team - 3rd in District*

# Men's Swimming

| Year | W - L | Coach | Captains | Misc. Information |
|---|---|---|---|---|
| 1921 | | H.C. Soucek | | Swimming introduced as sport. U. of I. Meet (State Meet then) Iowa City 2$^{nd}$ to West Des Moines |
| 1922 | | "      " | | 5$^{th}$ U. of I. State Meet |
| 1923 | | "      " | | |
| 1924 | | "      " | | Beat U-High in dual |
| | | | | |
| 1951 | | Chic Forwald Dwayne Draves | | 5$^{th}$ at State - 3 points, 8 on the team, Draves - student on U.I. swim team |
| 1952 | | NO TEAM | | |
| 1953 | | Arnold Fransen | | 5$^{th}$ at State - 4 points |
| 1954 | | "      " | | 5$^{th}$ at State - 6 points only meet entered |
| 1955 | 1-3 duals | "      " | | Failed to place at State |
| 1956 | 0-3 | "      " | | |
| 1957 | | **NO TEAM 1957-1964** | | |
| | | | | |
| 1965 | 1-7 duals | Dennis Vokalek | | 7$^{th}$ District, 13$^{th}$ State |
| 1966 | 4-4 | "      " | Bill Van Epps | 7$^{TH}$ MVC, 4$^{th}$ District, 6$^{th}$ State |
| 1967 | 0-11 | "      " | Bob Allen | 9$^{TH}$ MVC, No placers at State |
| 1968 | 1-10 | John Raffensperger | Steve Full | 9$^{th}$ MVC, 8$^{th}$ District |
| 1969 | 0-11 | Maurice LeVois | Ted Ostrem Jon Phillips | 6$^{th}$ District |
| 1970 | 0-11 | Ralph Kryder | Jerry Full | 6$^{TH}$ District |
| 1971 | 6-7 | "      " | Doug Ryan | 6$^{th}$ District, 13$^{th}$ State, Terry Riley 2$^{nd}$ State 100 breaststroke |
| 1972 | 4-6 | "      " | Jim Ahlgren | 6$^{th}$ MVC, 8$^{th}$ District |
| 1973 | 3-6 | "      " | Terry Riley Arturo Salinas | 7$^{th}$ District |
| 1974 | 8-3 | "      " | Jeff Whitebook | 8$^{th}$ MVC |
| 1975 | 5-6 | "      " | Bill Buxton Tracy Stamp | 6$^{th}$ MVC, 4$^{th}$ District |
| 1976 | 4-4 | "      " | Chuck Klasson Steve Noel Bruce Ogeson | 5$^{th}$ MVC, 3$^{rd}$ District, |
| 1977 | | "      " | John Chambers Mike Noel | 6$^{th}$ MVC, 3$^{rd}$ District, |
| 1978 | | "      " | Jim Heininger Paul Kienzle | 7$^{th}$ MVC, Dirk Wilkening MVP and 2$^{nd}$ State diving |
| 1979 | 4-7 | "      " | Steve Stein | 6$^{th}$ MVC, 7$^{th}$ District |
| 1980 | 2-11 | John Fitzpatrick | Ross Amundson John Clancy Kjell Holtsmark | 5$^{th}$ MVC, 8$^{th}$ District |
| 1981 | 3-5 | Paul Eaton | John Clancy | 8$^{th}$ MVC, 8$^{th}$ District MVP - Clancy |
| 1982 | 1-9 | Ian Bullock | Brian Kennedy | 8$^{th}$ MVC, Chris Nielsen MVP |

# Men's Swimming

| Year | Record | Coach | Captains | Notes |
|------|--------|-------|----------|-------|
| 1983 | 0-7 | Sue Chadima | Chris Nielsen<br>Tim Zaiser | 6th District, MVP Zaiser<br>2nd woman to coach Boys' sport |
| 1984 | 2-6 | " " | Mike Geraghty<br>Joe Hart | 4th MVC, 5th District,<br>Geraghty MVP |
| 1985 | 1-6 | " " | Scott Kisker<br>Ivan Lorkovic | 5th MVC, 5th Distict, MVP - Scott Kisker, 3rd State breaststroke Kurt Vanderhoef |
| 1986 | 0-7 | " " | Jay Dutton<br>Rod Lembke | 7th MVC, 5th District<br>MVP - Kurt Vanderhoef |
| 1987 | 0-7 | " " | | 5th MVC, 5th District, 11th State |
| 1988 | 2-3-2 | " " | | 5th MVC, 7th District |
| 1989 | 4-2 | Sue Chadima Chelf | | 5th MVC, 4th District, 11th State |
| 1990 | 7-0 | " " | | 2nd MVC, 2nd District, 3rd State, Jose Hildago State - Diving Champion |
| 1991 | 7-0 | " " " | | 2nd MVC, 2nd District , 3rd State, Hildago repeats 1st State Diving |
| 1992 | 7-1 | " " " | | 2nd MVC, 2nd District, 6th State |
| 1993 | 3-4 | Doug Helm | | 3rd MVC, 2nd District, 3rd State |
| 1994 | 7-1 | Derrick Abromeit | Jacob Everhart<br>Victor Sosa | 3rd MVC, 2nd District, 3rd State, 400 Free Relay State Champs (John Herr,Kamden Draper, Everhart, Sosa), Diving discontinued as an event after this season |
| 1995 | 3-5 | " " | Matt Hamer<br>Steve Tomblin | 5th MVC, 4th District, 12th State, Matt Hamer 1st State 100 breast-stroke, MVP - Kamden Draper |
| 1996 | 0-6 | Phil Luebke | Jon Brentner<br>Justin Kerstetter<br>Nate Kron | 8th MVC, 6th District<br>MVP - Justin Kerstetter |
| 1997 | 6-2 | " " | | 4th MVC, 4th District<br>MVP - Chris Andino |
| 1998 | 6-5 | " " | Chris Andino<br>Nathan Kron | Combined program with West, 3rd MVC, 3rd District, 12th State, MVP - Nathan Kron |
| 1999 | 4-3 | Phil Luebke | Andrew Talman | 7th MVC, MVP - Andrew Talman |
| 2000 | | " " | Zach White<br>Adam Yack | 3rd MVC, 3rd District, 7th State, MVP - Adam Yack |
| 2001 | 3-5 | Bogdan Deac | Dale Doershak | 7th MVC, 5th District<br>MVP - Keil Anderson |
| 2002 | 9-3 | Rob Meiezniowski | Brandon Fiagle | 1st MVC, 2nd District<br>MVP - Scott Stimmel |
| 2003 | 5-4 | " " | Scott Stimmel | MVP - Matt Shephard |
| 2004 | 6-3 | " " | Peter Cilek | 3rd District, 4th MVC |
| 2005 | | Matt Hamer | | |

# Wrestling 1954-2004

## 1950's

The wrestling program was started in the fall of 1953. No matches were held and Frank Bates was the coach of this first squad. The wrestlers did not have a place to wrestle so they moved mats into the attic of Central junior High School. With 20 boys taking part, things were fine until winter set in. Because there was no heat they were forced to find another practice room. The team was allowed to use the basement of Henry Sabin Elementary School for this purpose.

The next season practice sessions were moved to the all-purpose room at nearby Herbert Hoover Elementary School. This proved much better because of the close proximity to City High. That season, four matches were held and a record of 3-1 was achieved. Grant Grimm had the honor of recording the first pin in City High history. Dick Summerwill and Don Coulter also had wins in the first-ever match versus C.R. Wilson in 1954.

In 1955 the Little Hawks had a 3-3 record and the team finished fifth in the District meet. State qualifier Don Coulter recorded the first-ever pin for City High at State, but did not place.

The 1956 team had a full schedule of matches and practices moved back to the Junior High. In 1957 Clyde Bean replaced Frank Bates as the head coach and started a long (35 years) and successful tenure as coach of the wrestling program. His first team had a 1-14 record, but within four years had the first MVC wrestling championship in City High history.

Steve Machovic closed out the 50's by becoming City High's first State Champion wrestler when he won the 165-lb. title. A sophomore Butch Frantz placed second at 154 lbs. The team record was 17-1-1. The 1959 team finished second at the District and sixth at State.

## 1960's

The 1960's decade produced some excellent individuals and teams. In 1960 Don Westcott (154 lbs.) became the second Little Hawk to win a State title. That team had the first District title for City High and was third in both the MVC and State. Three Little Hawks placed second: Steve Weeber (112), Roy Frantz (165), and Steve Caldwell (Hwt.). The year 1961 saw the first MVC team title and a 12-2 record and the third individual State title as Butch Frantz won the 175-lb. crown. Kelly Donham, Steve Weeber and Tony Welt also placed.

In 1962 Jim Evashevski (second), Jim McGinness (third), and Don Hershberger placed. The next season the team had a third place finish. Steve Moss and John Rate were second and Bob Bream and Doug Woods were third. In 1964 Bob Bream became City

*Coach Bean and undefeated State Champ Bill Knight*

High's fourth State Champion and the team was sixth at State. In 1966 Bill Knight placed in his first-of-three State meets.

The 1967 and 1968 teams were the best of the decade. The Little Hawks just missed the State title in 1967 with a second-place finish. Heavyweight Roger Collins won a State title and Dennis Doderer (second) and Bill Knight (third) also placed. The 1968 team followed up with a third place finish, 112-lb. Bill Knight (29-0) and 154-lb. John Evashevski both won State titles. Doug Davis was third at 95. The 1969 squad finished the decade with a fifth place finish as Davis moved up to second at State as did Mike Bostwick (120) and Steve Barnes (138). The 1960's saw the Little Hawks with an 87-33-4 record, nine top 10 State finishes and six individual State Champions.

# 1970's

The early 70's saw the wrestling program faced with the same numbers problem that other Little Hawk programs faced. With enrollment in the 700 range, larger MVC schools had an advantage. Highlights of the early 70's were a 9-3 record in 1970, and Tom Lepic's 27-4 record and second in the State in 1971. Jim Aldeman (98) was also third that season. Rick Griffin (Hwt.) placed twice, in 1974 and 1975, and Bob Fobian, Bill Hoffman and Rob Myers also did well those years.

The last three seasons of the decade saw a dramatic turnaround with records of 10-1 (1977), 11-0 (1978) and 10-0 (1979). All three of these teams won MVC titles and the 1977 unit was District Champion as well. In 1977 Jay Hilgenberg (second), Tom Riley (third), and Eric Klasson (fifth) led the team. Heavyweight Eric Klasson and 126-lb. Tim

*1971 Coach Bean with wrestlers Lepic and Aldeman*

Riley were State Champions in 1978. Riley followed that with a repeat win at 126-lbs. in 1979 with Steve Klasson getting third at 185. The great finish brought the decade mark to 76-32-1 in dual competition and three MVC titles.

# 1980's

In 1981 the team was District Champion and third in the MVC. They followed in 1983 with an unbeaten MVC record (7-0), a 9-2 overall mark and MVC and District Championships. John Abadi (98 lbs.) won a State Championship and heavyweight Andy Haman finished second. The 1984 and 1985 teams were also MVC Champs to run the streak to three in a row. Andy Haman (Hwt.) was State Champ and Andy Petersen (171) was runner-up.

In 1986 the MVC title streak went to four and Pat Waters (138 lbs.) was an undefeated State Champ and recorded a record 25 pins. Kenny Stecher won the 105-lb. State title the following year (1987). The 1980's ended with a 75-36-6 dual mark, three MVC titles and four individual State winners.

# 1990's

The 1990's proved to be a true "golden" era for City High wrestling. The 1990 team kicked off the decade with a 13-7-1 mark, a District title and second in the State Dual Team tournament. Freshman Jeff McGinness began what would be one of the State of Iowa's most prolific careers with an undefeated State Championship at 103 lbs. Casey Hesseltine also won the 171-lb. title in 1990.

In 1991, the Little Hawks were MVC and District Champs and Jeff McGinness won his second straight title moving up to 112 lbs., but remaining undefeated. The team finished ninth in the State in the 35th and final season for Coach Clyde Bean.

Coach Bean's career record ended at 276-137-15, with nine MVC Titles, six District titles, and 17 individual State Champions.

Brad Smith, a highly successful coach at Lisbon, Iowa, succeeded Coach Bean in 1992. Coach Smith's first team had a 15-8 dual record, but won MVC, District and the Little Hawks' first-ever State Traditional and Dual Team titles. The team was led by 160-lb. State Champion Louis Pelsang and Jeff McGinness, who won his third consecutive State title, this time at 125 lbs.

In 1993 the Little Hawks had an undefeated regular season (16-0), and won the MVC for the third year in a row, but could not defend their State title, finishing fifth. Jeff McGinness however won his fourth consecutive State title (130 lbs.) and finished his career with a spectacular 172-0 record and 111 pins. Jeff went on to an outstanding collegiate career that included two NCAA titles for the Iowa Hawkeyes.

The years 1994 and 1995 resulted in District titles and MVC runner-up finishes. In 1996 the Little Hawks did not win the District title for only the second time in the 90's. Joe Lucchi at 103 lbs. won a State title. The following year, 1997, started another string of six straight District titles. The final three teams of the decade produced a 54-10 dual meet mark, three District titles and one

*First ever State Championship team, 1992*

State title. The 1997 season saw a then record 20-win season and a District Title. The 1999 team did even better, breaking that record with a 21-2 mark and won MVC, District and State titles. This squad also notched the Dual Team State title as well, the second time the Little Hawks had accomplished that double.

The 90's decade ended with a dual mark of 142-43-2 (76%) to account for the best winning percentage of any previous decade. The 90's also produced eight District titles, five MVC titles and two Traditional and Dual Team State titles. All but three of these wins were under the leadership of Brad Smith from 1992-99.

# 2000's

The first three years of the new century produced three more District titles, running the consecutive streak to six.

In 2000 the Little Hawks won the District and finished second in the State as 130-lb. Cory Connell won his division. Jacob Smith (third) and John Gabrielsen (fourth) also placed. In 2001 it was a repeat performance with a District win and runner-up finish in both the Traditional and Dual State meets. Johnny Galloway won the first of two State titles, Anthony Watson and Joe VeDepo were second, and Justin Jordan was fourth.

The 2002 season was a return to the "Throne Room" as the Little Hawks won their third Traditional and Dual State Championships. This was highlighted by three individual winners: Johnny Galloway repeated at 160 lbs., Anthony Watson won at 140 lbs. and freshman Kyle Anson was a winner at 119 lbs.

The 2003 squad set a new dual meet win mark with a 22-9 record. Kyle Anson did not defend his title, finishing second, but in 2004 he won his second title at 125 lbs. and posted a three-year record of 122-9. Fellow junior Zach McKray was runner-up at 130 lbs. The team posted a 20-6 record and finished 10th in the State meet.

In the 51 seasons (1954-2004) of Little Hawk wrestling, there have been just three coaches heading up the program: Frank Bates (1954-56), Clyde Bean (1957-91), and Brad Smith (1992-present). Those coaches collected 13 MVC titles, 15 District titles, three State titles and two State Dual crowns. In those years, 28 Little Hawks won individual State titles led by Jeff McGinness who won four in his brilliant 172-0 career.

**Jeff McGinness    Career Record 172-0**

*Jeff McGinness - 4 time State Champ, 172-0 record*

# Wrestling

| Year | W - L | Coach | Captains | Misc. Information |
|------|-------|-------|----------|-------------------|
| 1954 | 3-1 | Frank Bates | | Grant Grimm gets 1st pin in Iowa City history. |
| 1955 | 3-3 | "      " | | Don Coulter 1st pin at State. Team 5th in District |
| 1956 | 3-11 | "      " | | |
| 1957 | 1-14 | Clyde Bean | Paul Burgess Harold Krebs | Krebs qualified for State |
| 1958 | 4-8-2 | "      " | Loren Kober | Kober qualified for State |
| 1959 | 8-2 | "      " | Steve Machovec | 2nd District, 6th State   Machovec (165) 1st State Champ (17-1-1) Butch Frantz (soph) 2nd |
| 1960 | 10-3-1 | "      " | Don Westcott | 3rd MVC, 1st District, 3rd State Don Westcott (154) State Champ |
| 1961 | 12-2 | "      " | Roy Frantz Steve Weeber | 1st MVC,   5th State    Roy "Butch" Frantz (175) State Champ |
| 1962 | 10-3 | "      " | Jim Evashevski Jim McGinness | 2nd District,  8th State  = Kelly Donham - 2nd, Evashevski-2nd, McGinness - 3rd,  MVP - McGinness |
| 1963 | 9-2-1 | "      " | Steve Moss John Rate | 1st MVC, 1st District, 3rd State |
| 1964 | 9-3 | "      " | Bob Bream Tom Zeman | 6th State Bream (154) State Champ |
| 1965 | 5-6 | "      " | Larry Houser | Did not place at State |
| 1966 | 7-5 | "      " | Tom Bentz | 6th State - Placers = Bill Knight, John Houseal, Bud Maas,    MVP - Dennis Doderer & Dennis Smothers |
| 1967 | 8-4 | "      " | Dan Bell Dennis Doderer | 2nd State,  Roger Collins (hwt.) State Champ,  Placers were Bill Knight & Doderer,    Bean MVC Coach of the Year |
| 1968 | 9-2-1 | "      " | John Evashevski Bill Knight | Knight  (112) State Champ 29-0, Evashevski (154) State Champ, Team 3rd in State |
| 1969 | 8-3-1 | "      " | Dave Brender Doug Davis | 5th State - Doug Davis (95) 2nd Placers = Mike Bostwick & Steve Barnes,   MVP - Davis |
| 1970 | 9-3 | "      " | Mike Bostwick Barry Van Fossen Joe Williams | MVP - Tom Evashevski No placers at State |
| 1971 | 7-5 | "      " | Jim Aldeman Tom Lepic | Lepic (112) State 2nd   (27-4) Aldeman (98) 2nd MVP - Mark Phillips |
| 1972 | 5-5-1 | "      " | | No placers at State |

# Wrestling

| | | | | |
|---|---|---|---|---|
| 1973 | 2-9 | Clyde Bean | Ken Fobian | No placers at State |
| 1974 | 8-2 | " " | Bill Hoffman<br>Dean Smith | Hoffman (132) 6th State<br>Rick Griffin (hwt.) 6th |
| 1975 | 8-3 | " " | Rick Griffin<br>Robbie Myers | 9th State - Rob Myers (185) 2nd,<br>Griffin (Hwt) 3rd, Bob Fobian (138)<br>6th, MVP - Fobian |
| 1976 | 5-4 | " " | Rick Bostwick | Bostwick (126) 5th<br>Jay Hilgenberg (185) 6th |
| 1977 | 10-1 | " " | Steve Kurdelmeier<br>Tom Riley | 1st MVC, 1st District, 9th State, Jay<br>Hilgenberg (185) 2nd, Riley (119) 3rd,<br>Eric Klasson (hwt) 5th |
| 1978 | 11-0 | " " | Tom Cannon<br>Eric Klasson | 1st MVC, 7th State Klasson (hwt) &<br>Tim Riley (126) State Champs |
| 1979 | 10-0 | " " | Steve Klasson<br>Tim Riley | 1st MVC, 6th State Riley (126)<br>repeats as State Champ,<br>Steve Klasson (167) 3rd |
| 1980 | 3-8 | " " | Curt Radcliff | No State placers |
| 1981 | 8-3 | " " | Dave Klasson<br>Curt Radcliff<br>Barry Wyatt | 3rd MVC, 1st District |
| 1982 | 5-4-2 | " " | | |
| 1983 | 9-2 | " " | | 1st MVC(7-0), 1st District (164 pts),<br>8th State, John Abadi (98) State<br>Champ, Andy Haman (hwt) 2nd in<br>State, Soph. team MVC Champs 7-0 |
| 1984 | 9-1-1 | " " | John Abadi<br>Andy Haman<br>Andy Petersen | 1st MVC, 2nd Dist., 3rd State<br>Petersen & Haman MVP<br>Haman (hwt.) State Champ<br>Petersen 2nd & Pat Waters 6th State |
| 1985 | 9-2 | " " | Larry Knock<br>Dan Pelsang | MVC Co-champs,<br>MVP - Pat Waters |
| 1986 | 6-5 | " " | Andy Cooper<br>Pat Waters | 1st MVC, 3rd District, 11th State<br>Waters (138) State Champ,<br>undefeated, 25 pins, also MVP |
| 1987 | 6-4-1 | " " | | Kenny Stecher (105) State Champ,<br>**State Dual Team tournament<br>started** |
| 1988 | 14-3-2 | " " | | 10th in State |
| 1989 | 6-4 | " " | | |
| 1990 | 13-7-1 | " " | | 1st Dist.,5th State, 2nd State Dual Team<br>Jeff McGinness (103) & Casey<br>Hesseltine (171) State Champs |
| 1991 | 12-5-1 | Clyde Bean | | MVC Co-Champs (8-0-1), 1st<br>District, 9th State - McGinness (112)<br>State Champ, Coach Bean retires<br>after 35 years - record 276-137-15. |

# Wrestling

| Year | Record | Coach | Captains | Accomplishments |
|---|---|---|---|---|
| 1992 | 15-8 | Brad Smith | | MVC Co-Champs, 1st Dist., 1st State, McGinness (125) 3rd State Title, Louis Pelsang (160) State Champ |
| 1993 | 16-0 | " " | | 1st MVC, 5th State, McGinness (130) 4th State Title, Smith MVC Coach of the Year |
| 1994 | 12-5 | " " | | 2nd MVC (6-2), 1st District |
| 1995 | 13-4 | " " | Brad Eldeen<br>Travis Evans<br>Matt Peterson<br>Tyler Stein | 2nd MVC, 1st District<br>MVP - Travis Evans |
| 1996 | 4-4 duals | " " | Todd Barnes<br>Rob Kautz<br>David Kurth<br>Joe Lucchi | 5th MVC, 2nd District<br>Joe Lucchi (103) State Champ |
| 1997 | 20-3 | " " | Jon Blayer<br>Rob Knight<br>Anthony Maas<br>Zech Ziebarth | 2nd MVC, 1st Dist., 6th State<br>8 indiv. Qualified for State<br>MVP - Jesse West |
| 1998 | 13-5 | " " | Tony Brown<br>Walker Evans<br>Zach Evans<br>Rob Knight | 2nd MVC, 1st Dist., 12th State<br>MVP - Tony Brown |
| 1999 | 21-2 | " " | Nate Barnes<br>Cory Connell<br>Walker Evans<br>Zach Evans | 1st MVC, 1st District, 1st State (won State without individual winner), 1st State Dual Team<br>MVP - Walker and Zach Evans |
| 2000 | 17-6 | " " | Chris Campbell<br>Pat Campbell<br>Cory Connell<br>John Gabrielson | 3rd MVC, 1st District, 2nd State, 4th State Duals, Cory Connell (130) State Champ and team MVP, Anthony Watson 3rd, |
| 2001 | 19-5 | " " | Chris Campbell<br>Brian Ferentz<br>Jacob Smith<br>Anthony Watson | 2nd MVC, 1st District, 2nd State, 2nd State Duals,<br>Johnny Galloway (152) State Champ & MVP |
| 2002 | 21-2 | " " | Johnny Galloway<br>Mike Holm<br>Jacob Smith<br>Mike Somsky | 1st MVC, 1st District, 1st State, 1st State Duals, 9 State Qualifiers, 4 State Champs - Kyle Anson (119), Brad Stockton (130), Anthony Watson (140), Galloway (160)<br>MVP - Galloway |
| 2003 | 22-9 | " " | | 5th MVC, 3rd District,<br>Anson 2nd (38-4) |
| 2004 | 20-6 | " " | Kyle Anson<br>Greg Lalla<br>Zach McKray<br>Cody Smith | 3rd MVC, 2nd District, 10th State, Anson (125) State Champ (3 year record 122-9) also MVP, McKray (130) 2nd at State |

# Gymnastics 1972-1988

Gymnastics got its start in the 1971-72 school year, one of three sports added for women that year, volleyball and golf being the others.

Cheryl Neal was the first coach and the squad had a limited schedule and finished with a 1-3 record. The following season 17 girls were on the team, again under the direction of Cheryl Neal. The team had a 3-6 record, beating Linn-Mar twice and Iowa City West once.

Kay Lund took over for Coach Neal in 1974 and the team again won three contests. Melinda Stubbee and Dea Dea Mohr were co-captains.

In 1975, the fourth year of the program, the Little Hawks had their first State qualifier. Jill Strub placed 10th in the vault. The team, under the coaching of Kathy Stanley, finished sixth in the MVC, ninth in the District, and 10th at Regionals.

Carol Havens began a three-year stint as coach in 1976. The team had a 5-7 record and finished seventh in the MVC and fourth in the District. Angie Ward won the District vault and eight girls advanced to the Regionals. The 1977 squad moved up to sixth in the MVC. Angie Ward advanced to State in the all-around.

The 1978 squad, led by Barb Condon and Anne Scott, was seventh in the MVC and had its highest team finish ever in the District with a runner-up finish. Barb Condon finished 12th in the State in floor exercise.

In 1979, because of small numbers, the City High and West High teams combined into one squad. Anne Stokely and Val Nielsen coached them. The combined team won the District title and placed sixth at the Regionals. Cherie Connell qualified for State and placed fourth in the vault and fifth in the uneven bars.

The 1980 season began with another new coach, Bethany Schifflet. City High and West were not combined, but all practices and meets were held at West High (and this continued until the end of gymnastics). City High finished third at the District and ninth at Regionals in 1980.

*1979 combined team - District Champions*

In 1981 the term "team" was a misnomer as there were only two girls out for gymnastics, Sandy Hershberger and Patricia Buck. Both girls participated in the all-around. Hershberger's strongest events were vault and beam, while Buck received her most consistent scores in floor exercise.

In 1982 the squad numbers "swelled" to five and produced the first State Champion in City High gymnastics history. Sophomore Stephanie Smith won the vault competition with a score of 9.55. Stephanie also placed second on bars, third in tumbling and sixth in the all-around. Robyn Sekafetz finished second in tumbling, sixth on bars and third in the all-around. This was a great showing for a five-member team. Jill Schlott started a six-year stint as head coach, the longest tenure of any coach.

Practices were held before school at West High and Robyn Sekafetz had this comment regarding that, "I remember the first days when we were driving over to West at 5:30 in the morning and thinking how insane we were to do it. But looking back, it was worth it."

The 1983 team is considered one of the best ever at City High. Fourteen girls were on the squad and the team finished undefeated in dual meets. At the Regional meet they scored their highest point total of the season, yet missed qualifying for State as a team by a single point. At the State meet Stephanie Smith placed first in all-around and third in tumbling and vault. Robyn Sekafetz was third on the bars. Smith and Sekafetz were both named to the All-State team.

In 1984 the Little Hawks had their second straight undefeated regular season. The feat was especially noteworthy because defending all-around State Champion Stephanie Smith was forced to miss the season with knee surgery. The team won the District, but finished fifth at the Regionals with just the top four teams moving on to the State.

*Stephanie Smith - State Overall Champion*

Along the way the Little Hawks beat defending State Champion Linn-Mar.

With a 10-person squad the 1985 team had a 5-3 dual record and finished second in the District and sixth at the Regionals. Jenny Fugate was MVP. Jenny Schoen was MVP the following season (1986) as the team was ninth at Regionals.

In 1987, the next to last gymnastics team to represent City High, proved to be the most successful in state competition. The team finished second at the State meet and sophomore Dani Barr won the all-around championship. Leading the team was Coach Jill Schlott, in her sixth and final season as head coach. Coach Schlott was the only coach to head the program for more than three seasons.

Following the 1988 season, gymnastics was dropped as a sport due to decreasing numbers statewide and increased liability costs. The final team had a 3-6 dual record and the team finished fifth at the Regionals. Dani Barr repeated as State Champion in the all-around. Robyn Sekafetz, who captained the 1983 City High team, was the eighth and final gymnastics coach at City High.

In the short history of City High gymnastics (17 years) there have been eight different coaches. The team numbers ranged from 17 (1973) to a low of two (1981). The team did have two undefeated regular seasons (1983 and 1984) and produced four individual State champions, Stephanie Smith (1982 and 1983) and Dani Barr (1987 and 1988). The 1987 squad had the top State finish as they were the State runner-up.

# Women's Gymnastics

| Year | W - L | Coach | Captain | Misc. Info |
|------|-------|-------|---------|------------|
| 1972 | 1-3 | Cheryl Neal | | |
| 1973 | 3-6 | "        " | | |
| 1974 | 3-5 | Kay Lund | Dea Dea Mohr Melinda Stubbee | |
| 1975 | 4-6 | Kathy Stanley | Jill Strub | 6th MVC, 9th District,10th Regional Jill Strub to State - 10th in vault |
| 1976 | 5-7 | Carol Havens | Sue Hershberger | 7th MVC, 4th District, 8 advance to Regional |
| 1977 | 4-6 | "        " | Angie Ward | 6th MVC, 4th District |
| 1978 | 6-4 | "        " | Anne Scott | 7th MVC, 2nd District, 8th Regional, Barb Condon MVP |
| 1979 | 3-4 | Anne Stokely Val Nielsen | | City/West combine to form team 1st District, 6th Regional Cherie Connell to State - 4th vault, 5th bars |
| 1980 | 2-9 | Bethany Schifflet | | City/West no longer combined, but all practices and meets were at West, 3rd District, 9th Regional |
| 1981 | | "        " | Patricia Buck Sandy Hershberger | Only 2 girls on the "team" |
| 1982 | 0-6 | Jill Schlott | Stephanie Smith | 5th Dist (5 on the team), Smith was State Champ -vault, 2nd bars, 3rd tumbling, 6th all-around Robyn Sekafetz -2nd tumbling, 3rd all-around, 6th bars, |
| 1983 | 6-0 | "        " | Robyn Sekafetz Stephanie Smith | Stephanie Smith State Champ - all-around, 3rd tumbling and vault, Robin Sekafetz 3rd bars Smith & Sekafetz All-State team |
| 1984 | 7-0 | "        " | | 2nd year undefeated 1st District, 5th Regional |
| 1985 | 5-3 | "        " | Roxanne Addink Cammie Groenwold Sheri Sekafetz | 2nd District, 6th Regional MVP - Jenny Fugate |
| 1986 | 5-3 | "        " | Jenny Schoen | 3rd Sectional, 9th Regional, MVP - Schoen |
| 1987 | | "        " | | Team 2nd at State Dani Barr St. Champ all-around |
| 1988 | 3-6 | Robyn Sekafetz | | 5th Regional, Dani Barr repeats as State Champ all-around, Last Season for this sport. |

# Women's Golf 1972-2004

## 1970's

Women's golf had its official start in the 1971-72 school year, although Kandy Kellow represented City High in the Sectional meet in 1968 and finished first. She did not advance to the State meet.

Mary Foraker coached the team the first three seasons, but no information was available. Pam Hilgenberg had a one-year stint as coach in 1975 with Becky Bagford as the captain. The team was 10th in the MVC.

Ken Klein, previously the men's coach, was named the women's coach in 1976 and held the position for the next 14 seasons. Becky Bagford was again captain of that team as the Little Hawks moved up to seventh in the MVC. Julie Bean (twice) and Mary Wood led the last three teams of the 70's.

## 1980's

The 1980's saw steady improvement in the decade. Jane (1982) and Pam Bagford (1983) became the second and third Bagfords to be named captain. In 1984 the Little Hawks had their best showing to date with a third in the MVC, first Sectional championship and a second in the Regional. The 1985 squad repeated those finishes and had a 13-1 dual record. Amy Hagan was the MVP and Cathy ten Broeke was MVC medalist.

The 1986 and 1987 teams both had MVC runner-up finishes for the top MVC finish until 1997. Cathy ten Broeke was captain and MVP of the 1986 squad. These two teams had a combined dual meet record of 22-1. After the 1989 season, Ken Klein took three seasons off as coach before returning in 1993 for six more seasons.

*1997 team - District Champions*

## 1990's

In 1990 Bill Mitchell succeeded Ken Klein and coached one season. Cathy Hughes headed up the program in '91 and '92 before Ken Klein returned in 1993.

In 1994 and '95 the team finished third in the MVC and second in the Sectional. Sara Ribble and Kristy Sellers led those teams. In 1996, Sellers was the MVP and the team placed fifth (MVC), first (District), and second (Regional).

The 1997 team matched the highest MVC finish (second) and won the District. Katie Nolan and Jana Cumming were the leaders. In 1998, led by MVP Stacy Moss, the Little Hawks won the District championship for the third straight year and went on to finish sixth at the State meet for their highest finish ever to that point. Coach Klein retired after the season due to health reasons after a total of 20 seasons.

Dave Kriz succeeded Ken Klein and led the Little Hawks to three outstanding seasons. The 1999 team increased the District winning streak to four and was third at the MVC and Super meets and second at Regionals to again qualify for State. Stacy Moss was District medalist and Regional runner-up medalist. She shot 88-86 to tie for seventh at the State meet.

## 2000's

In 2000 the Little Hawks won their first MVC title ever and had a great postseason run as they won District and Regional titles and finished second at the State meet. Jill Frantz and Kelli Haught both shot 162 for 36 holes to lead City High at the State meet. Megan Hein, Haught, Amy Jehle and Frantz were the season leaders with Frantz named MVP. Jill Frantz and Ned Carter played at the State co-ed tournament in 2000.

*2000 team - MVC Champs & State Runner-up*

The 2001 team had an almost exact repeat of 2000 with the exception of the MVC where the Little Hawks finished second. The team, led by repeat MVP Jill Frantz, won its sixth consecutive District title and was again second at the State meet. Frantz finished third in the individual race with a 161 for 36 holes. Coach Kriz resigned to enter private business following the 2001 season.

Larry Pohren coached the next two seasons. In 2002 the District championship run ended at six as City High finished second. Krista Farnsworth and Lindsey Leonard were the leaders. Krista Farnsworth repeated as MVP in 2003, Pohren's last season.

In 2004 Jerry Hora became the eighth person to coach women's golf. Lindsay Leonard was named MVP in 2004 and the team finished fifth in the Super meet.

The Little Hawks have just one MVC title in their 1972-2004 history. That was in 2000. They do have five District titles, although spring records were sometimes not available because of spring publishing deadlines for yearbooks.

Ken Klein had the longest coaching tenure with 20 years. Seven others share the remaining 13 years of women's golf history.

# Women's Golf

| Year | W - L | Coach | Captain | Misc. Information |
|------|-------|-------|---------|------------------|
| 1968 | | NO TEAM | | Kandy Kellow 1st in Sectional |
| 1969 | | "        " | | |
| 1970 | | "        " | | |
| 1971 | | "        " | | |
| 1972 | | Mary Foraker | | First official team |
| 1973 | | "        " | | |
| 1974 | | "        " | | |
| 1975 | 1-6 | Pam Hilgenberg | Becky Bagford | 10th MVC |
| 1976 | 8-4-1 | Ken Klein | Becky Bagford | 7th MVC |
| 1977 | | "        " | Julie Bean | |
| 1978 | 0-9 | "        " | Julie Bean | 10th MVC |
| 1979 | 0-12 | "        " | Mary Wood | 8th MVC |
| 1980 | | "        " | | |
| 1981 | 3-10-1 | "        " | Beth Krieger | 8th MVC, 5th Sectional |
| 1982 | 4-3-1 | "        " | Jane Bagford | 5th Sectional |
| 1983 | 8-5 | "        " | Pam Bagford | 7th MVC, 5th Sectional, MVP Bagford |
| 1984 | 10-4 | "        " | Susie Gurnett | 3rd MVC, 1st Sectional, 1st Regional |
| 1985 | 13-1 | "        " | Amy Hagen Cathy ten Broeke | 3rd MVC, 1st Sectional, 2nd Regional, ten Broeke was 1st at MVC, MVP Hagen |
| 1986 | 11-0 | "        " | Cathy ten Broeke | 2nd MVC, 1st Sectional, 4th Regional, MVP Cathy tenBroeke |
| 1987 | 11-1 | "        " | | 2nd MVC, 2nd Sectional, 4th Regional |
| 1988 | 8-5 | "        " | | |
| 1989 | 7-5 | "        " | | 8th MVC, 2nd Sectional, 3rd Regional |
| 1990 | 5-14 | Bill Mitchell | | |
| 1991 | 3-11 | Cathy Hughes | | |
| 1992 | 1-11 | "        " | | 2nd Sectional |

# Women's Golf

| Year | Record | Coach | MVP/Players | Accomplishments |
|---|---|---|---|---|
| 1993 | 6-6-1 | Ken Klein | | |
| 1994 | 10-2-1 | " " | | 3rd MVC, 7th Super, 2nd Sectional, 3rd Regional |
| 1995 | 5-4 | " " | Sara Ribble, Kristy Sellers | 3rd MVC, 6th Super, 2nd Sectional, MVP - Sellers |
| 1996 | 8-7 | " " | Kristy Sellers | 5th MVC, 1st District, 2nd Regional, MVP - Sellers |
| 1997 | 13-5-1 | " " | Katie Nolan | 2nd MVC, 1st District, 3rd Regional, MVP - Jana Cumming |
| 1998 | 9-11 | " " | Stacy Moss | 3rd MVC, 1st District, 2nd Regional, 6th State, MVP - Moss, Coach Klein retires due to health reasons |
| 1999 | 41-9-2 | Dave Kriz | Stacy Moss | 3rd MVC, 3rd Super, 1st District, 2nd Regional, Moss was District medalist and runner-up Regional medalist, Moss 7th at State and team MVP |
| 2000 | 11-4 | " " | Meagan Hein, Amy Jehle | 1st MVC, 2nd Super, 1st District (5th straight), 1st Regional, 2nd State, MVP - Jill Frantz |
| 2001 | | " " | Jill Frantz | 2nd MVC, 2nd Super, 1st District, (6th straight), 1st Regional, 2nd State, Frantz 3rd All-State and MVP |
| 2002 | | Larry Pohren | Krista Farnsworth, Lindsey Leonard | 2nd District, 5th Regional MVP - Farnsworth |
| 2003 | 4-44 | " " | Krista Farnsworth | 6th MVC, 9th Super, 5th District MVP - Farnsworth |
| 2004 | 39-11 | Jerry Hora | Lindsay Leonard | 5th Super, MVP Lindsey Leonard and Alecia Tank |

# Men's Tennis 1923-2004

## 1923-1927

In searching City High yearbooks, the first year that turned up information on men's tennis was 1923. There was mention of Richard Boyles and Imy Albert playing both singles and doubles at the University of Iowa Tourney. No coach was mentioned or team record. In 1925 Albert and Boyles were listed as first in doubles at the Iowa meet.

The next mention is 1929 where Horace Redman and John Boyles were listed as representing Iowa City High school at the State Tourney.

## 1930's & 1940's

The first year that a coach is listed is 1931 when Howard Orvis, described in the yearbook as a freshman at the University of Iowa, was the coach. George Wells, who coached football, basketball and track, was the coach in 1932 and 1933. Con Chapman and Henry Soucek,Jr. (son of famed coach of pre-1920's) represented Iowa City High at the State Tourney in 1932.

Irvin Keeler had a one-year term as coach in 1934 and Wagner and Mann qualified for State. Herb Cormack began an 11-year stint as head tennis coach in 1935 (interrupted by a two- year WWII break).

Limited information is available on many seasons because of spring publishing deadlines for yearbooks. In 1939 the team was third in the MVC and fifth in the District. The 1942 team, headed by all-around athlete Dave Danner, was MVC champions and Danner is listed as only losing one match all year. Earl Cathcart lost only to Danner all year. No mention of the State meet was found. The 1943 team was District champions and runner-up in the MVC. Following the season the Navy took Coach Cormack for the next two seasons.

Francis Merten was coach the next two seasons when Cormack was in the Navy. His 1945 team was third in the MVC. No report for 1944. In 1946 Coach Cormack returned from WWII and the Little Hawks were MVC Champs. Bruce Higley was State Singles runner-up.

In the 1948 season Robert Pendleton was named coach. Henry Rate and Keith Boyle were State Doubles Champions and the team finished as MVC Champs. The last year of the decade saw the team win both the District and State titles. Henry Rate and Ed Duncan were State Doubles Champions. The Little Hawks also won the MVC title for the third time in four years.

## 1950's

In 1951, under the coaching of Robert Pendleton, the team had another MVC title and started the "Andrews era" as Jamie Andrews won the State Singles crown.

For five consecutive years either Jamie or his brother Art won State Tennis Championships. Jamie repeated in 1952 with brother Art and Ted Dunnington winning doubles that year. In 1953 Art won the first of his three straight singles titles. The team also won the MVC Championship.

In 1954 Art again was State champion and won the National Boys' Indoor Singles Championship. The team

*Jamie Andrews - 2 time State Singles Champion (1951-52)*

won the MVC title for the fourth consecutive year. The following year (1955) City High swept MVC, District and State honors and Art Andrews was again State Singles Champion. Art also had the rare honor for a high school student in that he was selected for the Davis Cup trials. The MVC title was the fifth consecutive for the Little Hawks and eighth in the last 10 years. Art was undefeated as the number two player as a freshman and three years at number one for a brilliant career.

An unusual fact regarding these eight MVC titles is that they came under the direction of five different coaches: Herb Cormack (1946), Robert Pendleton (1948-49, 1951), Gene Peisner (1952-53), Bob Shultz (1954), and Frank Bates (1955).

Jack Cody was the new coach in 1957 and led the Little Hawks to two more MVC titles in 1957 and 1958. In 1959 Dave Strauss and Gary Lubin became State Doubles Champions.

*Art Andrews - 3 time State Singles Champion (1953-55)*

## 1960's

In 1960 John Gearhart succeeded Jack Cody as coach and his 1960 team became MVC Champions, giving the Little Hawks 11 of the last 15 MVC titles under the tutelage of seven different coaches. John Wilmeth was State runner-up in singles the following year (1961).

In the 1962 season, Richard Strauss and John Wilmeth were State Doubles Champions. The following year (1963) Jack Boal started a 10-year stint as head coach. Richard Strauss completed a perfect 21-0 season with the State Singles title. In 1964 Stauss had his 40-match winning streak stopped in the State Championship match and finished second.

The 1965 squad was undefeated and notched an MVC title, the first since 1960. In 1966 Steve Houghton, the current University of Iowa coach, was the District Champ in singles and was the State runner-up. In 1968 Bill Randall and Bruce Nagel were State Doubles Champions. Nagel went on to two State titles playing for West High when that school opened in 1969.

## 1970's

The first six years of the 70's saw only one winning season (1970). Garl McLaughlin was named coach in 1975 and started to turn the program around. Just prior to the start of Coach McLaughlin's career, the duo of Patsy Donelson and Stuart Dryer won the 1974 State Co-ed Doubles Championship.

Coach McLaughlin remained as head coach for 25 years and his career was highlighted with the City High tennis courts being renamed in his honor in 2001. Coach McLaughlin's second team (1976) finished second in both the MVC and District. In 1978 the team of Dave Talbott and Bill Burger finished third in State Doubles. Talbott followed that up by teaming with Cory Vorheis to finish second the next season.

## 1980's

In 1982 City High scored a double-double so to speak as Mike Cram and Steve Molen were the State Doubles Champions and then Cram and Michele Conlon won the State Co-ed Doubles Championship. In 1984 junior Steve Molen was second in the State Singles as the Little Hawks were third in the MVC. The following spring the team put together a 13-1 record and an MVC Championship. Molen again was State runner-up. The 1980's saw three State runner-up finishes in the State co-ed meet: 1980 and 1981 Cram and Conlon and 1983 Conlon and Steve Molen.

## 1990's

The 1993 squad turned in a 16-4 record and the first MVC Championship since 1985. The team also finished fourth at the State meet. The 1996 team repeated that fourth place finish. The

*First ever State Championship team, 1999 (16-1)*

final three years of the century saw an outstanding trio of seasons. In 1997 the 17-2 team won MVC and District titles and finished third at the State. Rob Fumerton, Leif Johnson and Rob Weingeist were the leaders. In 1998 the squad won a record 18 matches, repeated the MVC and District wins and moved up to second at the State Tourney. Weingeist repeated as MVP. The team of Ross Cram and Kris Tiedt finished second at the State co-ed tournament.

The 1999 team ended the twentieth century with a 16-1 record and MVC runner-up finish. The post season was even better as the Little Hawks won the District title and then won the State Championship. Cousins Jon and David Houghton were State Doubles Champions.

*1999 - David & Jon Houghton - State Doubles Champs*

## 2000's

The first year of the new decade saw Coach McLaughlin coach his 25th and final team. The team had a 15-4 record and a District Championship. The team went on to a third place finish at the State. Brett Green and Dave Balmer were State runner-up in Doubles. A Garl McLaughlin scholarship is awarded each spring to a Little Hawk senior tennis player.

In 2001 the successor to Coach McLaughlin was City High graduate and former player, Chris Hall. Coach Hall's first team had a 14-1 record and won the MVC Championship.

The 2002 squad led by MVP Scott Houghton finished third in the District meet. In 2003 Houghton repeated as MVP and following the 2004 season Coach Hall resigned to take a teaching and coaching position in Davenport. Madison Brigham and Alex Howe were co-MVP's on the 2004 squad.

# Men's Tennis

| Year | W - L | Coach | Captains | Misc. Information |
|------|-------|-------|----------|-------------------|
| 1923 | | | | Apparently at least one meet U. of I. Tourney - Richard Boyles and Imy Albert played both doubles & singles |
| 1924 | No | information found | | |
| 1925 | | | | Alberts and Dick Boyles 1st place Doubles |
| 1926 | No | information found | | |
| 1927 | " | " " | | |
| 1928 | " | " " | | |
| 1929 | | | | Horace Redman and John Boyles, Represented I.C.H.S. at State Tourney, First time sponsored by State Association |
| 1930 | No | Information found | | |
| 1931 | | Howard Orvis | | Coach was freshman at University of Iowa |
| 1932 | | George Wells | | Don Chapman & Henry Soucek, Jr. represented I.C.H.S. at State Tourney |
| 1933 | | " " | | Had 4 meets |
| 1934 | 2-1 | Irvin Keeler | | Wagner & Mann qualified for State |
| 1935 | | Herb Cormack | | |
| 1936 | | " " | | |
| 1937 | | " " | | |
| 1938 | | " " | | |
| 1939 | | " " | | 3rd MVC, 5th District |
| 1940 | | " " | | |
| 1941 | | | | |
| 1942 | | " " | | 1st MVC, Dave Danner 1st State. He only lost 1 match all year. Crain & Cathcart qualified for State doubles |
| 1943 | | " " | | 2nd MVC, 1st District, Danner lost in 1st round at State, Cormack enters the Navy |
| 1944 | | Francis Merten | | |
| 1945 | | " " | | 3rd MVC |
| 1946 | | Herb Cormack | | 1st MVC, Cormack returns, Bruce Higley 2nd at State |
| 1947 | | " " | | No State qualifiers |

# Men's Tennis

| Year | Record | Coach | Player | Notes |
|------|--------|-------|--------|-------|
| 1948 | | Robert Pendleton | | 1st MVC, Henry Rate & Keith Boyle State Champs Doubles |
| 1949 | | "      " | | 1st MVC, Undefeated, 1st District, 1st State, Henry Rate & Ed Duncan State Champs Doubles |
| 1950 | | "      " | | |
| 1951 | | "      " | | 1st MVC, Jamie Andrews State Singles Champ |
| 1952 | 16-1 | Gene Peisner | | Coach Pendleton to the Navy 1st MVC, 1st District, Jamie Andrews repeats State Champ, Art Andrews & Ted Dunnington Doubles Champs |
| 1953 | 9-5 | "      " | | 1st MVC, Art Andrews State Singles Champ |
| 1954 | | Bob Schulz | | 1st MVC, Art Andrews repeats State Champ also National Boys' Singles Indoor Champ |
| 1955 | 14-1 | Frank Bates | | 1st MVC (5th straight, 8 out of last 10), 1st District, 1st State, Andrews repeats State Champ - 4 years undefeated in singles, also picked for Davis Cup Trials. |
| 1956 | 5-0-1 | "      " | | |
| 1957 | 4-1 | Jack Cody | | 1st MVC |
| 1958 | | "      " | | 1st MVC |
| 1959 | 7-1 | "      " | | Dave Strauss & Gary Lubin State Champs Doubles |
| 1960 | 2-5 dual | John Gearhart | John Conwell Dave Strauss | 1st MVC (11th MVC title in last 15 years) |
| 1961 | 5-2 dual | "      " | John Wilmeth | Wilmeth 2nd at State |
| 1962 | | "      " | John Wilmeth | Richard Strauss & John Wilmeth State Champs Doubles |
| 1963 | 3-3 | Jack Boal | | Richard Strauss State Champ Singles, he had a 21-0 record |
| 1964 | 8-6 | "      " | Richard Strauss | Richard Strauss 2nd in State; 40-match streak broken |
| 1965 | 5-0 dual | "      " | | 1st MVC - undefeated |
| 1966 | 6-2 | "      " | Terry Paul | Steve Houghton won District, 2nd at State |
| 1967 | | "      " | Steve Houghton | |

# Men's Tennis

| Year | Record | Coach | Player | Notes |
|------|--------|-------|--------|-------|
| 1968 | 6-2 | Jack Boal | Scott Beckett | Bill Randall & Bruce Nagel State Champs Doubles |
| 1969 | 3-11 | " " | Bill Randall | |
| 1970 | 8-5 | " " | Randy Dryer | |
| 1971 | 2-12 | " " | Tom Lepic | |
| 1972 | 2-12 | " " | Jim Fransen | |
| 1973 | 1-9 | Bob Farnsworth | Jeff Wilson | |
| 1974 | 2-9 | " " | | Stuart Dryer and Patsy Donelson win Co-ed State Doubles |
| 1975 | 6-7 | Garl McLaughlin | Stuart Dryer | 4th District |
| 1976 | 12-1 | " " | Dave Mauer | 2nd MVC, 2nd District |
| 1977 | 12-0 | " " | Bart Goplerud Doug Swisher | 1st MVC, 2nd District |
| 1978 | 7-5 | " " | Bill Burger Scott Franklin | Dave Talbott & Bill Burger 3rd in State Doubles |
| 1979 | 11-2 | " " | Mark Dreusicke | 4th MVC, Dave Talbott & Cory Vorheis 2nd State Doubles, Vorheis and Shelly Freeman 3rd. State co-ed |
| 1980 | 4-7 | " " | Blaine Pass Bill Daniher | Mike Cram & Michele Conlon 2nd at State co-ed meet, MVP - Mike Cram |
| 1981 | 4-6 | " " | Randy Hester | Mike Cram & Michele Conlon repeated as 2nd at State co-ed meet |
| 1982 | 9-3 | " " | Mike Cram | Mike Cram & Steve Molen State Champs Doubles, Cram and Michele Conlon win State co-ed Doubles. |
| 1983 | 8-3 | " " | Matt Kienzle | Steve Molen & Michele Conlon 2nd at State co-ed meet |
| 1984 | 6-4 | " " | Jim Dreusicke | 3rd MVC, 2nd District Steve Molen 2nd State Singles |
| 1985 | 13-1 | " " | Steve Molen | 1st MVC, Steve Molen repeats 2nd State Singles, team qualified for State, MVP - Molen |
| 1986 | 7-5 | " " | Tom Nielsen Jack O'Brien | 3rd District MVP - Alexi Abras |
| 1987 | 9-3 | " " | Chris Hupfeld Tom Jordon | 2nd District, Alex Abras 3rd at State and team MVP |
| 1988 | 7-4 | " " | Alexi Abras | 3rd District, Ross Cram & Kris Tiedt 2nd at State co-ed meet, MVP Abras |

# Men's Tennis

| Year | Record | Coach | Players | Accomplishments |
|------|--------|-------|---------|-----------------|
| 1989 | 5-6 | Garl McLaughlin | Braden Neiman<br>Jeff Nielsen | 2$^{nd}$ District,  Nielsen 4$^{th}$ singles and MVP |
| 1990 | 11-4 | "   " | Bob Whiteis<br>Rob Woolson | 2$^{nd}$ District,<br>MVP Josh Field |
| 1991 | 6-7 | "   " | Adam Henn | 3$^{rd}$ District |
| 1992 | 7-4 | "   " | Josh Field<br>Braxton Neiman | 3$^{rd}$ District, Andy Downer & C.J. Thielke 4$^{th}$ State doubles |
| 1993 | 16-4 | "   " | Andy Downer<br>C.J. Thielke | 1$^{st}$ MVC,  1$^{st}$ District,  4$^{th}$ State |
| 1994 | 9-6 | "   " | Chad Carson | 3$^{rd}$ District, MVP - A.J. Johnson |
| 1995 | 10-5 | "   " | Ben Folsom<br>A.J. Johnson | 4$^{th}$ District<br>MVP - Rob Weingeist |
| 1996 | 11-6 | "   " | Jeff Houghton | 2$^{nd}$ District, 4$^{th}$ State<br>MVP - Jon Houghton |
| 1997 | 17-2 | "   " | Rob Fumerton<br>Leif Johnson | 1$^{st}$ MVC, 1$^{st}$ District, 3$^{rd}$ State MVP - Rob Weingeist, Jon & David Balmer 5$^{th}$ State doubles |
| 1998 | 18-1 | "   " | Rob Weingeist | 1$^{st}$ MVC (13-0),1$^{st}$ District,  2$^{nd}$ State,  MVP - Weingeist,  Jon & David Balmer 5$^{th}$ State doubles, Ross Cram & Kris Tiedt 2$^{nd}$ State co-ed  doubles |
| 1999 | 16-1 | "   " | David Houghton<br>Jon Houghton | 2$^{nd}$ MVC, 1$^{st}$ District, 1$^{st}$ State The Houghtons were State doubles Champs, Brett Green & David Balmer 3$^{rd}$ doubles, MVP - The Team |
| 2000 | 15-4 | "   " | Brett Green | 1$^{st}$ District, 1$^{st}$ Sub-State, 3$^{rd}$ State,  Brett Green & Dave Balmer 2$^{nd}$ State doubles,  MVP - Balmer,   Coach McLaughlin retires after 25 years. |
| 2001 | 14-1 | Chris Hall | | 1$^{st}$ MVC,  Only loss to C.R. Kennedy |
| 2002 | 10-6 | "   " | Dan Hansen<br>Scott Houghton<br>Jeremy Kraus | 3$^{rd}$ District<br>MVP - Scott  Houghton |
| 2003 | | "   " | Scott Houghton<br>Ned Pirotte | MVP - Scott Houghton |
| 2004 | 2-13 | "   " | Brett Chiles<br>Alex Howe | Madison Brigham and Alex Howe MVP,  Coach Hall leaves to take coaching and teaching job in Davenport. |

# Women's Tennis 1966-2004

Women's tennis has the honor of being the first sport recognized for women in the history of City High. As chronicled in the introduction, Mona Schallau, an outstanding tennis player in Iowa and a junior at City High, petitioned the Board of Education in 1966 to allow her to participate in the District Tennis Meet sponsored by the Girls High School Athletic Union. Mona entered and won the District title and the ensuing State Singles title and became the first woman athlete from City High to win an individual State Title.

## 1960's and 1970's

The following season (1967) City High fielded an entire team under the coaching of Marianne Lentz, with a full schedule of meets. Schallau repeated as State champion that season and went on to a successful college and professional career on the women's pro circuit. In 1968 Nancy Nagel won the District title but did not place at the State.

Marianne Lentz coached for five seasons and had the longest tenure as coach until Shelly Freeman-George stabilized the program with 18 years at the helm starting in 1987. The Little Hawks had nine coaches in the first 21 years of the program and one the last 18.

Cheryl Neal, Larry Brown, Marie Theobald, Larry DeHann, Paul Ginter, Jean Dobyns, and Alan Vandeventer all headed up the women's tennis program for short periods between 1972 and 1986.

*Mona Schallau - First State Tennis Champion, 1966*

*First Women's Tennis team, 1967*

## 1980's

City High went from Mona Schallau's second State singles title in 1967 until the 1981 season before a second Little Hawk won a State crown. Sophomore Michele Conlon, a multiple sport athlete and one of City High's best all-time athletes, won the State Singles crown in 1981 with an undefeated season. Michele was upset the following year, but came back as a senior to win her second State singles title. Michele is currently the head Women's Tennis coach at Iowa State University.

Although denied a State Singles title in 1982, Conlon teamed with Michael Cram to win the State co-ed Doubles crown. This was the second

*Michele Conlon - 2 time State Singles Champion*

co-ed crown for City High as Stuart Dryer and Patsy Donelson won the crown in 1974. The Little Hawks also had three runner-up finishes in the 1980's; Conlon and Cram in 1980 and 1981 and Conlon and Steve Molen in 1983.

In 1987 Shelly Freeman-George, a 1979 City High graduate and former Little Hawk basketball and tennis standout, took over as head coach and remained in that position until the end of the 2004 season.

## 1990's and 2000's

City High's first MVC team title came in 1993 under the direction of Coach Shelly Freeman-George. That team won a-then-record 16 matches. The 1995 team finished second in the MVC and the Regionals. Katy Balmer and Jenny Shultz led that squad.

The 1997 and 1998 teams both recorded 13-0 regular season records and were MVC Champions. In 1998 the Little Hawks finished as State runner-up to Bettendorf 5-1, with Emmy and Kate Cilek winning the State Doubles title. In 1998 Kris Tiedt and Ross Cram were second at the State co-ed Championship.

In 1999 the team won both the MVC and District titles and repeated as State runner-up, once again losing to Bettendorf, this time 5-3. That team established the City High record for wins in a 20-1 season. The Cilek sisters, Emily Rowat, Katie Bossen and Elena Woodhead were the leaders. Jenny Schulte had an outstanding two-year career as she placed sixth at State as a junior (2000) and fourth as a senior (2001).

The 2004 team, which was Freeman-George's 18th and final season, was MVC Champions with Megan Gatens repeating as team MVP. Freeman-George coached squads won five MVC titles and had two State Runner-up Teams (1998 and 1999). In a five-year span from 1995-99 her teams had a combined record of 78-8 with three MVC tittles and two State runners-up.

Because spring sports' records were difficult to research, due to yearbook publishing deadlines, the number of MVC and District team titles may not be totally inclusive. We do know

*1998 - MVC Champions and State Runner-up*

that since 1993 the Little Hawks have won five MVC titles. There have been four individual State singles titles won, two by Mona Schallau and two by Michele Conlon. One doubles title, Kate and Emmy Cilek (1998) and two co-ed titles, Patsy Donelson and Stuart Dryer (1974) and Michele Conlon and Michael Cram (1982)

Nine coaches have headed the women's teams 1967 to 2004 with Shelly Freeman-George having the longest tenure of 18 years.

*1998 - Emmy & Kate Cilek - State Doubles Champions*

# Women's Tennis

| Year | W - L | Coach | Captain | Misc. Information |
|------|-------|-------|---------|------------------|
| 1966 | | | | No Team<br>Mona Schallau Singles State Champion |
| 1967 | | Marianne Lentz | | Mona Schallau repeated State Champion |
| 1968 | 7-1 | " " | Nancy Nagel | Nancy Nagel 1st at District |
| 1969 | | " " | | |
| 1970 | 11-1 | " " | Connie Murphy | |
| 1971 | 10-1 | " " | Mary Randall | |
| 1972 | 13-0 | Cheryl Neal | Mary Randall | |
| 1973 | 7-3 | " " | Carole Kron | |
| 1974 | 5-6 | Larry Brown | Patsy Donelson | Donelson and Stuart Dryer won State co-ed doubles |
| 1975 | 4-6 | " " | | |
| 1976 | 2-9 | " " | | |
| 1977 | | | Lisa Karlin | |
| 1978 | 4-6 | Marie Theobald | | 5th MVC |
| 1979 | 3-10 | " " | Shelly Freeman | 7th MVC, Freeman & Cory Vorheis 3rd State co-ed doubles |
| 1980 | | Larry DeHann | | Michele Conlon and Mike Cram were 2nd at State co-ed |
| 1981 | 4-5 | " " | | Michele Conlon undefeated State Singles Champion, Conlon & Cram repeated 2nd at State co-ed meet |
| 1982 | 3-6 | " " | Ann Terry | Michele Conlon and Mike Cram won State Co-ed Doubles |
| 1983 | 5-5 | Paul Ginter | Michele Conlon | Michele Conlon Singles State Champion, Conlon & Steve Molen 2nd at State co-ed |
| 1984 | 5-6 | Jean Dobyns | | |
| 1985 | 6-5 | " " | Sandy Chen | 4th MVC, 3rd Sectional<br>MVP - Sandy Chen |
| 1986 | 5-6 | Alan Vandeventer | | |
| 1987 | 2-3 | Shelly Freeman-George | | |
| 1988 | 7-4 | " " | | 4th MVC |
| 1989 | 12-3 | " " | | |
| 1990 | 8-5 | " " | | |
| 1991 | 8-5 | " " | | |
| 1992 | 10-3 | " " | | |
| 1993 | 16-4-0 | " " | | 1st MVC |
| 1994 | 9-7 | " " | | 5th MVC |

# Women's Tennis

| 1995 | 13-3 | Shelly Freeman-George | Katy Balmer<br>Chris Bricker | 2nd MVC, 2nd Regional<br>MVP - Balmer & Jenny Shultz |
|------|------|------|------|------|
| 1996 | 12-2 | "        " | Bren Landon<br>Chris Bricker | MVP - Beth Cooper & Kris Tiedt |
| 1997 | 17-2 | "        " | Bren Landon<br>Jenny Shultz | 1st MVC (13-0),   lost both matches to State Champ Bettendorf |
| 1998 | 16-0 | "        " | Beth Cooper<br>Kris Tiedt | 1st MVC (13-0), State Runner-up to Bettendorf,  Emily Cilek and Kate Cilek  State Doubles Champions, MVP - Kris Tiedt, Tiedt & Ross Cram 2nd at State co-ed meet |
| 1999 | 20-1 | "        " | Katie Bossen<br>Emily Rowat | 1st MVC, 1st District, Runner-up again to Bettendorf,<br> MVP - Emmy Cilek |
| 2000 | 9-5 | "        " | Betsy Balmer<br>Erin Doolin | Jenny Schulte 6th State Singles & MVP |
| 2001 | 6-11 | "        " | | Jenny Schulte 4th State Singles |
| 2002 | 10-10 | "        " | Kelly Ferentz<br>Nora Lawrenson | MVP - Lawrenson |
| 2003 | | "        " | Erin Alward<br>Jaime Watts | MVP - Megan Gatens |
| 2004 | 14-5 | "        " | Erin Alwood<br>Megan Gatens<br>Lindsay George | 1st MVC,  MVP Megan Gatens repeats, after 18 years Coach Freeman-George retires |

*2004 MVC Champions - Coach Freeman-George's last team*

# Men's Track and Field 1906-2004

City High has a storied history in men's track dating to 1908, with its first individual champion, to 2004 when the Little Hawks won their 11th State Team Title, which ranks fourth all-time in Iowa history.

As in football, basketball and baseball there are indications that City High did have athletes participating in track and field prior to 1906, but these were not sanctioned by the Board of Education. There have been 15 head coaches at City High with Chic Forwald (20) and John Raffensperger (34) having the longest tenures.

## *Pre-1920's*

The first sanctioned team apparently was fielded in 1906. It was coached by Mr. Siepert and captained by weight man Charles Hazard. The 1907 team was the first to score points in the State meet, which had its start in 1906, as Yetter placed third in the mile and fourth in the 880. The 1908 team had the first individual State Champ when Arlo Wilson won the high jump. The team finished fourth with 14 points. Adding to Wilson's points were Leo Keppler with seconds in the 100 and 220 dashes and Yetter was second in the mile. John Jewell was the coach.

In 1910 and 1911, under the coaching of Mr. Barnes, the team had some outstanding success. In 1910 Paul Hoerlein (high hurdles) and Charles Parson (440) were state champions and the team won two major meets. The 1911 season saw Parson repeat as 440 champion and Edwin Shrader win both the high jump and the pole vault. Shrader's 5'10" high jump equaled the best in

*1912 team - Coach George Bresnahan, first salaried track coach*

the nation in 1911. Both Parson and Shrader were invited to the Stagg meet in Chicago after the season. That 1911 team also recorded the first-ever Drake Relays winner (the 2-Mile relay) with a time of 8:57.6.

George Bresnahan, in 1912, became the first salaried coach for City High. Coach Bresnahan went on to be the head coach for the Iowa Hawkeyes for 28 seasons and was named an assistant coach of the 1932 Olympic team. He is the author of one of the most widely used textbooks on track and field. He coached the Little Hawks for three seasons.

In 1916 H.C. Soucek started a 10-year (1916-1925) stint as the head coach. During that time some very outstanding individuals were members of the Little Hawk track and field teams, including City High's only two Olympians, Eric Wilson and Chan Coulter!

In 1917 Ken Hicks, second in the mile, and Percy Osborne, fifth pole vault, placed in the Stagg meet in Chicago. The 1919 season saw future Olympian Eric Wilson as State champion in the broad jump, as it was called in those days, with a 20' 9" jump. Wilson was also third in the 220. Eric was a multiple Big 10 Champion at Iowa and briefly held the World Record in the 440 that he set in winning the U.S. Olympic Trials in 1924. He participated, but did not win a medal in the 1924 Olympics.

## 1920's

As the 20's began Henry Soucek was in his fifth year at the helm. Versatile Chan Coulter, who would join his former teammate Eric Wilson on the 1924 Olympic team, was a two-event winner at the 1921 State meet. He won the 100 and 440 dashes. Coulter was invited and placed third in the Stagg meet in both the 440 and 220. His 220 time of :22.1 is still number eight on the all-time list at City High as of 2004. Xavier Boyles won the State pole vault title establishing a then record of 10' 11-1/8".

*Chan Coulter & Eric Wilson - on the 1924 Olympic Team*

In 1924 Wallace Elliott became the 11th Little Hawk to win a state title winning the mile run. In an earlier meet he tied the then National Interscholastic record with a 4:23.7 time. His converted time (4:21.40) puts him seventh on the All-Time list of 1600 runners in City High history. Chic Forwald, future coach of the Little Hawks, finished second at the State meet in the shot put and went on to a fine career at Iowa.

John Weismann was named to succeed Soucek in 1926 and coached two seasons. George Wells, who also coached football, basketball and tennis during his career at City High, began a six-year term as head coach in 1929. Jaro Soucek was District Champion in the javelin in 1929.

## 1930's

The 1930 season saw the first MVC Indoor meet held at the University of Iowa. In that meet Howard Moffit was the first ever-indoor champion for the Little Hawks when he won the long jump. Bob Kittredge also won the 440 in that meet. Howard Moffit would return in 1947 to be the head coach at City High.

In 1931, 1932, and 1935 there were no teams. Spring football was added in its place. George Wells coached in 1933 and 1934 with Dale Marshall setting the MVC record in the javelin with a throw of 163' 4-1/2" in 1934.

Francis Merten replaced Wells in 1936. The next three seasons had mixed results before again the sport was dropped for four seasons (1939-1942),

## 1940's

The first three years of the 40's there was no official team, but in 1941 Paul Ware entered both the MVC Indoor and State Indoor meets. He won the MVC 880 and the State 440 in :51.8.

In 1943 the sport was reestablished with Wally Schwank as the coach. The 1944 team was fifth in the MVC and John 'Tug' Wilson became the first outdoor State champion since 1924 when he won the pole vault (11' 3"). The next season, 1945, Wilson followed that up by winning both the State pole vault and long jump championships. The team finished second at the MVC Indoor with Tug Wilson winning three events.

The 1946 squad posted a win in the State Indoor 880 yd. relay with the team of Coulter, Fliss, Bob Wilson, and Fryauf running a time of 1:38.2. In 1947 City High grad Howard Moffit was named coach. Virgil Troyer won the State Indoor 440 title and was part of the outdoor State champion mile medley team (3:37.6). Other runners were Dick Williams, Chug Wilson and Jack Davis.

In 1948 the squad was District champions. Bill Reichardt placed in four events. The team of Williams, Spaan, Ebert and Troyer won the Drake Relays mile relay in 3:31.9. The 1949 squad finished off the 40's with several top performers. Keith Hemingway, Stan James, Leroy Ebert, Jim Bradbury, Jerry White and Bob Kacena were the leaders. James, Bradbury, Kacena and Ebert were 2-mile relay State champions in 8:21.7.

## 1950's

The 1950's kicked off the A.C. 'Chic' Forwald era in City High track. For the next 20 seasons the very popular Forwald, a 1924 City High graduate, headed the Little Hawk track and field program.

His first squad, 1950, finished third in the MVC Indoor, third in the District, and fourth in the MVC Outdoor. The mile medley team of Bob Moore, Jerry White, Dick Oliphant and Leroy Ebert won the State Indoor championship. That same quartet with Duane Davis replacing White won the Drake Relays in 3:47.4. Ebert, who had numerous sub-two-minute anchor legs, went on to an outstanding track career at Iowa. Ebert also won the State Indoor 440 title in a fine :51.8.

The remaining years of the 50's showed moderate success. The 1951 team was fourth (MVC) and third (District) and the 1952 squad was third MVC and second District. These were possibly the top teams in a very competitive MVC. The throwing events were the top individual events during the 50's. Mike Korns was second in the State Indoor shot put and won several major meets in the discus also. The following year, 1952, saw Jim Freeman go a step further as he won both the Drake and State Outdoor shot put titles. His throw of 54' 8" earlier in the season still is seventh on the all-time list at City High as of 2004.

The 1954 squad finished third MVC and second District. In 1955 the Little Hawks had an excellent District showing of third with five winners: Jim Wilker (shot put), Bill Scott (discus), Don Coulter (pole vault), Bill Thomas (880), and the mile relay team (Thomas, Taylor, Scott, Shima).

In 1957 junior Bill Housel had an undefeated year in the shot put, winning the State at 55' 11". That throw is still fifth all-time at City High as of 2004. In 1958, Housel did not repeat his Drake and State wins, but did win the District.

## 1960's

The 1960's began the same way the 50's did, with an outstanding mile medley relay. Field events also dominated the 60's. Dick Corso, who also was second in the State Indoor mile, anchored the medley team that went undefeated all season. Corso's 1:58.7 anchor at Drake brought the Little Hawks from behind for the victory. The State Champion team, 3:39.1, consisted of John Stevens, Mike Wilkinson, Bob McCool, and Corso.

In 1961 the Little Hawks had two State champions in field events. Phil Minnick won the high jump, 6' 2", and Gary Snook the football throw, 237' 5". The team was fourth in both the MVC and District. Joel Jensen had one of the state's top shot put efforts with a 56' 6" at the Cornell Relays. That is still number three all-time in City High history.

Again in 1962 there were two field event champions. This time Gary Gordon won the high jump and Snook repeated in the football throw. Snook went on to play quarterback for the Iowa Hawkeyes.

The 1963 and 1964 teams were led by sprinters Bob Mauseth and John Kelley along with high jumper Chuck Coulter. Kelley scored a trifecta in the District in 1964 by winning the 100, 220 and 440. His 440 time is still eighth on the all-time list as of 2004. John went on to finish second at State in the 440 and fourth in the 220. He later competed for Iowa.

The 1966 squad was highlighted by another field event standout. Larry Wilson won the State Indoor title in the high jump. An injury hampered his success in the outdoor season. The 1967 team's showing gave an indication of how tough the MVC was in track and field. They finished 10th in the MVC, but second at the District meet.

Bill Asprey, Dave Eastland and Steve Zerwas were the leaders. Eastland won both the MVC and District mile titles and Asprey went on to place at State in the 100 and 220.

In 1968 seniors Mike Wilson and Tom Finley both finished second at the State meet and set school records in the process. Finley ran a school record :09.9 and lost in a photo finish in the 100. Wilson set school records in both hurdle races. He was second at :14.7 in the high hurdles and third at :19.8 in the 180 low hurdles.

Sophomore Mike Holm won the District 440 title but did not place in the State meet. Jim Russell set a school record in the discus, 144' 8".

The 1969 season not only ended the 60's but the 20-year coaching career of Chic Forwald. Chic, who was a 1924 City High graduate and top shot putter, retired following the season. He coached two State champion shot putters along with five other field event State champions. One of the top relay meets in eastern Iowa is named the Forwald Relays in his honor and in 1978 he was inducted into the Iowa Track Coaches Hall of Fame.

*54 years of City High Track & Field coaching:*
*Chic Forwald 1950-69, John Raffensperger 1970-2003*

# 1970's

Assistant coach John Raffensperger, known as Coach Raff, was named to succeed Chic Forwald and headed the program for the next 34 years until his retirement following the 2003 season.

Jim Housel and Jim Knoedel captained the first squad of the 70's. Knoedel became the first of three Knoedel brothers to be named captain of the Little Hawks. The 2-mile run was added as an event and Jim Knoedel was the first school record holder in that event.

The 1971 team had its highest District finish (third) since 1967. Mike Gratz, Bill Binney, Rob Naggatz and Bill Knoedel were the leaders with Gratz the MVP.

In 1972 Bill Knoedel became the first State champion in the Coach Raff era winning the State Indoor high jump with a jump of 6' 5-3/4". Bill jumped 6' 7" in the outdoor season as he won 15 of 16 high jump competitions. He had a great career at Iowa and later jumped 7' 4-1/2", one of the top jumps in the world at that time. The 1972 team had many outstanding performers. School records were set in the high jump (Bill Knoedel, 6' 7"), pole vault (Mike Mueller, 13' 0"), long jump (Knoedel, 21' 3"), discus (Steve Mauseth, 152' 8"), 2-mile (Roy Clancy, 9:56.5), plus two relay records (mile and 440). Carl Hargrave, Jim Kafer, Jeff Blank, Dick Evans, Denny Aubrecht, Rob Rew and Steve Dean all made great contributions as the team had its highest MVC finish since 1961 and a 10th place State finish.

The 1973 squad had another outstanding year finishing just nine points out of first in the MVC and finishing seventh place at State. At the State meet Roy Clancy was second in the 2-mile run with a school record 9:20.7. Mike Mueller was third in the pole vault with a school record 14' 3", Jim Edwards third in the mile, and the mile relay team of Aubrecht, Rew, Bruce Carew and Dean finished fourth. That group established the school record earlier at Ft. Madison, 3:27.5. Also setting a record was the 2-mile relay team of Clancy, Burke, Evans, and Edwards with an 8:14.8.

A significant event of the 1973 season was the inaugural A.C. Forwald Relays held the week prior to the Drake Relays. This meet has developed into the premier co-ed relay meet in eastern Iowa and regularly produces some of the top men's and women's times and distances in the state.

The 1974 squad led by captains and three-year veterans Denny Aubrecht, Steve Dean, Rob Rew and Jim Edwards had a second place at the District and a fourth at the MVC. The Forwald Relays was held on the U. of Iowa all-weather surface and the Little Hawks were second. The 2-mile relay team of Bob Wilson, Jim Wilson, Jim Edwards and Steve Dean shattered the old school record with a 7:56.0 time. That record, which converts to 7:53.2 in meters, held up until the State Champion 2000 team ran 7:52.85. Aubrecht and Dean both broke the school points record.

The 1975 and 1976 teams, although not placing above sixth in the MVC, were highlighted by outstanding individuals. In both years middle and long distance runners dominated. The 2-mile relay again was outstanding as the Wilson twins returned and were joined by Devon Cancilla and Randy Jackson. They ran 7:57.1 and just missed the 1974 record. Junior Randy Jackson ran 9:34.2 in the 2-mile run and Jim Wilson set a new 880 record with his 1:59.2.

In 1976 six school records were set. Randy Jackson, by being a part of four of those records, certainly stamped himself as the premier distance runner in City High history and possibly the state. Jackson set records in the 880 (1:57.7), mile (4:16.3), and 2-mile (9:00.2). His 2-mile time winning the state is still the second best in Iowa history as of 2004. He also anchored the school record mile medley team of Randy Miller, Steve Carew and Kevin Michel with a 1:53.8, 880 leg. Michel became the only Little Hawk to be named captain for two years.

Following the season Jackson finished fifth in the National High School meet in Chicago. As a collegian he went on to several Drake Relays wins in the 3000 steeplechase and was 1980 NCAA Champion and fifth in the Olympic Trials running for Wisconsin.

In 1977 Randy Miller broke Mike Mueller's pole vault record with a jump of 14' 7-1/4", which remains the record because the pole vault was discontinued as an event in 1988. Miller was also a top 10 all-time performer in the 100 as he was named the team's MVP.

The 1978 season produced an unusual happening regarding the annual Forwald Relays. Due

118

to a schedule mix-up the Iowa track became unavailable and, after several days of negotiating, the Forwald Relays was moved to Muscatine. This meet was the first time the Forwald meet was run in meters.

During that same season Matt Trimble set a new school indoor record in the mile (4:30.3) and his 4:19.5 outdoor time was second all-time to Randy Jackson. Jim Schnoebelen recorded top 10 times in the 2-mile and 880. Trimble was named MVP.

In 1979 Matt Trimble broke his own indoor record for the mile (4:25.7). An injury kept him out of the outdoor season. Sophomore Norm Balke set a new school record in the discus (153' 9") and junior Mike Vermace established a new record in the 400 low hurdles (:55.9). State qualifiers Kevin Drake (440) and Eric Christner (high hurdles) both had top 10 performances. The MVC Indoor meet was discontinued in 1979.

## *1980's*

The 1980 team was probably the best team until the 1986 MVC champions. Five school records were established including a State Champion high jumper in Paul Marchael. He was the first state champion since 1976. This team had third (District) and fourth (MVC) showings. School records were: Marchael (6' 10" high jump), Norm Balke (170' 10" discus), Mike Vermace (:54.5 low hurdles), mile relay 3:24.1 (Vermace, Jon Horick, Bryant Robinson, and Kevin Drake). Also the high-low hurdle relay of Vermace, Robinson, Dan Wilson and Mark Grenko set a school record.

The 1981 season also had another state champion as Norm Balke won the State shot put crown with an outstanding 58' 1" throw. Balke also set a school record with his 180' 5" discus throw. These records still stand today and Balke is currently the weight coach for the Little Hawks, after a fine collegiate career at Iowa. Jeb McWilliam (:49.9, 400), Mark Grenko (:15.0, high hurdles), and Bill Schoderbek (:58.0) all had top three all-time performances. Grenko also anchored the second best all-time shuttle hurdle relay.

Bad weather hampered the 1982 season as snow and cold cancelled three meets. The highlight was a District title in the 4 x 400 with the third best time in history. Jeb McWilliam ran a tremendous come-from-behind :48.9 anchor leg to bring home the victory. Steve Semken, Craig Hagen and Robb Fluent were the other runners. McWilliam had a :49.8 open 400 also. Tom Ward (high jump), Bill Schoderbek (low hurdles), and Leon Davis (long jump) all had top three all-time marks. This was the final year of District competition until reinstated in 2004.

In 1983 Erik Miller ran the second all-time mark in the 110 high hurdles (:14.9) and Leon Davis set a new school record in the long jump (21' 7-1/2"). In 1984 Tim Smith broke that mark with a 21' 9-3/4" leap. The high jump duo of senior Tom Ward (6' 7") and junior Mike Raffensperger (6' 4") dominated the event with Raffensperger winning the MVC.

Smith, in addition to his long jump, ran 1:58.6 in the 800 and :50.8 in the 400. The Little Hawks won their first-ever Forwald Relays title and had several outstanding freshman and sophomore efforts.

The 1985 squad is generally credited with being the catalyst for the track and field turnaround for City High despite not winning many meets. The combination of seniors and underclassmen seemed to set the stage for the future. Senior Mike Raffensperger won his second MVC high jump championship and also became number two all-time at City High with a 6' 7" jump. Other seniors - Ivan Lorkovic (3200), Brad Lake (high hurdles), John Ruth (low hurdles, 800), and Terry Keefer (long jump, 400) - made major contributions. The freshman-sophomore team was undefeated including winning the MVC Sophomore title.

In the post season Mike Raffensperger, competing in the National Junior Olympic meet, placed sixth in the high jump and sixth in the javelin with a 180' 5" throw breaking the City High record of 170' 0" set in 1936. He went on to a fine track career at Northern Iowa.

The 1986 Little Hawk squad won the first MVC title in school history by winning the 56th annual meet with two photo-finish victories in the last two events. The MVC title capped an undefeated regular season (11-0) and set the stage for an unprecedented run in which City High would win 18 of 19 MVC titles up through 2004.

Five school records and 31 Top 10 additions were established in the undefeated '86 season. In addition eight sophomore and12 freshman records were set. Nine Little Hawks scored over 100 points with junior Brad Gehrke totaling 208. Seniors Mark Dawson, Kelly Durian and Wade Sass, along with juniors Gehrke, Gerry Coleman, and Joe Ruth, were the leaders. Brent Roth and Tim Vermace became the first freshman since the 50's to get varsity letters.

The 1987 edition of City High track and field duplicated the three-point victory in the MVC and picked up a fourth-place finish at the State meet. Six new records were set: Gerry Coleman (100, 200), Brad Gehrke (400), Brent Roth (high hurdles), the 4 x 100 team of Roth, Gehrke, Darin Zapf, and Coleman, and the 4 x 200 team of Roth, Bryan Dixon, Gehrke and Coleman. Six indoor records were set as well. Sophomore Brent Roth set a new school scoring record with 274 points. Senior Brad Gehrke established the career point record with 526 points. Gehrke finished his career by winning the State Pentathlon, scoring 3,339 points. He also finished second all-time in the 200 (:21.98), first in 400 (:49.16), and fifth in high jump (6' 6"). John Lopos and Tim O'Donnell finished fourth and fifth all-time in the discus. Joe Ruth, who went on to run at Northwestern, had an outstanding year in the 800 and 1600.

The year 1987 marked the end of the pole vault as an event in Iowa high school track and field. Dave Raffensperger became the last City High athlete to compete in the pole vault. Raffensperger finished in a tie for sixth at the State meet. Iowa remains one of only two states that do not have the pole vault.

## *First All-Weather Track*

One of the highlights of the 1988 season was the construction of the new eight-lane all-weather track at Bates' Field. The condition of the cinder track at City High was such that no home meets had been held since 1985. The $165,000 track was a great additon to the athletic facilities at City High and greatly contributed to the future success of the Little Hawks' track programs.

In 1988 the Little Hawks continued their MVC title runs, this time by a dominating 31 points. The team capped the year by finishing fifth at the State meet as Glen Lomenick capped a fantastic end of the season by winning the 1600 crown in 4:21.33. Brent Roth had a hand in 15 of City High's 22 State meet points with a second in the low hurdles (:53.43), third in high hurdles (:15.01), and a :48.99 anchor for the third place 4 x 400 team (Bryan Dixon, Kenny Williamson, Mark Palmberg). Lightning and heavy rain forced the cancellation of the first Forwald Relays to be held on the new all-weather track at City High.

At the MVC meet Lomenick had what Coach Raff describes as the "most spectacular one meet performance" of all the Little Hawks he has coached. That is saying something since Tim Dwight had State meets where he had four firsts! Lomenick won a rare distance triple by winning the 3200, 1600, and 800 in a span of three hours. He started by winning the 3200 in 9:35.8, then followed up with state leading times of 4:18.0 (1600) and 1:56.6 (800). Lomenick was not a one-man show as junior Brent Roth won the high hurdles, low hurdles, and anchored the 4 x 400 in :49.3. The 4 x 100 and 4 x 200 teams also were winners. Coach Raff was named MVC Coach of the Year for the third consecutive season.

An undefeated regular season and a fourth consecutive MVC title highlighted the 1989 season. Brent Roth, MVP for the season, again broke his 400 hurdle school record (:53.25) as he won the MVC Athlete of the Year honors. He won his seventh MVC title with victories in the highs, lows and 4 x 400 relay. The field events also saw outstanding performances by Greg Kruse jumping (6' 5-1/2" high jump), and Andy White throwing (53' 8" shot put, 161' 7" discus).

Donnie Stecher (:10.79, 100), Mark Palmberg (:50.8, 400), and Brad Dawson (4:29.72, 1600) also had an outstanding year. Coach Raff was again named MVC Coach of the Year. Brent Roth (second, low hurdles) and Andy White (third, discus) were the top State meet placers. Roth went on to a fine career in the hurdles for Purdue.

## 1990's

The 1990 team, with just seven letter winners back, was a surprise second place in the MVC and eighth at the State meet. This would be the last year the Little Hawks did not win the MVC or Forwald Relays up through the 2004 season. Junior Pete Simons was an upset winner of the 3200 at State in 9:30.77. He followed that up with a second in the 1600 (4:22.82) and a sixth in the 800 (1:59.31). Another junior Donnie Stecher finished third in the 100 and Brad Kelley seventh in the 400.

Andy White had a Drake Relays winning discus throw of 167' 2", which put him second all-time behind his coach Norm Balke. With an outstanding group of freshman, sophomores, and juniors Stecher, Kelley and Simons returning things looked bright for 1991.

## The Tim Dwight Era

The 1991 season kicked off the 'Tim Dwight era' in City High track and field and what an era it was! The Little Hawks had a 9-1 regular season, then set a record by scoring 63 points at the State meet and still only getting second (71-63 loss to Ames).

The team set five indoor and five outdoor school records. Freshman Tim Dwight had a hand in six of those 10 records. Dwight became the first freshman in memory to win an event in 4A State Track as he won the first of his four 200 meter titles. He also set school records in the 400 (:49.12) and long jump (22' 5-1/4"). His 437 points established another school record. Sophomore Jason Keese scored 301 and five others scored over 200 in a great team effort.

With just three seniors the Little Hawks set the stage for several great years to come. Those seniors were Donnie Stecher, who lost just one 100 meter race and was second in the State 200, Pete Simons State champion in the 1600 and runner-up in the 3200, and Brad 'The Destroyer' Kelley who was sixth at State in the 400 and part of several relays.

Juniors Joey Woody (third lows, fourth highs, second 4 x 400), Josh Briggs (fourth 1600), and Dave Novotny (2:00.60, 800) along with sophomore sensation Jason Keese, who ran everything from 100 to 800, all made great contributions.

Pete Simons was the MVC Athlete of the Year capturing three firsts at the conference meet. Coach Raff was MVC and Regional Coach of the Year.

After a State runner-up finish in 1991 and with all but three major contributors returning City High was one of the favorites for the State title in 1992. The Drake Relays seemed to jump -start the title run. Five Drake titles (long jump, 4 x 200, low hurdles, 4 x 800, 4 x 400) and Joey Woody winning the MVP award stamped City High as the state favorite.

The John Ask Relays followed and the Little Hawks had one of their brightest days ever. Woody set an all-time Iowa record in the 400 hurdles

*Joey Woody - Iowa Record Holder - 400 hurdles*

(:51.71) and a state leading :14.31 in the highs. Tim Dwight set school records in the long jump (23' 3-1/2"), 400 (:48.19), 200 (:22.09) then ran a :48.18 anchor on the 4 x 400 relay. That unit just missed the all-time Iowa record as they ran 3:17.7. The other runners were Jason Keese (:49.3), Chad Pate (:50.9) and Woody (:48.57). That time remains second all-time in Iowa as of 2004.

The MVC title followed (the sixth in the last seven years). Just prior to the MVC meet Joey Woody, running in what turned out to be his last meet, ran the 800 for only the second time in his career and shattered the school record with a 1:53.24. He also earned an invitation to the National High School meet in California in June. Prior to the state meet an auto accident took Woody out of the lineup.

At the State meet City High rallied behind sophomore Tim Dwight, who won three events, to post a 21-point victory over Davenport Central. City High won five events and added two seconds, a third and a fifth to dominate, despite not having Joey Woody. Dwight had wins in the 200 (:21.59), 400 low hurdles (:52.95), and long jump (23'3-1/4"). Jason Keese won the 400 (:49.11) and the 4 x 800 team of Josh Briggs, Dave Laughlin, Nile Heefner, and Dave Novotny won in 7:55.55, as they stayed undefeated for the season.

The 4 x 400 team of Heefner, Chad Pate, Corey Honore and Keese was third, the 4 x 200 team of Ben Ringena, Pate, Keese and Dwight was second in 1:28.93. The 1600 medley team started off the scoring on Friday with a second in 3:31.95. Honore, Ben Waterbury, Pate and Novotny were the team members. Novotny anchored in 1:55.7. Andy Luett placing fifth in the shot put (50' 1") scored the final points. The 1992 State Championship was the first ever for City High. Coach Raff won his first State Coach of the Year award.

Joey Woody went on to win a NCAA Championship in the 400 hurdles for Northern Iowa, was fourth in the 200 Olympic Trials and second in the World Championship in Paris in 2002. As of 2005 he is still competing on the professional circuit.

In regards to his track career, Woody noted; "There's no doubt in my mind that I would not have been as successful in my track and field career if I had not had the opportunity to compete for City High, and be coached by some of the best coaches ever in the state of Iowa. I still represent the Little Hawks in every competition I'm in throughout the world because that is where I learned how to become a great competitor."

The 1993 Little Hawks were undefeated for the second year in a row bringing the unbeaten string to 20 as they defended their state title. Dwight broke his own scoring record for the third year (533) and Jason Keese (346) and Corey Honore (308) broke the 300 mark. Twelve school records were set with Dwight figuring in 11 of them. There were 36 additions to the Top 10 list and some very outstanding freshmen and sophomores, who were major varsity contributors.

In winning the Forwald Relays the Little Hawks scored a record 155-1/2 points. An April snowstorm postponed the meet one day. Both MVC titles went to City High as Dwight set MVC records in the long jump (23' 6-3/4") and the 200 (:21.54) and also won the low hurdles and ran a :20.9 anchor leg on the 4 x 200. Keese had :48.2 (400) and 1:56 (800) splits, Jason Frahm had two 1:58 (800) races. Honore, Nile Heefner, Ben Ringena and Erik Frank also had excellent races.

At the MVC Super meet Keese and Dwight combined for 56 points which matched the team total of runner-up Dubuque Senior. At Drake Dwight won the MVP award and the team had four winners (long jump, low hurdles, 4 x 400, Medley).

At the State meet the Little Hawks were again led by junior Tim Dwight and senior Jason Keese. Dwight and Keese figured in 57 of the 60 points scored. Dwight won the 200 for the third straight year (:21.63), the long jump for the second straight year (23' 5-3/4") and anchored a 4 x 400 win with a :47.96 leg. Other members of the 4 x 400 were Ben Ringena, Rob Thein and Corey Honore. Keese repeated as 400 champion (:49.61) and had a great 1:53.59 anchor to win the 1600 medley. Also on that relay were Ringena, Honore and Merrill Coleman.

The 4 x 800 team of Jason Frahm, Kjell Aamodt, Nile Heefner, and Keese (8:00.61) and the 4 x 200 team of Ringena, Honore, Mike Richards, and Dwight (1:29.42) earned second places. Dwight anchored in :20.93. City High's other points came from a fourth by Jason Frahm in the 800 (1:58.58).

Keese and Frahm represented Iowa on a USA Track and Field-sponsored trip to China following the season. Coach Raff was an assistant coach on that trip. He was also chosen MVC and State Coach of the Year.

The 1994 season marked the end of Tim Dwight's fabulous career. The team had another undefeated season running the streak to 28 straight meets and won their third straight State title with a 60-53 margin over Davenport Central.

Thirteen school records were set and again Dwight had a hand in 11 of them. Dwight's 15th MVC title was one of his best as he blazed a :46.86 anchor leg to help City High win the 4 x 400 in a MVC record setting 3:18.29. Rob Thein added a :49.7 leg. Scott VeDepo, John McMurray, Steve Kurth, Merrill Coleman, Mike Richards, Jeremy Harrod, Corey Honore, Andy Johnson, Dan Joyner, and Cory Kendall all made significant contributions.

The Little Hawks again had a great Drake weekend. The team had four wins (long jump, 4 x 100, 4 x 400, medley) and Dwight won his second MVP award. He finished his career with 10 Drake titles.

*Tim Dwight - 12 time State Champion*

During the regular season, Dwight set all-time Iowa best marks in the indoor 400 (:48.73), 100 (:10.19), and 200 (:20.72). He went on to All-American status in both football and track at Iowa and was the MVP of the Big 10 Track meet his senior season prior to joining the NFL.

At the State meet Dwight won a record fourth consecutive 200 title (:21.90), his third straight long jump (23' 11") and anchored the winning 4 x 200 and 4 x 400 relays. He had fantastic relay legs of :20.83, :20.32, :47.23, and :46.72 in the two-day meet. Other members of the 4 x 200 were Jason Ringena, Mike Richards and Merrill Coleman. The 4 x 400 team was Richards, Rob Thein, and Corey Honore. The medley champions (3:28.93) had Ringena, Coleman, Honore, and Jason Frahm, who anchored in a 1:54.35. Other place winners were: third, 4 x 100 (43.60) Jeremy Harrod, Coleman, Korey Kendall and Scott VeDepo; fifth, Jason Frahm 800 (1:58.74); fifth Richards long jump (21' 10-1/2"); fifth, freshman Jason Ringena 200 (:22.66); and sixth, Thein 400 low hurdles (:54.69).

Tim Dwight finished his career with 12 State titles, the most in State history (eight individuals and four relays). Following the season Dwight competed at the National High School meet in North Carolina where he finished second in the long jump and fifth in the 200 (his only 200 defeat ever).

In 1995, the first year of the Post-Dwight era, it was a continuation of previous years. A fourth straight unbeaten season ran the string to 36. Sophomore Jason Ringena led the scoring with 299, with Merrill Coleman at 251 and Jess Holland (228) close behind. The Little Hawks won Forwald by 79 points and the MVC and Super meets by 62 and 43 points.

Three relay wins (4 x100, 4 x 200, 4 x 400) and two third places at Drake again marked City High as the team to beat in the State. At Drake the Little Hawks won their fourth straight 4 x 400 and third straight medley title. Junior Merrill Coleman had two great anchor legs in the sprint relays to bring victories.

The jumping events were also outstanding with underclassman Joel Johnson (6' 7", high jump), Jess Holland (23' 0", long jump) and Mike Richards (22' 3-1/4", long jump) all ranking among the state's best. Seniors John McMurray and Rob Thein went on to fine collegiate careers.

At a very rainy State meet the Little Hawks won three events and placed 10 times as they scored 61 1/2 points to second place Ames with 34. A surprise win in the 4 x 800 was a special victory. The team of Rory Triplett, Sean Triplett, Scott Gordon and John McMurray won in 8:00.17. McMurray anchored in 1:58.6. Also winning was the all underclassmen 4 x 200 team of Dan McMahon, Mike Richards, Merrill Coleman and Jason Ringena in 1:29.61. Dan McMahon upset teammate Merrill Coleman in the 100 as the Little Hawk duo went 1-2 for 12 big points. The 4 x 100 team was second with McMahon, Scott VeDepo, Kory Kendall and Coleman in :42.80.

Picking up thirds were Ringena (:22.27, 200), Rob Thein (:53.80, low hurdles), Jess Holland (21' 4-1/2", long jump), and the 1600 medley of Kendall, Richards, Thein and McMurray in 3:33.83. Placing fourth was the 4 x 400 team of Holland, Richards, Thein and Ringena in 3:21.65. The 61-1/2 -34 victory over Ames was the second largest margin of victory in the history of the State meet. Coach Raff was again chosen State Coach of the Year.

With many returning state champions and place winners the Little Hawks went into 1996 as again the state favorite. This certainly was the best team yet and arguably one of the top of all time. The winning streak reached 44 with major meet point totals of 149 (Forwald), 178 (Waterloo West), 138 (MVC), 98-1/2 (Super) and capped off with a State meet record total of 78, doubling the score on second place Dubuque Senior. This record still stands as of 2004. The margin of victory (39) is the largest ever.

Merrill Coleman edged Mike Richards 317-315 in scoring with Ringena, McMahon, Holland and Kahlil Hill all scoring over 200 points. Seven school records were set and one all-time Iowa record. The 4 x 100 team (McMahon, Ringena, Richards, Coleman) running at the National High School meet set the record of :41.33, which also still stands.

City High again was outstanding at the Drake Relays with four titles, including three relays. This was the fifth straight 4 x 400 and the third straight 4 x 100 win. Merrill Coleman became the fourth Little Hawk in five years to be named MVP. MVC Division and Super titles followed, as did the fifth straight unbeaten season and State title.

The State meet was a show of depth. City High placed in 10 of the 17 events, winning five and getting four seconds. Twelve different Little Hawks were fourth or above.

Winning events were: Dan McMahon, a repeat winner in the 100 (:10.95); Jason Ringena 400 (:48.63); Jess Holland long jump (23' 1-1/2") and 4 x 200 relay team of McMahon, Kahlil Hill, Richards, and Coleman (1:27.96). The 4 x 100 win was with the same group except for Ben Fraga replacing Richards (:42.82).

Picking up seconds were: Richards long jump (22' 0"); Ringena 200 (:22.20); Joel Johnson high jump (6' 4") and the 4 x 400 team of Jason Dwight, Holland, Richards, and Ringena in 3:20.23. In another show of depth, Rory Triplett, and Mark Dendinger ran in the preliminary race, saving Dwight and Holland for other prelims. Coleman picked up a third in the 100, the medley team was third with Holland, Dwight, Richards, and Triplett and the 4 x 800 finished fourth with Triplett, T.J. Elbert, Jesse Ammerman, and Scott Gordon. Coach of the Year honors were awarded to Coach Raff and his assistants following the season.

Great senior leadership from Sean and Rory Triplett, Richards, McMahon, Coleman, Ben Fraga, Jesse Ammerman, and Tim Ocheltree allowed the seniors to go seventh grade through graduation without a loss of any kind.

A sixth consecutive unbeaten season in 1997 ran the winning streak to 51 meets. Jason Ringena led in scoring (349) with Jess Holland close behind at 302. Jason Dwight, Nikolai Hill, Kahlil Hill and T.J. Elbert all scored over 200. Ringena went over 1000 for his career, the third Little Hawk ever to do that (Jason Keese and Tim Dwight were the others).

In the Super meet win City High scored a record 123 points to 50 for runner-up Cedar Falls. The MVC title was the 11th in the last 12 seasons. The highlight of the MVC was setting the all-time Iowa record in the 4 x 200 relay. The Little Hawks became the first Iowa school to ever break 1:27 as they dashed to a 1:26.38 time. Nikolai Hill, Jess Holland, Jason Dwight and Jason Ringena were the runners. This record still stands as of 2004.

Another highlight of the season was senior Jason Jordan, in his first year of any competitive athletics. He joined the track team and eventually ran a 1:55.6 in the 800 and anchored a State Championship 4 x 800 and a third place on the medley team.

At Drake the Little Hawks won five titles. The MVP award went to Jason Ringena, the fifth MVP award in six years for someone on the City High team. The 4 x 400 won the Drake event for the sixth straight year. The 4 x 100 won for the fourth time and the 4 x 200 for the third straight year.

Quality and depth again brought a sixth straight-State title to tie the All-Time Iowa mark. City High doubled the score of the second place team and won six events and had 11 placers as they scored 71-1/2 points.

Jason Ringena was a triple winner as he won the 200 (:21.57), 400 (:48.73), and anchored the 4 x 400 with a :47.65. T.J. Elbert, Jason Dwight and Jess Holland also ran on that relay. The Little Hawks won four of the five relays. The others were 4 x 800 (7:58.56), Scott Gordon, Joe Colangelo, Elbert and Jason Jordan; 4 x 200 (1:27.67) Nikolai Hill, Holland, Dwight, Kahlil Hill and the 4 x 100 (:42.42), the same group as 4 x 200 except T.J. Kempf replaced Dwight.

Nikolai Hill was second in the 100 (:10.86) and Holland was third in the long jump (22' 4-3/4") with Kahlil Hill sixth in that event. Joel Johnson was fifth in the high jump (6' 4") and the medley relay (3:30.67) picked up third with Kempf, K. Hill, Dwight and Jordan. Jordan, in his first year of track, anchored in 1:55.6.

Coach Raff and his staff won their sixth State Coach of the Year award and Coach Raff was inducted into the Iowa Track Coaches Hall of Fame at the end of the year.

In 1998 the State Title winning streak was stopped at six, but the Little Hawks won both the MVC and Super meets. The winning streak reached 53 before being snapped.

One of the highlights was beating Cedar Falls 84-81 in the Super Meet after losing to them by 18 and 40 points in earlier meets. Field events were key as Tony Burrier (high jump), Justin Coyer (shot put), and Andy Stewart (discus throw) came through. Scott Gordon (800), Roberto Moreno (1600, 3200), Burrier (high hurdles), and all five relays had season bests. Tony Burrier had the highest finish at the State meet, third in the 110 high hurdles.

The 1999 season proved to be as Coach Raff said, "one of the most exciting and rewarding seasons of my career." With the six-year streak broken in 1998 and almost no seniors on the squad, the 1999 Little Hawk team appeared to be a year away from state contention. Instead the development of some outstanding underclassmen and a very balanced State meet brought about the most improbable State title for City High.

Drake was not the usual springboard as the Little Hawks won no events and had only one finish as high as third. Four invitational meet wins preceding the MVC and Super meets were close but victories. The MVC win was the ninth in a row and 13th of 14 for City High. Junior Ryan Strang had a breakout meet as he won the 110 high hurdles and had a :48.9 split in the 4 x 400. Roberto Moreno had career best times in the 1600 and 800. Sophomore Hakim Hill had four firsts and Justin Coyer recorded the state's top shot put throw of 57' 5" as the Little Hawks appeared to be peaking.

At the State meet the chance for a top-five finish was the best bet and a scoreless first day backed that idea up. As the Saturday portion of the meet unfolded the Little Hawks slowly crawled into contention. Justin Coyer picked up a second in the shot put (56' 8"), the 4 x 800 picked up a surprising fourth (8:02.98) with Jacob Smith, Joe Colangelo, Hugh John Barry and Skyler Moss. Then the 4 x 200 team also got a valuable fourth place (1:29.87) with the best time of the season. The team was Ryan Strang, Kevin Grifhorst, Calvin Davis, and Hakim Hill. Hill also picked up a fourth in the long jump to add three more points. Roberto Moreno repeated his third place finish from Drake in the 1600 (4:20.45). At that point it still seemed a third place finish was most likely.

In the next to last event the 4 x 100, the Little Hawks who were seeded fifth, got a great anchor by Hakim Hill to get third and six big points. City High needed to win the final event, the 4 x 400, to tie for the title. The Little Hawks, anchored by a :49.44 from junior Ryan Strang, came from behind to win in 3:22.25 and set off the victory celebration. Others on the 4 x 400 were freshman Calvin Davis, junior Kevin Brewer and senior Joe Colangelo. Inspirational races from seniors Hugh John Barry, Andy Litton and Colangelo were especially important in the state victory.

## 2000's

With many returning place winners, City High started the 2000 season as the State favorite. With an undefeated season and a new streak now at 15, the Little Hawks did not disappoint. Record point totals at the MVC (144) and Super (132) meets and a near state record long jump of 24' 4" by Hakim Hill were regular season highlights.

Three Drake champions and two runners-up helped offset a disqualification of the winning 4 x 400 team. Hakim Hill with 394 and Ryan Strang with 348, led the team with points for the season. Calvin Davis, Roberto Moreno, Matt Wooldrik and Kevin Brewer all had more than 180 points.

Ryan Strang and Hakim Hill were chosen co-most valuable of the MVC meet. Hurdlers Brian Barry and Jim Croker along with sprinters Matt McCracken, Adam Smith and John Skay helped provide depth all season.

Once again City High had a dominating State meet, scoring 72 points, all but one on the second day, and winning by a 32-point margin. The Little Hawks won six events including four of five relays and placed a total of 12 times. Hakim Hill had part of four titles, winning the 100 (:10.88), long jump (22' 6"), and anchoring the 4 x 100 and 4 x 200 relays. Others running on the 4 x 200 were Strang, Wooldrik, and Davis. The 4 x 100 was the same except Sumaster Newell replaced Strang. Other winning relays were the 4 x 800 (7:52.85) with Skyler Moss, Jeremy Mims, Dave Keitel, and Kevin Brewer breaking the oldest school record on the books, and the 4 x 400 with Tim Triplett, Brewer, Moss and Strang in a State meet record time of 3:18.01.

Other place winners were Davis, second in the 200; Moreno third in the 1600; Strang third in the 110 high hurdles; Mims sixth in the 800; and the 1600 medley sixth. The 72 points were the third highest in state history. City High's title was the eighth in the last nine years. The 4 x 100 team of Sumaster Newell, Calvin Davis, Ryan Strang, and Hakim Hill finished third at the Addias High School National Championship meet in a time of :42.16 in North Carolina in June.

The National Federation of High School Coaches Association named Coach Raffenperger National Coach of the Year for 2000 for his longevity of success.

## New Red All-Weather Track

The 2001 season saw the resurfacing of the 12-year-old all-weather track. The new red and white surface, an upgrade from the previous track, made the Little Hawk facility one of the best in eastern Iowa.

With only six seniors on the 2000 team, City High was again the favorite in 2001. Another unbeaten season (10th in the last 12) brought the current win streak to 24 straight. The MVC win was the 11th straight and the Super meet win was the ninth of nine.

Hakim Hill led in scoring with 354 points and the Little Hawks made 28 Top 10 additions. The 155-1/2 points at the Forwald Relays tied the scoring record. The Drake Relays again was a showcase as the Little Hawks won three relays (4 x 800, 4 x 200, 4 x 400), the latter two being anchored by Calvin Davis. Davis also ran on the second place 4 x 100 relay and was selected by the media as the outstanding performer at Drake. He became the sixth Little Hawk to win this honor.

Seniors Skyler Moss, Jeremy Mims, and Tim Triplett were season-long inspirational leaders and other seniors like Jim Croker, Jeff Gilmore and Sumaster Newell contributed vital points. These along with a top group of juniors helped City High to 54 and 72 point victories in the MVC and Super meets respectively, prior to another smashing State meet victory. Mim's 1:53.55 in the

800 almost broke Joey Woody's school record, and Hakim Hill's :10.42 in the 100 was second only to Tim Dwight.

The highlight of this year's State meet was the Little Hawks winning all five relays, only the third time in State history this had been accomplished. City High broke the 70 point mark for the third straight year with 71. City High also won two individual events to total seven wins in the meet.

*Members of the 5 winning relays at the 2001 State Meet*

Individual winners were Jeremy Mims 800 (1:56.21) and Hakim Hill long jump (22' 11-1/2"). Winning relay teams were: 4 x 800 (8:00.12) Skyler Moss, Dave Keitel, John Williams, Colin Swaney; 4 x 200 (1:27.69) Sumaster Newell, Matt Wooldrik, Calvin Davis, Hill; 4 x 400 (3:19.68) Tim Triplett, Moss, Mims, Calvin Davis; 4 x 100 (:41.89, State Meet Record) same team as the 4 x 200; 1600 medley (3:31.40) Newell, Moss, Triplett, and Mims.

Other place winners were: Hill third in the 100 and Warren McDuffie fourth in discus. The title was the ninth of the last 10 and third in a row. Following the season the 1600 medley won the National Championship (3:22.69) at the Addias National High School Track Meet and set an all-time Iowa record. That team was Sumaster Newell, Hakim Hill, Calvin Davis, and Jeremy Mims. Mims anchored in a 1:51.9. That brought to three the number of relays in which the Little Hawks have set all-time Iowa records. They all stand as of 2004.

Coach Raff and his staff were again selected as MVC and State Coaches of the Year.

For the first time since at least 1998 the 2002 Little Hawks were not a solid favorite to win the State title but with Calvin Davis to build around the Little Hawks kept getting better all season.

John Williams started the season out by setting the indoor 800 school record (1:58.76). Greg Deal led in scoring with 250 points edging Davis (237), who missed two meets with a mid-season injury. Tyler Gerard, a senior out for track for the first time, was the surprise of the year as he scored 217 points and ran on two State Champion relays. Junior Rob Duwa was also a major contributor.

At Drake Calvin Davis won the 100 and anchored the 4 x 200 to victory. The Little Hawks won the MVC by 56 points and the Super meet by 34. Davis was named MVC Athlete of the Year. It was the 15th title in the last 16 years for City High.

At the Forwald Relays City High unveiled a new state of the art scoreboard and automatic timing system that was primarily purchased with money donated by City High graduate and current NFL player, Tim Dwight. Dwight also purchased an entire set of hurdles as he continued to give back to the program.

At the State meet Calvin Davis was outstanding, picking up wins in the 100 (:10.73), 200 (:21.37) and then a spectacular come-from-behind anchor leg of :20.81 for a victory in the 4 x 200. Others on that team were Greg Deal, Rob Duwa, and Tyler Gerard (1:28.14). Also picking up a win was the 1600 medley of Deal, Gerard, Colin Swaney, and John Williams (3:31.58). Williams' anchor was 1:56.20.

A second place and school record time in the 4 x 800 brought eight more points. Swaney, Dave Keitel, Jay Herlein, and Williams ran 7:50.93 with everyone at 1:58.4 or better. Greg Deal added four points with his third in the long jump (22' 0"). Jon Lamb pulled a nice surprise as he added a sixth in the 1600 with a personal record of 4:28.42.

With Davis out of events, the Little Hawks needed at least a fifth place in the 4 x 400 and to beat West D.M. Valley to win the title. With two unheralded runners, who were strictly junior varsity at the middle of the season, the Little Hawks did just what they needed. Adam Smith, Connor Jostes, Phil Kenney, and Phil George ran 3:24.47 to finish fifth and clinch a five-point victory over Valley. Jeremy Rew set a school record and finished third in both the 100 and 200 wheelchair events. The undefeated season ran the current winning streak to 33 straight wins.

*2002 team - 10th State Title for City High*

Coach Raffensperger became the first coach in Iowa history to win 10 State Titles. Calvin Davis later set an all-time Iowa Best of :47.01 in the 400 at the National meet in North Carolina. John Williams ran 1:55.47 in the 800 at the same meet for the third best in City High history.

Matt Wooldrik won his 12th varsity letter and later added his 13th in baseball to become the all-time leader in varsity letters won at City High.

The 2003 season marked the 36th and final season for Coach Raff. Juniors Ryan Grenko (191) and Colin Swaney (172) led in scoring as the team, dominated by underclassmen, won both Valley conference titles and finished fifth in the State meet.

In a rain-drenched Forwald Relays the Little Hawks put up 131 points and won for the 13th straight year. The Drake Relays saw City High win the medley relay with Rob Duwa, Aaron Grove, Grenko and Swaney running. Grenko's :48.6 in the 400 put City High in the lead and Swaney finished the 800 in 1:57.

The Little Hawks won the 11th and final Super meet by 17 points. Weight men Ben McCracken and Michael Sabers were key. The MVC meet followed and City High won for the 13th straight year (17 of last 18) scoring 146 1/2 points. Coach Raff was named MVC Coach of the Year for the 15th time. Colin Swaney's quote epitomize the City High attitude, "We do pride ourselves on always turning out our best, no matter what the meet is."

At the State meet the medley team was third (3:31.77), Michael Sabers was fifth in the discus (157' 11"), the 4 x 800 of Pat Barry, Curt Steyers, Corey Mims and Swaney were second (7:59.15) with each running personal bests. Junior Ryan Grenko had a fourth place (:49.46) in the 400 and Swaney (800), Deal (long jump), and the 4 x 200 team pulled off sixth-place finishes.

*Coach John Raffensperger - Iowa Track Coaches Hall of Fame*

Coach Raff ended his career with 10 State titles, the most of any Iowa coach, 17 MVC titles, 119 major meet wins, 56 State Champions, 36 Drake Champions, one National Champion and six other National place winners. He was elected to the Iowa Track Coaches Hall of Fame and received one National Coach of the Year award.

The most rewarding honor was the naming of the new City High track as the John Raffensperger Track in 2000. Also at that time a scholarship fund was set up in his name. Other very rewarding and special experiences over the years for Coach Raff have been, "Having former athletes Jim Kafer, Norm Balke, Mike Moore, Jim and Andy Knoedel and my sons Mike and Dave helping me coach."

The "Beat goes on" might easily be the slogan of the 2004 season. Tom Carey, an assistant coach with Coach Raff, took over and continued the Little Hawk track tradition with an undefeated season and the 11th State title in City High history.

Three invitational wins, including the 14th straight Forwald Relays, led up to the Drake Relays. The Little Hawks repeated as Medley Champions and set a Drake record of 3:27.18, with Ben Evans, Phil Kenney, Ryan Grenko, and Colin Swaney. Sophomore Ben Evans also won the long jump (22' 7-1/2").

Rain, lightning, and hail forced cancellation of the MVC meet at the mid-point of the meet. The title was awarded to City High on the basis of seed times. Due to the resumption of District meets, the Super meet was discontinued after 11 years, all City High victories.

For the first time since 1982, District track meets were held to determine the state qualifiers. City High won, scoring 124 points. The Little Hawks qualified in 15 of the 17 events, including double qualifiers in three events (high hurdles, 1600, 3200).

At the State the Little Hawks prevailed 61-56 over Ankeny. Winning events were the 1600 medley of Evans, Scott Knight, Grenko and Swaney (3:28.75); long jumper Evans (22' 9-1/2") and 1600 Swaney (4:19.21). Picking up seconds were the 4 x 400 (Swaney, Jack Butler, Knight, Grenko) in 3:21.31, and high jumper Spencer Langtimm (6' 4"). Getting a third was the all underclassmen 4 x 100 (:43.00). Sean Deal had a fourth in the 110 high hurdles as did the 4 x 200 team. Phil Kenney gave up his spot in the medley to pick up valuable fifth-place points in the 200. Sophomore Josh Koeppel finished the scoring with an eighth in the discus, this being the first year that points were given for eight places.

The State Championship earned Tom Carey, a much deserved, State Coach of the Year award. Long-time assistant and former City High state shot put champion (1981) Norm Balke was selected as the Assistant Coach of the Year for the state of Iowa.

In the 95 years of City High track and field there have been a number of notable accomplishments. This would include 11 State team championships, 81 individual and relays wins at State, 50 Drake Relay titles, plus six individuals selected as the outstanding performer at Drake. Three coaches and three athletes have been voted into the Iowa Track Coaches Hall of Fame: Chic Forwald (1978), Bill Knoedel (1991), Bud Williams (1995), Eric Wilson (1997), John Raffensperger (1997), and Joey Woody (2002).

Two City High individuals made the U.S.A. Olympic team, Eric Wilson (400) and Chan Coulter (400 hurdles), which was held in Paris in 1924. Coach Bresnahan was an assistant coach for the 1932 Olympic team. Three graduates won NCAA titles: Eric Wilson 1921 and '23 for the University of Iowa in the 220, Randy Jackson 1980 for University of Wisconsin in the 3000 steeplechase, and Joey Woody 1996 for the University of Northern Iowa in the 400 hurdles. Woody also has a Gold (4 x 400) and a Silver (400 hurdles) medal in the World Championship competition.

# Men's Track & Field

| Year | W - L | Coach | Captains | Misc. Information |
|------|-------|-------|----------|-------------------|
| 1906 | | A. F. Siepert | Charles Hazard | Hazard ranked 3rd in Shot Put |
| 1907 | 0-2 dual | " " | Hans Hoerlein | Hoerlein 3rd LJ at State<br>Mile Relay 3rd at State |
| 1908 | | John J. Jewell | Leo Keppler | Won Marion Central & UI Invit., 4th State (14 pts), Arlo Wilson wins State HJ, Keppler 2nd 100, 220 |
| 1909 | | " " | Leslie Yetter | Yetter 4th 880 at State |
| 1910 | | Mr. Barnes | Charles Parson | Parson wins State 440, Paul Hoerlein wins State 120 HH, Hoffman 2nd Hammer Throw |
| 1911 | | " " | Edwin Shrader | 2-Mile Relay winner at Drake First Drake title for City High. Team second at State, Parson wins 440 again, Shrader wins HJ and PV |
| 1912 | | George Bresnahan | Robert Yetter | First salaried Coach |
| 1913 | | " " | | |
| 1914 | | " " | | 2nd Marion Central, 3rd U of I Interscholastic meet |
| 1915 | | W. E. Beck | | 2nd Marion Central, 4th U of I meet |
| 1916 | | H. C. Soucek | Lyle Brigham | |
| 1917 | | " " | Percy Osborne | Ken Hicks (2nd Mile) & Percy Osborne (5th PV) at the Stagg Meet in Chicago |
| 1918 | | " " | Ken Hicks | |
| 1919 | 1-0 dual | " " | Eric Wilson | Wilson - State 1st LJ, 3rd 220 |
| 1920 | | " " | | No report in yearbook Chan Coulter 4th SP - Iowa Interscholastic Meet |
| 1921 | | " " | | Xavier Boyles wins State and sets record, 10' 11 1/8" Pole Vault, Coulter wins 100 and 440 and at Stagg Meet places 3rd in the 220 (:22.4) & 440 |
| 1922 | | " " | | |
| 1923 | | " " | | Wallace Elliott 2nd mile at State |
| 1924 | | " " | Wallace Elliott | Chic Forwald -2nd State Shot Put, Wallace Elliott wins Mile at State, Elliott ties National HS Mile Record (4:23.7) (not at the State meet) |

# Men's Track & Field

| 1925 | 1-0 dual | H. C. Soucek | Reilly | 4th at Grinnell Relays<br>Beat U-High Indoor 52-42 |
|------|----------|--------------|--------|-------------------------------------------------|
| 1926 | 1-0 dual | John Weismann | Robert James | Cadwallader high point man at State Indoor meet (12pts.) |
| 1927 |  | "       " | Fremont Isaacs | Isaacs wins 440 at Iowa Interscholastic |
| 1928 | 1-1 dual | Walter S. Knox |  | Frank Clark 3rd 880 Indoor |
| 1929 | 1-1 dual | George Wells | Jaro Soucek | Soucek 1st in Javelin at District |
| 1930 |  | "       " | Howard Moffit | First MVC Indoor held<br>Howard Moffit won Long Jump |
| 1931 |  | NO TEAM |  |  |
| 1932 |  | NO TEAM |  |  |
| 1933 | 0-5 dual | George Wells |  | Dale Marshall 1st MVC Javelin, MVC 6th of 6 |
| 1934 | 0-3 dual | "       " |  | Marshall sets MVC Javelin Record 163' 4 1/2 " |
| 1935 |  | NO TEAM |  | Track dropped in favor of Spring football |
| 1936 | 1-2 dual | Francis Merten | Dick Amerine<br>Jerry Pooler | 6 meets |
| 1937 | 2-3 dual | "       " |  |  |
| 1938 | 3-1 dual | "       " |  | Jack Fertig (javelin), DeWayne Justice (PV), and Herman Miller (PV) qualified for State |
| 1939 |  | NO TEAM |  |  |
| 1940 |  | NO TEAM |  |  |
| 1941 |  | NO official TEAM |  | No Team - Paul Ware only entry in MVC Indoor - wins 880, Entered State Indoor - wins 440 (:51.8) |
| 1942 |  | NO TEAM |  |  |
| 1943 |  | Wally Schwank |  | Bucky Walter wins MVC Indoor 880 |
| 1944 | 0-1 dual | "       " |  | Full Team reestablished.<br>5th MVC Indoor, won 2-mile Relay at District, Tug Wilson won State Pole Vault (11' 3") |
| 1945 | 2-2 dual | "       " | Dean Housel<br>Tug Wilson | 2nd MVC Indoor, Wilson wins PV and LJ at District and State |
| 1946 | 3-0 dual | "       " | Bill Olson | 4th MVC Indoor, 1st 880 relay at State indoor |
| 1947 |  | Howard Moffit | Wayne Fliss<br>Chug Wilson | 3rd MVC Indoor, State champs sprint medley (3:39.6), Virgil Troyer 1st 400 State Indoor :52.4 |

# Men's Track & Field

| 1948 | 1-1 dual | Howard Moffit | | District Champs, 7 qualified for State, 7th MVC Indoor, 5th MVC, Won Drake Mile relay |
|------|----------|---------------|---|---|
| 1949 | 0-2 dual | " " | | 5th MVC Indoor, 8th State 2-Mile Relay = State Champs (8:21.7) |
| 1950 | 1-5 | Chic Forwald | Leroy Ebert Bob Kacena | 3rd MVC Indoor, 4th MVC, 3rd Dist. Medley relay Won State Indoor |
| 1951 | 2-5 | " " | | 5th MVC Indoor, 4th MVC, 3rd Dist. |
| 1952 | 2-5 | " " | | 4th MVC Indoor, 3rd MVC, 2nd Dist., Jim Freeman State Champ SP (52' 2 1/4") |
| 1953 | 2-3 | " " | | 6th MVC Indoor, 6th MVC, 4th District |
| 1954 | 1-6 | " " | | 3rd MVC Indoor, 3rd MVC, 2nd District |
| 1955 | 2-7 | " " | | 5th MVC Indoor, 6th MVC, 3rd District |
| 1956 | 3-7 | " " | | 8th MVC Indoor, 7th MVC 4 qualified for State, No placers |
| 1957 | 6-4 | " " | | 3rd MVC Indoor, 6th MVC, 2nd District, Bill Housel undefeated in Shot Put won at State ( 55' 11") |
| 1958 | 4-5 | " " | Jerry Gingerich Bill Housel | 5th MVC Indoor, 7th MVC, 4th District, Housel District Champ SP (53' 1") |
| 1959 | 2-5-1 | " " | | 4th MVC Indoor, 5th MVC, 3rd District |
| 1960 | 4-3 | " " | | 5th MVC Indoor, 5th MVC, 2nd District, Medley Relay undefeated - Won State (3:39.1) |
| 1961 | 2-7 | " " | Phil Minnick | 6th MVC Indoor, 4th MVC, 4th District, State Champs: Phil Minnick HJ (6' 2") & Gary Snook FB Throw (237' 5") |
| 1962 | 0-7 | " " | | 7th MVC Indoor, 6th MVC, 3rd Dist. 7th State, Gary Gordon wins State High Jump (6' 0"), Gary Snook wins State FB Throw (228' 9"), MVP Snook |
| 1963 | 1-8 | " " | | 8th MVC Indoor, 8th MVC |

# Men's Track & Field

| Year | Record | Coach | Captains | Notes |
|---|---|---|---|---|
| 1964 | 0-9 | Chic Forwald | Charles Coulter | 8th MVC Indoor, 9th MVC, 4th District, John Kelley wins 100, 220, 440 at District Meet |
| 1965 | 2-8 | " " | Mike Luther<br>Alan Stelpflug | 9th MVC Indoor, 10th MVC, 5th District |
| 1966 | 1-11 | " " | Pat Holland | 9th MVC Indoor, 9th MVC, 4th District, Larry Wilson HJ wins State Indoor |
| 1967 | 1-8 | " " | Bill Asprey<br>Dave Eastland<br>Steve Zerwas | 9th MVC Indoor, 10th MVC, 2nd Dist., 8 qualified for State, Bill Asprey 5th State 100 |
| 1968 | 1-8 | " " | Mike Wilson | 10th MVC Indoor, 9th MVC, 4th District |
| 1969 | 2-8 | " " | John Wilson | 11th MVC (scored 1 pt. in meet), 7th District, Coach Forwald retires after 20 years |
| 1970 | 2-9 | John Raffensperger | Jim Housel<br>Jim Knoedel | 8th MVC<br>Housel MVP |
| 1971 | 4-7 | " " | Bill Binney<br>Mike Gratz | 10th MVC, 3rd District<br>Gratz MVP |
| 1972 | 4-9 | " " | Ed Evans<br>Carl Hargrave<br>Jim Kafer<br>Bill Knoedel | 5th MVC Indoor, 4th MVC, 4th Dist., 10th State, Bill Knoedel MVP and State Indoor Champ HJ & record (6' 5 3/4") |
| 1973 | 1-11 | " " | Bruce Carew<br>Roy Clancy<br>Mike Mueller | 3rd MVC Indoor, 4th MVC, 4th Dist., 7th State, Clancy MVP<br>**First Forwald Relays** held (will be annual event, week before Drake) |
| 1974 | 4-9 | " " | Denny Aubrecht<br>Steve Dean<br>Jim Edwards<br>Robbie Rew | 6th MVC Indoor, 4th MVC, 2nd District, Aubrecht MVP Forwald Relays on West's all-weather track. |
| 1975 | 0-13 | " " | Jeff Marner<br>*Kevin Michel<br>Jim Wilson | 3rd MVC Indoor, 6th MVC, 3rd District, *Michel only Junior to be captain<br>Randy Jackson (Jr.) MVP |
| 1976 | 0-16 | " " | Randy Jackson<br>Kevin Michel | 4th MVC Indoor, 6th MVC, 8th District, Randy Jackson wins State 2-Mile and MVP again |
| 1977 | 1-13 | " " | Andy Knoedel<br>Randy Miller<br>John Stille | 8th MVC Indoor, 9th MVC, 6th District, Miller MVP, Beat West in Dual |

# Men's Track & Field

| 1978 | 0-11 | John Raffensperger | Jim Schnoebelen<br>Pete Wilson<br>Jim McMillin | 8th MVC Indoor, 10th MVC, 4th Dist.   Matt Trimble MVP Forwald Relays moved to Muscatine when UI track is unavailable. |
|------|------|--------------------|------------------------------------------------|-----------------------------------------------------------------------------------------------------------------------------|
| 1979 | 0-14 | "            " | Eric Christner<br>Todd Seaton<br>Matt Trimble | 8th MVC, 6th District Christner MVP <u>Indoor MVC Discontinued</u> |
| 1980 | 4-6 | "            " | Kevin Drake<br>Bryant Robinson<br>Mike Vermace | 4th MVC, 3rd District, Paul Marchael State HJ champ, Drake & Vermace were co-MVP |
| 1981 | 2-13 | "            " | Norm Balke<br>Brian Boersma<br>Mark Grenko | 7th MVC, 2nd District (5 Champs) Norm Balke wins State Shot Put (58' 1"),   Balke MVP |
| 1982 | 1-9 | "            " | Scott Brooker<br>Craig Hagen<br>Jeb McWilliam | 7th MVC, 5th District (last year District meets held) McWilliam MVP |
| 1983 | 2-9 | "            " | Derek Davis<br>Leon Davis<br>Mike Edwards | 8th MVC,   Leon Davis MVP Qualify for State by Season Long Performances |
| 1984 | 5-6 | "            " | Erik Miller<br>Tim Smith<br>Tom Ward | 6th MVC,    Tim Smith MVP Win Forwald Relays for first time. |
| 1985 | 1-8 | "            " | Mike Raffensperger<br>John Ruth | 7th MVC Mike Raffensperger MVP |
| 1986 | 11-0 | "            " | Mark Dawson<br>Kelly Durian | 1st MVC (first championship ever),  Raff MVC Coach of the Year |
| 1987 | 8-3 | "            " | Gerry Coleman<br>Brad Gehrke | 1st MVC, 4th State,  Gehrke MVP,  Raff MVC Coach of the Year |
| 1988 | 10-1 | "            " | Bryan Dixon<br>Glenn Lomenick<br>Kenny Williamson | 1st MVC, 3rd State, Lomenick  wins State 1600 Raff MVC Coach of the Year |
| 1989 | 9-0 | "            " | Brent Roth<br>Greg Schnetzler | 1st MVC  (4 in a row),  Roth MVP,  Raff MVC  C.O.Y. |
| 1990 | 5-3 | "            " | Jamie Keefer<br>Andy White | 2nd MVC, 8th State, Pete Simons State Champ 3200 |
| 1991 | 9-1 | "            " | Brad Kelley<br>Pete Simons | 1st MVC, 2nd State,  State champs were: Tim Dwight 200, Pete Simons 1600. And 4 x 200, Raff MVC Coach of the Year |

# Men's Track & Field

| Year | Record | Coach | Athletes | Notes |
|------|--------|-------|----------|-------|
| 1992 | 9-0 | John Raffensperger | Chad Leistikow<br>Chad Pate<br>Joey Woody | 1st MVC, 1st State (first time IC team wins State) 62 pts., 5 Champions at State & Drake, Woody MVP, Raff MVC & State Coach of the Year |
| 1993 | 9-0 | " " | Erik Frank<br>Nile Heefner<br>Jason Keese | 1st MVC, 1st Super (first meet), 1st State - Won 5 events (60 pts.), Jason Keese MVP, Raff MVC & State Coach of Year |
| 1994 | 8-0 | " " | Tim Dwight<br>Jeremy Harrod<br>Corey Honore | 1st MVC, 1st Super, 1st State (57 pts.), 4 Drake and 5 State Champions, Tim Dwight MVP and finishes with 12 State titles, Raff MVC & State Coach of the Year |
| 1995 | 9-0 | " " | Cory Kendall<br>John McMurray<br>Rob Thein<br>Scott VeDepo | 1st MVC, 1st Super, 1st State (61 1/2 pts.), 3 Drake & State Champions, MVP - Thein & McMurray, Raff MVC & State Coach of the Year |
| 1996 | 8-0 | " " | Merrill Coleman<br>Dan McMahon<br>Mike Richards<br>Rory Triplett | 1st MVC, 1st Super, 1st State (78 pts.), All-time Scoring Record at State, 5 State Champions, MVP - Senior Class, All-time Iowa Best 4 x 100 (:41.33), Raff MVC & State Coach of the Year |
| 1997 | 7-0 | " " | Jason Dwight<br>T. J. Elbert<br>Jess Holland<br>Jason Ringena | 1st MVC, 1st Super, 1st State (6 in a row), Won 6 events at State (71 1/2 pts.), Scoring Record at Super-123 pts., All-time Iowa Best 4 x 200 (1:26.38), MVP Ringena (running) & Holland (field), Raff MVC & State Coach of the Year |
| 1998 | 5-3 | " " | Tony Burrier<br>Scott Gordon<br>T.J. Kempf<br>Mat Saur | Winning streak snapped at 53 consecutive, 1st MVC, 1st Super, MVP - Burrier (running) & Andy Stewart (field), Raff MVC Coach of the Year |
| 1999 | 8-1 | " " | Hugh John Barry<br>Joe Colangelo<br>Justin Coyer<br>Nick Linder | 1st MVC, 1st Super, 1st State (39 pts.), 4 x 400 won at State, MVP - Coyer (field) & Colangelo (running), Raff State Coach of the Year |

# Men's Track & Field

| | | | | |
|---|---|---|---|---|
| 2000 | 9-0 | John Raffensperger | Brian Barry<br>Kevin Brewer<br>Ryan Strang | 1st MVC, 1st Super, 1st State (72 pts.),  Won 6 events at State, Record Points at MVC (144) and Super (132),  Strang MVP |
| 2001 | 9-0 | "          " | Jeremy Mims<br>Skyler Moss<br>Tim Triplett | 1st MVC, 1st Super, 1st State (71 pts. ) Champions - All 5 Relays - Only 3rd team in Iowa history to win all 5,  MVP - Mims, National Champions and All-time Iowa Best 1600 Medley (3:22.69), Raff MVC & State Coach of the Year |
| 2002 | 9-0 | "          " | Calvin Davis<br>Adam Smith<br>John Williams<br>Matt Wooldrik | 1st MVC, 1st Super, 1st State, 49 pts. (4 in a row, 10 out of last 11)  First Coach in Iowa to win 10 State titles,  Calvin Davis sets Iowa 400 record (:47.01), MVP Davis, Raff MVC & Regional Coach of the Year |
| 2003 | 5-3 | "          " | Aaron Grove<br>Jon Lamb | 1st Forwald Relays (13 in a row), 1st MVC (13 in a row, 16 of last 17), 1st Super (all of them, 11 in a row), 5th State,  Rob Duwa MVP<br>Coach Raff retires after 36 years. |
| 2004 | 9-0 | Tom Carey | All Seniors | MVC rained out, 1st District (Districts reinstated this season, held with girls), 1st State (61 pts.), co MVP  Ryan Grenko, Colin Swaney (running) Michael Sabers (field), Coach Carey State Coach of the Year |

# Women's Track and Field 1973-2004

Women's track and field had its start in the spring of 1973. There were 38 participants on that first team and was coached by Paul Havick. That first squad did not win a meet. The following season, also under the direction of Coach Havick, the team won two meets and finished ninth in the District meet.

*First Women's Track team ever, 1973*

In 1975 veteran coach Orrie Rew, who was also the women's softball and men's cross country coach, took over the program. Coach Rew coached for the next six seasons. Because of spring yearbook deadlines information is sparse for those years, but 1977 was a very good year with nine school records set.

Lori Springer (400) and Jodi Hershberger (1500) had an outstanding season in 1979 as they set school records and went on to the State meet.

## 1980's

In 1981 and 1982 John Clark was the coach with Phyllis Burnett, Sheral Oliver and Denise Organ as outstanding athletes. In 1983 Carol Lumpa was the coach and Denise Organ was sixth in the State 400 hurdles.

The 1984 season was the first of seven seasons under the leadership of Bud Williams. Helene Wieting had an outstanding career in the distance events and was MVP in 1985. The 1986 team had the highest MVC finish (fourth) and won the District for the first time. Heather Paul was fifth in the State long jump. Sophomore Leslie Brown had the first of two MVP awards.

The 1987 season was a break through year as the Little Hawks won the MVC for the first time and were second in the District. Bud Williams was selected MVC Coach of the Year and Heather Paul was the MVP. The 1988 squad repeated as MVC Champions, were third at the District and had their highest State finish (eighth). Leslie Brown was fourth in the 400 hurdles. Brown was also the MVP.

In 1989 the team accomplished the three-peat by winning the MVC and moved up to fifth in the State meet. The '89 team also won the first-ever event at the State, claiming the 800 medley title. Ingrid Friesen, Carrie Shurr, Lesley Kennedy and Darcie Dotson were the members of that team. Williams won his third MVC Coach of the Year award and Sharie Brooker and Ingrid Friesen were co-MVP's.

# 1990's

The Little Hawks followed up the State relay win in 1989 with another in 1990 as the 4 x 800 team of Mindy Visser, Jenny Miller, Anya McMurray and Michelle Nason won the title. The team won both the MVC and District crowns and finished ninth at the State. This was the seventh and last season for Bud Williams as coach.

Randy Jackson, a City High graduate and former State Champion, took over in 1991. That season (1991) saw the MVC streak end, but only because the meet was cancelled due to bad weather. The team was fifth at the State and had the first individual State champion as sophomore Jill Myatt won the first of her three titles in the 400.

The 1992 team won both the MVC and District and was seventh at State. Jill Myatt repeated as 400 champion. In 1993 the team won the school's sixth MVC title and also the first-ever MVC Super meet. Randy Jackson was named MVC Coach of the Year and the team had the highest finish ever, runner-up at State. The squad won three events including Jill Myatt's third consecutive 400 title in :57.9. The team also won the 800 medley (Tanya Gatlin, Jann Duffy, Venice Monagan, Jill Myatt) and the 4 x 800 (Janet Koberg, Rachel Briggs, Cara Wolf and Missy Novotny).

The year 1994 marked the first year since 1986 that City High did not win the MVC as they finished second in both the Divisional and Super meets. They did win the District meet. Keely Barnett won the State Indoor 800 in March.

The 1995 squad started another MVC winning streak as they won the MVC, Super and District meets and followed that up with a third place finish at the State, winning two relays. The 800 medley of Erica Davis, Kenna Long, Jann Duffy and Venice Monagan and the 1600 medley of Sara Nordquist, Duffy, Monagan and Keely Barnett were winners. Barnett also earned points in the 800. Monagan and Barnett shared the team MVP honors. This was Coach Jackson's final season.

Steve Sherwood, who had been coaching at Regina, took over in 1996. MVC and District titles were added and a repeat third place finish at State. Keely Barnett added another indoor 800 title, and ran on a State indoor winning 4 x 400 along with Jenny Mulder, Kelly Triplett, and Teesa Price. Barnett added the State outdoor 800 to her collection, then anchored the distance medley to a win. Others on that team were Sara Nordquist, Anessa Sloan, and Kelli Chestnut.

*Teesa Price - 5 time State Champion 1996-99*

The 1997 season saw the first undefeated season as the Little Hawks swept all meets including their first ever-State Championship. City High scored 51 points and won three events: Keely Barnett (800), Teesa Price (100 hurdles) and Kristin Knight (200). With one event remaining City High trailed Ankeny by four points. After a great :59 lead-off leg by Kelly Triplett, Teesa Price, Kelli Chestnut and Keely Barnett brought the baton around the track in second place for eight points and the team title. Keely Barnett ended her fabulous career with part of seven state titles in track and one individual title in cross country (1995).

City High lost two regular season meets in 1998 but came into the State meet as a favorite to repeat. Kristin Knight, who won the Drake 100, repeated in the 200 at State and Teesa Price won the 400 hurdles. Although those were the only two Little Hawk wins, tremendous depth allowed the team to place in eight other events to win by a 55-35 score. Alison Nair, Amanda Nerad, Nicole Gatens, Kelli Chestnut and Anne Heefner played major roles.

The 1999 season certainly appeared to be the best year yet for City High as every point scorer from the 1998 State Champions returned. The Little Hawks swept through the MVC, Super and Districts, but lost two-time 200 champion Kristin Knight to a season ending hamstring injury.

City High trailed cross-town rival West High much of the State meet, but took the lead with double victories from Teesa Price (100 and 400 hurdles) and Michelle Lilienthal (1500 and 3000). The Little Hawks scored a 61-51 win over West for their third straight title. Lilienthal's 1500 time of 4:34.01 established a State Record; her winning 3000 time was a State Meet Record. Placing in all but two relays supplied vital points.

Coach Sherwood resigned following the season and assistant Terry Coleman was named his replacement. Coach Coleman remains to the present time.

## 2000's

In Coleman's first season the Little Hawks won four events at the State meet but finished second behind Iowa City West. The team did notch a District win. Coach Coleman was named Regional Coach of the Year. Michelle Lilienthal certainly stamped herself as the premier Iowa distance runner of all time as she repeated as champion in both the 1500 and 3000 races. She was also a two-time Drake Relays winner in the 3000, establishing the Iowa Record of 9:47.53.

*Michelle Lilienthal - All-time Iowa Record 1500 & 3000*

She went on to a fine career at the University of Wisconsin.

The 2001 team was again runner-up to Iowa City West, but this time by a single point. After a one-year absence, the Little Hawks again won the MVC and District. The Little Hawks won two relays at State: 800 medley with Morgan Rohrbach, Maya Monitto-Weber, Virginia Dreier, and Monica Mims and the distance medley with Rohrbach, Elizabeth Matzen, Mims and Nelle Trefz. Molly Gable, Kelsie Linder, Jennie Funk and Maureen O'Sheridan-Tabor also were major contributors. Coach Coleman was named State Coach of the Year.

The 2002 season saw the Little Hawks return to the throne scoring 65 points and setting a record margin-of-victory (26 points) at the State meet. The team had an undefeated 13-0 record and qualified in 17 of 19 events for the State meet.

City High won just two events at State. Sophomore transfer Jennie Funk won the 3000 and the team of Virginia Dreier, Heaven Tutson, Elizabeth Matzen, and Monica Mims won the 800 medley relay. The Little Hawks' great depth supplied places in a total of 12 events. The team won three events at Drake also: Jennie Funk (3000), 4 x 800 relay team of Mims, Nelle Trefz, Funk and Meggan Reed, and the shuttle-hurdle relay quartet of Emily Triplett, Katy Fraga, Tara Whiting and Maya Monitto-Weber. Coach Coleman repeated as State Coach of the Year.

The 2003 team is what many believe to be the best team in State history. With 58 points returning from the 2002 Championship team, that was a great starting point. Led by talented seniors Monica Mims, Jessica Elliott and Meggan Reed the team was again undefeated, a streak of 26 meets now. Two Drake wins helped establish state leadership: Nelle Trefz in the 3000 and the 4 x 800 team of Mims, Trefz, Funk and Reed.

*2003 - State 4 x 800 Relay Champions*

At the State meet the Little Hawks won five events and scored a state record 82 points. Winning events were Nelle Trefz (1500 and 3000), the 4 x 800 team of Maggie Leyendecker, Funk, Reed and Trefz; the distance medley team of Virginia Dreier, Camille Jordan, Monica Mims, and Reed and the final event of the day the 4 x 400 (Mims, Katie Krei, Dreier, and Reed). This capped off a record-setting meet and season for the Little Hawks. Coach Coleman was named MVC and State Coach of the Year following the season. Nelle Trefz, Jennie Funk and Monica Mims are all currently competing collegiately.

After winning State titles in 2002 and 2003, the pressure was on the 2004 Little Hawk squad to match the three State titles won by teams from 1997 through 1999. The 2003 squad won the State title with a talented group of seniors. The 2004 squad also had a talented group of seniors to rally behind. The distance duo of Nelle Trefz and Jennie Funk would be together for the first time since their freshman season and sprinters Emily Triplett, Camille Jordan, Virginia Dreier, and Ashton Strickland provided a nice balance. Added to this group of seniors was the most talent-laden freshman class to enter City High. The stage was set for a title defense.

City sailed through the first part of the regular season undefeated, beating rivals Iowa City West and West Des Moines Valley at invitational meets. The Drake Relays saw City High claim a second and fourth in the 3000 with Nelle Trefz and Jennie Funk, a first place in the 4 x 800 relay, fifth place in the sprint medley relay, and fourth place in the 4 x 100 relay. Conference rival Cedar Falls performed even better than City High. The state didn't have to wait long to see City High and Cedar Falls run head-to-head at the MVC conference meet. A close meet throughout saw Cedar Falls nip the Little Hawks by three points in the end to take the conference title. How would the Little Hawks respond to this unexpected defeat? That question

*2003 - State Distance Medley Relay Champions*

was answered one week later at the district meet. For the first time in City High history (and possible state history) a single school qualified for state in all 19 events, erasing the memory of the 2nd place conference finish and setting up a great battle at Drake Stadium in Des Moines.

The 2004 State meet looked to be a battle between City High, Iowa City West, Cedar Falls, and West Des Moines Valley. Each school had qualified more than enough events to put them over the top, but the key would be who could make it happen during the course of the two-day State meet. City High began the meet by getting big second place points out of the distance medley

141

relay team and finished the first day with a dramatic win by Jennie Funk over defending Drake Champion Sarah Wickman in the 3000. Even with this City High ended the day in second place behind Iowa City West. However, the big point-scoring day would be Saturday. What a great Saturday it was! The morning session saw City High with seconds in the 4 x 800 relay and the sprint medley relay taking the lead in the team standings after the morning session. City would not relinquish its lead in the afternoon. City's 4 x 200 relay won the first title in that event, Emily Triplett placed 6th in the 100 hurdles, Nelle Trefz won her fifth State title by winning the open 800 and placed fourth in the 1500. A third place in the 4 x 100 relay and fifth place in the 4 x 400 relay rounded out the scoring for the Little Hawks. In the end, City High won its sixth State title with 62 points over West Des Moines Valley and Iowa City West. A large and talented group of seniors walked off of the Drake track with their third consecutive State title and a suitcase full of memories of the 2004 season. Coach Coleman was voted Regional Coach of the Year following the season.

In the 32-year history of City High Women's track and field, the team has won 14 MVC titles and six State Championships under eight different coaches.

*2003 State Championship team - State Record 82 points*

# Women's Track & Field

| Year | W - L | Coach | Captain | Misc. Information |
|---|---|---|---|---|
| 1973 | 0-5 | Paul Havick | | First year for this sport, 38 on the team |
| 1974 | 2-1 duals | " " | Mary Clancy<br>Carol Lepic | 9th District |
| 1975 | 4-1 duals | Orrie Rew | | 6th MVC, 9th District |
| 1976 | | " " | | 7th MVC |
| 1977 | | " " | | 9 School Records Set |
| 1978 | 1-3 duals | " " | | 10th MVC |
| 1979 | 0-5 | " " | | 8th MVC |
| 1980 | | " " | | |
| 1981 | | John Clark | Phyllis Burnett<br>Sheral Oliver | 7th MVC |
| 1982 | 0-3 | " " | | 6th MVC, only 14 out for the team, MVP - Denise Organ |
| 1983 | 0-4 | Carol Lumpa | | 6th MVC, 5th District |
| 1984 | 2-9 | Bud Williams | Denise Organ | 7th MVC, 10th District |
| 1985 | 6-6 | " " | Kirsten Gisolfi<br>Valerie Honohan | 6th MVC, 4th District<br>MVP - Helene Wieting |
| 1986 | 6-4 | " " | Tanya Gisolfi | 4th MVC, 1st District<br>MVP - Leslie Brown |
| 1987 | 8-4 | " " | Helene Wieting | 1st MVC, 2nd District, MVP - Heather Paul, Williams MVC Coach of the Year |
| 1988 | 8-3 | " " | Heather Paul | 1st MVC, 3rd District, 8th State, MVP - Leslie Brown, Williams MVC Coach of the Year |
| 1989 | 6-3 | " " | Sharie Brooker<br>Ingrid Friesen | 1st MVC, 3rd District, 5th State, State Champion in sprint medley relay, Co-MVP Brooker and Friesen, Williams MVC Coach of the Year |
| 1990 | 8-2 | " " | Michelle Nason | 1st MVC, 1st District, 9th State, State Champion in 4 x 800 Relay, MVP - Jenny Miller |
| 1991 | | Randy Jackson | | 2nd District, 5th State (MVC rained out),Jill Myatt State Champion 400 m. |
| 1992 | 5-2 | " " | | 1st MVC, 1st District, 7th State, Jill Myatt State Champion 400 again |

# Women's Track & Field

| 1993 | | Randy Jackson | Jill Myatt | 1st MVC, 1st Super (first Super Meet), 2nd State, Jill Myatt 400 Champion :57.9 (3rd year in a row), also State Champions 4 x 800 and sprint medley, Jackson MVC Coach of the Year |
|---|---|---|---|---|
| 1994 | 5-3 | " " | | 2nd MVC, 2nd Super, 1st District, |
| 1995 | 7-1 | " " | Jann Duffy Tammy Frantz Venice Monagan | 1st MVC, 1st Super, 1st District, 3rd State, State Champions in sprint medley & distance medley, MVP - Monagan & Keely Barnett |
| 1996 | 5-4 | Steve Sherwood | Chris Kjonass Sara Nordquist Katie Sidwell Kelly Triplett | 1st MVC, 2nd Super, 1st District, 3rd State, State Champions - Keely Barnett 800 & distance medley (anchored by Barnett), MVP - Keely Barnett & Teesa Price |
| 1997 | 9-0 | " " | Keely Barnett Erica Davis Angie Madlock Kelly Triplett | 1st MVC, 1st Super, 1st District, 1st State, First Girls' State Team Title (51 pts.), State Champion Keely Barnett repeats 800, Kristen Knight 200, Teesa Price 100 LH, MVP - Keely Barnett |
| 1998 | 6-2 | " " | Kelli Chestnut Olivia Mills Alison Nair Kaye Sparks | 1st MVC, 1st District, Repeat State Champions (55 pts.), State Champions Kristin Knight repeats 200, Teesa Price 400 LH, MVP - Knight |
| 1999 | 8-1 | " " | Anne Heefner Teesa Price Kristin Knight Kaye Sparks | 1st MVC, 1st Super, 1st District Repeat State Champions (61pts.), State Champions - Teesa Price 100 & 400 LH, Michelle Lienthal 3000 & 1500 (4:34.01) State record, distance medley sets State record (4:03.56) but not at State meet, MVP - Kristin Knight |
| 2000 | 6-3 | Terry Coleman | Nicole Gatens Michelle Lilienthal Molly Meng Amanda Nearad | 2nd MVC, 2nd Super, 1st District, 2nd State, State Champions - 4 x 100, distance medley, Lilienthal repeats in 1500 & 3000, MVP - Gatens, Lilienthal, & Nearad Coleman - Regional Coach of the Year |

# Women's Track & Field

| Year | Record | Coach | Captains | Accomplishments |
|------|--------|-------|----------|-----------------|
| 2001 | | Terry Coleman | Molly Gable<br>Kelsie Linder<br>Morgan Rohrbach<br>Maureen O'Sheridan-Tabor | 1st MVC, 1st District, 2nd State State Champions - sprint medley and distance medley, MVP - Jennie Funk, Monica Mims, & Nelle Trefz, Coleman - State Coach of the Year |
| 2002 | 13-0 | " " | Katie Fraga<br>Katie Funk<br>Elizabeth Matzen<br>Erilynn Russo | 1st MVC, 1st Super, 1st District (12 champions), 1st State (65 pts.), State Champions - Funk 3000 and sprint medley, MVP - Jessica Elliott, Monica Mims, & Jennie Funk, Coleman - State Coach of the Year |
| 2003 | 13-0 | " " | Jessica Elliott<br>Monica Mims<br>Megan Reed<br>Maya Monitto-Webber | 1st MVC, 1st Super, 1st District, 1st State (82 pts. State Record) (5 out of last 7 State meets), State Champions Nelle Trefz 1500, 3000 (undefeated), and 4 x 400, 4 x 800, Distance Medley, MVP - Nelle Trefz, Coleman State Coach of the Year |
| 2004 | 12-1 | " " | Jennie Funk<br>Virginia Dreier<br>Nelle Trefz<br>Emily Triplett | 2nd MVC, 1st District, 1st State (62 pts.) (6 of last 8 State meets), Co-MVP's - Sarah Anciaux, Jennie Funk, Camile Jordan, Nelle Trefz, Emily Triplett, Coleman Regional Coach of the Year |

# Men's Soccer 1984-2004

Men's soccer was the last sport added on the men's side with the first team playing in the spring of 1984. Tim Zweiner, a City High graduate, was the first coach. The State Athletic Association did not sanction soccer until the 1994-95 school year.

The first squad had a 7-5 record. John Stellwagon was named MVP. In 1985 the team won eight matches with Corby Stone the MVP. The following season reflected more improvement with an 11-5-2 record with Sean McNulty the MVP.

The last three years of the decade showed steady improvement with the 1989 team finishing 14-8-1.

## 1990's

In 1990, Tim Zweiner's seventh year as head coach, the Little Hawks had a 17-2 record, losing only to Bettendorf and Iowa City West. In 1991 there was again a 17-win season and second in the MVC, the highest conference finish up to that point.

The 1993 season was a break through year as the Little Hawks won their first MVC title in men's soccer. The following year City High finished second in the MVC.

*First Soccer team to qualify for State Tourney, 1995*

The year 1995 was Coach Zweiner's 12th year as head coach and he retired following that season as the only coach in City High history at that point. The Little Hawks won their second MVC title and went on to finish second in the State meet. This was the first officially sanctioned State meet for IHSAA soccer. Jason Witt was the MVP of the 12-4-1 squad. Coach Zweiner remains the all-time winningest soccer coach with 145 career wins.

In 1996 Tom Kaut took over for Zweiner and his first team had a 13-3-1 record and beat West in the District tournament. Jason Abbott, Shawn Conklin, Brandon Courtney and Todd White were co-captains. The 1997 squad had an undefeated MVC season (13-0) and suffered its only loss (after 15 straight wins) to West in the District. The final record was 15-1 and Nate Lawler was named to the All-State team.

In 1998 the Little Hawks repeated as MVC Champs and finished 17-3-2. The team qualified for the State for just the second time by beating West, Muscatine and C.R. Jefferson. At the State, Sioux City West fell, but then a loss to Urbandale in the semi-final put the Little Hawks into the consolation game, where they lost to Des Moines Roosevelt to finish fourth. Junior Wade Murray made the All-State squad.

*1998 team - MVC Champs - 4th at State*

In the last year of the decade City High finished second in the MVC, but qualified for the State tournament where they lost in the first round to MVC rival Dubuque Hempstead. The team set a one-game record of 19 goals against East Waterloo and Matt Landers was named All-State. Tom Kaut left after the season with a four-year coaching record of 60-10-6 (79%).

# *2000's*

Ian Parratt coached in 2000 (10-6-2) with Gavin Whiting MVP and Dusty Villhauer and Will Wheaton the co-captains. Allen Kuelomovic coached the next three seasons. The 2001 team set the single season mark for wins with 18. That squad won the MVC and finished third in the state. At State, City High defeated Marshalltown, but lost to West Des Moines Valley to put them into the consolation game where they defeated Sioux City North to pick up the third place trophy. Mo Payne, Joe Pfaller and John Ostola were the leaders with Payne making All-State.

The next two seasons (2002 and 2003) had a combined record of 25-9-1 and the Little Hawks were led both years by co-MVPs Ian LeMaster and Matt Mobily. The 2003 squad just missed the State, losing to West in the Sub-State.

Henry Aiyenero replaced Kuelomovic and stayed one season,. Joe McAndrew and Chris Penick were co-MVPs as the 2004 team lost to C.R. Kennedy in the Sub-State. Jose Fajardo, who was the women's coach for eight seasons, was named the new men's coach for the 2005 season.

The Little Hawks have a 267-96-24 record in the 21 seasons of men's soccer. That includes four appearances in the State tournament with a second place finish in 1995 as the best finish.

Soccer was sanctioned by the IHSAA in 1995. The MVC recognized soccer in 1984. City High has won five MVC titles.

# Men's Soccer

| Year | W - L | Coach | Captain | Misc. Information |
|------|-------|-------|---------|-------------------|
| 1984 | 7-5 | Tim Zweiner | | First time for this sport<br>Not State recognized sport<br>MVP - John Stellwagon |
| 1985 | 8-8-1 | "         " | | MVP - Corby Stone |
| 1986 | 11-5-2 | "         " | | MVC 5-3, MVP - Sean McNulty |
| 1987 | 10-7 | "         " | | |
| 1988 | 12-5 | "         " | | |
| 1989 | 14-8-1 | "         " | | |
| 1990 | 17-2 | "         " | | |
| 1991 | 17-5-2 | "         " | | 2$^{nd}$ MVC |
| 1992 | 16-4-1 | "         " | | MVC (7-1-1) |
| 1993 | 11-3-5 | "         " | | 1$^{st}$ MVC |
| 1994 | 10-2-3 | "         " | | 2$^{nd}$ MVC |
| 1995 | 12-4-1 | "         " | Ezra Eash<br>Adam Murray<br>Jason Witt | First year sanctioned by IHSAA<br>1$^{st}$ MVC, 2$^{nd}$ State, MVP Jason Witt,<br>Zweiner retires after 12 yrs. 145 wins |
| 1996 | 13-3-1 | Tom Kaut | Jason Abbott<br>Shawn Conklin<br>Brandon Courtney<br>Todd White | Beat I.C. West in District |
| 1997 | 15-1 | "         " | | 1$^{st}$ MVC (13-0), Nate Lawler All-State, Only loss was to I.C. West in District |
| 1998 | 17-3-2 | "         " | Jonas Benson<br>David Boothroy<br>Andy Watson | MVC (11-0-2), 4$^{th}$ State<br>MVP - the Team<br>Wade Murray All-State |
| 1999 | 15-3-2 | "         " | Matt Landers<br>Ned Le Blond<br>Wade Murray<br>Tyler Witt | 2$^{nd}$ MVC, 1$^{st}$ District, Lost first round at State (Hempstead), Landers - MVP and All-State, Most goals in one game - 19 |
| 2000 | 10-6-2 | Ian Parratt | Dusty Villhauer<br>Will Wheaton | MVP - Gavin Whiting |
| 2001 | 18-4 | Allen Kuelomovic | Joe Pfaller<br>John Ostola | 1$^{st}$ MVC, 3$^{rd}$ State, Mo Payne MVP and All-State |
| 2002 | 11-6 | "         " | Chris Jensen<br>John Ostola | MVP - Ian LeMaster & Matt Mobily |
| 2003 | 14-3-1 | "         " | Ian LeMaster<br>Matt Mobily<br>Jeff Ploessl | Lost in Sub-State to I.C. West, MVP - LeMaster & Mobily, Coach Kuelomovic leaves after season |
| 2004 | 9-9 | Henry Aiyenero | Jon Bassett<br>Joe McAndrew | Lost to C.R. Kennedy in Sub-State, Joe McAndrew and Chris Penick MVP, Coach Aiyenero leaves |
| 2005 | | Jose Fajardo | | |

# Women's Soccer 1985-2004

Soccer was the last sport added for women (1985). A West High student took the Iowa City school district to court in 1985 to allow her to play soccer on the men's team since there was no women's team. As a result, women's soccer teams were set up at both schools. Because of the small turnout it was decided to combine the schools' two teams. The schools remained combined until the 1993 season.

The Girls Athletic Union did not officially sanction soccer until 1998. The Union had a policy that until a certain percentage of the school districts had a sport, it could not be officially recognized. This happened in 1998. This program was added officially as a summer program, with the starting date in May.

Soccer has been one of the most successful sports for women at City High with the most losses ever in a season being four, and that not occurring until the 17th season of the sport. The first eight seasons (1985-92) there was a City High/West High combined program. Then 1993 became the first year both West and City High had their own programs.

The first 10 seasons of soccer saw seven different coaches head up the program. Since that time just two coaches led the Little Hawks through a much more stable period.

## 1980's and 1990's

In the first year of the program (1985) Keith Marcus was in charge of the combined program and the record was a perfect 12-0. Maurien Champion was the captain. The team wore black and gold uniforms to avoid favoring either high school. Margaret Beals coached the next two squads to 10-1 and 9-0 records. Maurien Champion was MVP in '86 and the unbeaten '87 team gave up only two goals the entire season.

Nelson Logan coached the next three seasons. The 1989 team was 17-1, which included the first MVC title (8-0).

*1998 team - Undefeated regular season (16-1-0)*

Then 1990, Logan's last year, saw a repeat title and 18-0 record. In 1991 Diane Huston became the first of four straight new coaches for the program. That team had a 17-0 record and scored 114 goals while giving up just nine.

Cathy Nielsen coached the next season (1992), and the Little Hawks won 21 straight matches before losing the final match to finish 21-1 (that broke a 58-match streak). The only loss was to Council Bluffs St. Alberts. The State still did not recognize soccer.

In 1993 the Little Hawks began their own program as the combined City-West program was discontinued. There was another new coach and another outstanding season (15-0-1) in 1993. Iran Castro was the coach of the MVC Champion Little Hawks. In the first competition with West, City High won both matches.

Diane Delozier became the fourth new coach in four seasons in 1994. Coach Delozier remained for three seasons, winning MVC titles two of the three seasons. The 14-0-1 record in 1994 gave the Little Hawks a phenomenal six-year record of 102-2-3 in women's soccer (95%). The 1994 team gave up just one goal the entire season.

The 1995 team did not win the MVC but led by Natalya Anthony and Krista Leistikow, had a 14-3-1 season. The following season led by Sarah Hurley and Beck Rosenthal, they won the MVC in Delozier's last season with a 13-1-2 record.

Jose Fajardo was hired in 1997 and started an eight-year career as head coach. His first team was MVC runner-up (12-1) and finished 17-2 overall. Michelle Mobily, Dawn Siberts and Martha Kelch were the leaders.

The year 1998 was the first year the Girls' Athletic Union recognized women's soccer. The Little Hawks had an undefeated MVC season and a Divisional title before losing to Pleasant Valley in the Regional tournament. Martha Kelch, Michelle Mobily, and Claire Galluzzo were the leaders with Mobily being named All-State.

The last year of the 90's saw another MVC title and a 15-2 record. Alison Crosby and E.B. Slouka shared the MVP award and Teesa Price was named second team All-State. Price returned to City High as head coach in 2005 after an outstanding collegiate career at the University of Iowa.

## *2000's*

In 2000 Alison Crosby, Nicole Gatens and Lindsay Sickels led the squad, with Gatens named to second team All-State. The 2001 Little Hawks won the MVC and qualified for the State Tournament where they finished fourth, losing to Iowa City West in the consolation game. Kelsie Linder, Lindsay Sickels, E.B. Slouka and Jessica Villhauer were the team leaders with Villhauer and Slouka named All-State.

In 2002 it was a repeat MVC title with Lauren Hartson, Stephanie Bissell, E.B. Slouka and Jessica Villhauer leading the way. The Little Hawks qualified for the State again where they beat Bettendorf, lost to Dubuque Wahlert, then beat West Des Moines Valley in the consolation game to finish third. Villhauer was named to the Elite All-State team and Slouka to the second team.

In 2003 with Bissell, Hartson and Villhauer again leading, City High qualified for the State for the third consecutive season. They lost a heart breaking two overtime shootout to Urbandale in the first round of the State to end the season. Elizabeth Nerad and Lauren Hartson shared the MVP award and Jessica Villhauer repeated on the All-State Elite team. This was the third time Villhauer was named All-State.

The 2004 season, which was Coach Fajardo's last as women's coach, ended with a Sub-State final loss to Iowa City West. Coach Fajardo was later named to coach the City High men's team for the 2005 season. Former City High All-Stater and Hawkeye star Teesa Price Vitense was named to succeed Fajardo.

In the 20-year history (1985-2004) of women's soccer at City High, there have been six undefeated seasons and five with just one loss. Included was a 58-match winning streak, 1989-92. Only four times in history have the Little Hawks lost more than three matches. The 20-year record is 288-38-7, a winning percentage of 86%. Eight different coaches have led the Little Hawks to these wins. There has been three State tournament appearances, all since 2001. The Iowa Girls' Athletic Union first sanctioned women's soccer in 1998.

*2002 - MVC Champs - 3rd at State*

## Women's Soccer

| Year | W - L | Coach | Captain | Misc. Information |
|------|-------|-------|---------|-------------------|
| 1985 | 12-0 | Keith Marcus | Maurien Champion | Not State recognized Sport First year for sport   MVP - Tracey Olson,  Combined program with West High |
| 1986 | 10-1 | Margaret Beals | | MVP - Maurien Champion |
| 1987 | 9-0 | "        " | | Only gave up 2 goals all season |
| 1988 | 9-2-3 | Nelson Logan | | |
| 1989 | 17-1 | "        " | | MVC (8-0) |
| 1990 | 18-0 | "        " | | |
| 1991 | 17-0 | Diane Huston | | 114 goals , only 9 scored against |
| 1992 | 21-1 | Cathy Nielsen | | 21 straight wins,  scored 88 goals, the last match broke the 58 -game winning streak |

# Women's Soccer

| 1993 | 15-0-2 | Iran Castro | | MVC Champs |
|------|--------|-------------|--|-----------|
| 1994 | 14-0-1 | Diane Delozier | | Repeat 1st MVC, undefeated, gave up just 1 goal |
| 1995 | 14-3-1 | "      " | Natalya Anthony Krista Leistikow | MVP - Leistikow |
| 1996 | 13-1-2 | "      " | Sarah Hurley Beck Rosenthal | 1st MVC, MVP - Rosenthal |
| 1997 | 17-2 | Jose Fajardo | Michelle Mobily Dawn Siberts | 2nd MVC (12-1), Martha Kelch MVP, Both losses to Dubuque Wahlert |
| 1998 | 16-1-0 | "      " | Martha Kelch Michelle Mobily | **IGA Union recognized women's soccer.** 1st MVC (13-0), lost in Regional to Pleasant Valley, Mobily All-State, MVP - Claire Galluzzo |
| 1999 | 15-2 | "      " | Alison Crosby Helen Spencer | 1st MVC (12-1), Teesa Price 2nd All-State, MVP - Crosby & Elizabeth Slouka |
| 2000 | 16-3 | "      " | Alison Crosby Nicole Gatens | MVP - Gatens & Lindsay Sickels, Gatens 2nd team All-State |
| 2001 | 17-4 | "      " | Kelsie Linder Lindsay Sickels E.B. Slouka | 1st MVC, 4th State (lost to I.C. West in consolation game), Slouka and Jessica Villhauer All-State, MVP - Sickels &Villhauer |
| 2002 | 15-4 | "      " | Lauren Hartson E. B. Slouka Jessica Villhauer | 1st MVC, 3rd State (beat West D.M. Valley in consolation game, Villhauer Elite All-State, Slouka 2nd team All-State, MVP - Hartson & Stephanie Bissell |
| 2003 | 15-4 | Jose Fajardo | Stephanie Bissell Lauren Hartson Jessica Villhauer | Jessica Villhauer - All State Elite Team, lost 2 OT shootout in 1st round of State, co- MVP - Hartson & Elizabeth Nerad |
| 2004 | 8-9 | "      " | Jamie Frantz Kelsie Full | Lost in Sub-State final to I.C. West Coach Fajardo becomes Men's coach |
| 2005 | | Teesa Price Vitense | | Former City High athlete hired as new coach |

152

# Baseball 1906-2004

City High baseball had its start in 1906, the same as football, basketball and track. Limited information is available for the first few years. As with football and basketball there apparently was "Club or Town team" type of activity involving City High athletes prior to 1906.

In that first official team of 1906 Mr. Siepert, who also coached basketball, was the coach. No record is listed for that first team, but the 1907 team is listed at 2-2 and 1908 at 1-4. Captains were listed for those three teams. Lee (first name not listed) was captain in 1906 and 1907 and Don Crissinger for 1908. There were 35 practicing in 1908.

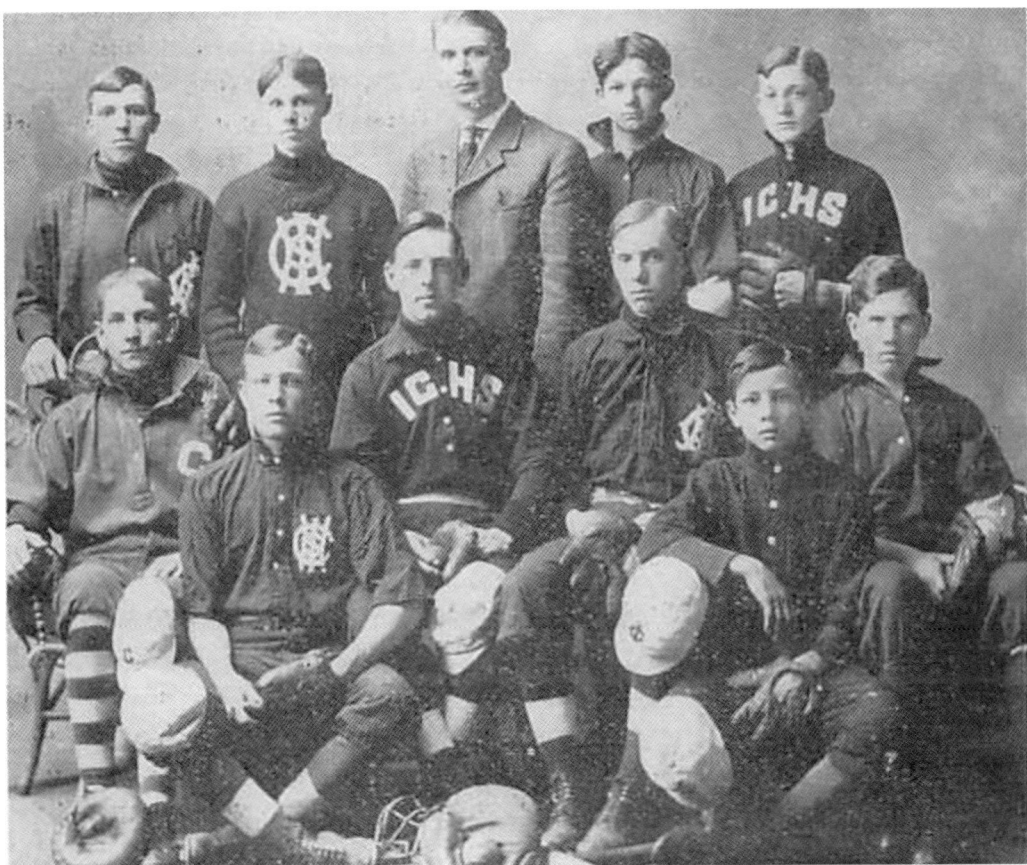

*1907 - Second Baseball team ever at City High*

In 1910 the team had a 2-1 record and Earl Sangster was credited with both wins. Rusty Gordon took the loss in the other game, despite striking out 15 batters.

The 1911 yearbook states that baseball was dropped in favor of track. Yearbooks only list one other season with baseball information until 1945 and that was in 1921. Five games were scheduled that season. Three were reported, those being victories over St. Patrick's, St. Mary's and U-High.

In 1945 the baseball program was reinstated by Earl Sangster, who had been a member of the 1910 team at City High. Thirty-five players reported for the team. Eleven games were scheduled. Only three scores were listed, victories over Cotter and Durant and a loss to Solon. The City High baseball field was later named after Earl Sangster.

Gil Wilson took over the next season (1946) and remained one season. Frank Bates, who was also the football and wrestling coach, took over in 1947 and remained for the next seven seasons. Earl Sangster continued as American Legion coach during the summers.

No information was found on the 1947 and 1948 squads, but the 1949 team had a 20-5 record and won its first three games in the tournament. A loss to C.R. Franklin, a team City High beat four times earlier, knocked them out. In a 4-3 extra inning victory over St. Ambrose Academy of Davenport, Dick Doran was credited with 20 strikeouts.

In baseball, the Little Hawks were playing in what was known as the Little Six Conference, since the MVC did not start playing baseball as a league until 1959. The Little Six included Muscatine, Ft. Madison, Keokuk, Burlington, Fairfield, and Washington.

## *1950's*

In 1950 Ed Morgan had a 17-strikeout no hitter against New London. Second baseman Bill Faemon helped save the no hitter, according to Morgan by "stopping a blue darter with his forehead". Morgan, the starting pitcher in 1950 and 1951, was credited with 21 victories those two seasons.

The 1952 team was 8-8 and finished fourth in the Little Six. The 1953 squad was 12-5 and lost to Ft. Madison in the District final, 5-4 in 10 innings. That was the seventh and final year for Frank Bates as coach.

Bill Holmstrom was named the coach in 1954 and started a 15 year career as the head coach. His first year included a 13-4 record and second in the Little Six. The team lost in the finals of the District.

The only losing record in Holmstrom's 15-year career came in 1955. The Little Hawks lost to Van Horne in the tournament.

In 1956, the Eddie Watt era of City High baseball began. Freshman Eddie Watt was the mainstay of the pitching staff as the Little Hawks had a 14-4 record and finished second in the Little Six conference. Watt had a 13-strikeout game among his accomplishments that season. After shutting out their first three foes in the District, the team lost to Pella (3-2) in the District final.

In 1957 the Little Hawks had a 13-3 record with all three losses coming to State Champion Muscatine. In one of those games sophomore Watt struck out 13, but still lost 2-0. The team was again runner-up to Muscatine in the Little Six. Muscatine won the District tournament game 5-3 in ten innings. City High had games of 24 and 20 runs that season.

*1959 team - State Runner-up - Ed Watt pitches 5 no-hitters*

The year 1958 was a carbon copy of 1957. The record was 14-4 with all four losses coming at the hands of State Champ Muscatine. That gave City High a 27-7 record for the last two seasons with all seven losses coming to Muscatine. The Little Hawks did manage to snap the Muskies 40-game winning streak with a 4-3 triumph in the fourth game of the season. Muscatine won the District tournament game 1-0 to end the City High season.

The 1959 season finally saw redemption against Muscatine. The Little Hawks lost only one regular season game (2-0 to Muscatine) and stormed through the District tournament to qualify for the State Tournament where they lost a heart breaking 2-0 game to Council Bluffs Thomas Jefferson in the State Championship game.

In the State Championship game Ed Watt threw a 2-hitter and struck out 15, but the Little Hawks could not put across a run and lost 2-0.

Ed Watt had a spectacular senior year capped by an equally spectacular tournament stretch. His final season was 12-2, both losses being 2-0 games. His ERA was 0.56 with 206 strikeouts in 98 2/3 innings. He also batted .529 for the season.

Watt started the tournament series with a no-hitter and 17 strikeouts vs. Solon. He followed that with a no-hitter against Regina, where he also was 4 for 4 at the plate. He beat C.R. Regis with 11 strikeouts, then pitched another no-hitter vs. Fairfield, where he struck out 19 of 21 batters.

In the Sub-State tournament he beat Shell Rock 3-0 with a one-hitter, again recording 19 of 21 outs by strikeouts. The above-mentioned State Championship game followed. He allowed just two hits and struck out 15 in a losing effort.

Watt's catcher Bill Slaymaker hit .390 and infielder Gene Rarick hit .372 to back up the great pitching. The Little Hawks outscored their opponents 137-16 in 19 games. Ed went on to star at Northern Iowa for two years before signing a pro contract with the Baltimore Orioles. He pitched in the World Series for Baltimore and also hit several homeruns as a pitcher in the major leagues.

## 1960's

In 1960 a 10-5 record again included three losses to nemesis Muscatine, including a 1-0 loss in the District final game. The 1961 team actually beat Muscatine in their only meeting, but lost to Columbus Junction in the opening tournament game. John Oakes was the MVP.

The 1962 team had a successful 18-5 season and a nice tournament run. Tournament wins over West Branch, CR Prairie, Solon, Mt. Vernon, Clinton and Davenport West put the Little Hawks in the State Tournament.

A 4-0 loss to Williamsburg in the State ended the run. Excellent pitching highlighted the team. ERA's of the pitching staff were as follows: Donn Haugen (0.00), John Rhoades (1.62), and Dave Moss (2.61). Ken Richard (19) and Moss (17) led in RBI's and Skip Hohle had 20 stolen bases to lead the Little Hawks offense.

No details were available in 1963, but Don Rhoades was one of the captains and he returned to his alma mater in 1979 as the head baseball coach. The 1964 team, led by Donn Haugen, was 19-5 and lost in the finals of the District.

In 1965 the team had a 13-8 mark and was fourth in the MVC and District Champs before losing in the Sub-State final. Mike Wymore was the MVP of that squad.

No win-loss records were found for 1966-1970. The 1968 team was the last for coach Bill Holmstrom. He left after 15 seasons, to become Athletic Director for the Clinton schools. Gary Smothers and Dave Wooldrik were the leaders of that team with Wooldrik, just a junior, named MVP and also All-State.

In 1969 Ron Schnack was hired to succeed Bill Holmstrom. Ward Stubbs and Dave Wooldrik led Schnack's first team.

# 1970's

Only one won-loss record was found between 1966 and 1980 (12-12 in 1971). (Yearbook deadlines often prevented summer sports from being published.) Captains for that period included: Bob Schultz ('70), John Piro ('71), Jim Kafer ('72), Joe Leone ('73 and also All-State), Mike Hoffman ('75), Tom Frantz and Dan McKenzie ('76), Doug Dunham and Tim McDaniel ('77), and Mike Hoogerwerf and Jerry Johnson ('78). Glenn Moss ('75) and Tony Powell ('79) were also named to All-State teams.

Ron Schnack coached through 1974, John Vanni from 1975-78, and Don Rhoades in 1979. In 1979 the local Kiwanis Club donated a beautiful electric score board in honor of longtime supporter of Iowa City baseball, Carroll Wooldrik. Wooldrik's son (Dave) and grandson (Matt) were both All-State baseball players at City High.

# 1980's

Bob Rasley, former star outfielder for the Hawkeyes, was named head coach in 1980 and stayed three seasons. His 1980 team was eighth in the MVC. Jeff White and Mike Conlon were All-MVC. The 1981 squad was sixth in the MVC and, with a late season run, made it to the Sub-State where they lost a 3-2 decision to Mason City. Jeff Canfield was named to the All-State team in 1982.

Ron Adams had a three-year term as head coach starting in 1983. His first squad was 14-15 and fifth in the MVC. Scott Flynn was named All-State and Terry Allen All-MVC. The 1984 team had one of the best records ever at 24-8 to finish third in the MVC (the team started the season 14-1). Pitcher Scott Flynn repeated as All-State. Mark Lumpa also made All-State.

Coach Adams' final team in 1985 featured Mark Lumpa and Jim Duthie, who both later played for the Northern Iowa Panthers. Duthie returned as pitching coach for the Little Hawks in the 1990's. Lumpa was named All-State and also MVP of the Iowa Senior All-Star game. Lumpa's All-State honor matched his previous All-State selection in football and basketball. He was arguably the best all-around athlete at City High in the 1980's.

In 1986 Marty Lantz was named to succeed Ron Adams. The Little Hawks won their first ever MVC title with a 23-7 record. Coach Lantz was named MVC Coach of the Year. Steve Bradley and Cole Runge were All-MVC selections.

Randy Norton coached the next two seasons before Marty Lantz returned for three more years. The 1989 squad had the best record at 22-15 during this time period.

# 1990's

In 1992 City High grad Jay Chelf was named coach and led the program for the next nine seasons for the second longest tenure among baseball coaches.

The 1992 team proved to be one of the best teams and started a four-year reign as MVC Champs. Adam Hanrahan and C.J. Thielke were named All-State and led the team to the third State tournament for City High. The team made it all the way to the Championship game before losing to Ankeny. In the title game City High blasted out 14 hits but made four errors and had five wild pitches to hurt their cause. Jeff Lantz had a record tying four hits in that game.

The 1993 season saw a repeat MVC title and a 24-win season. C.J. Thielke was again All-State, along with Brian Mitchell. They both went on to outstanding careers at the University of Iowa and brief pro careers.

The 1994 team won a record 31 games and had three All-State players; Brian Mitchell, Brad Seaton, and Zach Grabinski. A loss to Burlington in the District ended the season. Mitchell established a state record when, in a game against Cedar Falls, he hit two grand slam homers in the same inning.

In 1995, in what was probably the best team ever at City High, the Little Hawks won their fourth consecutive MVC title, won a record 36 games, finished the season ranked number one, and went to the State title game for the second time in four years. Victories over C. R. Jefferson and Ames at State put them in the championship game.

They lost to West Des Moines Valley, 6-5, in the title game. Four Little Hawks were named All-State. Pat Gavin (P), Zach Grabinski (1B), Jeremy Loria (C), and for the third year in a row, Brian Mitchell (3B). Mitchell was also honored as MVC Baseball Player of the Year. The 36-5 record remains the best as of 2004.

The MVC streak ended at four as the 1996 team had a 21-16 record. Dan Heefner and Mitch Price both were named All-State. The 1997 team started a five-year MVC title streak and also returned to the State tournament, where they lost to Sioux City East in the semi-finals after an opening round win over Mason City. Mark Seaton and Mitch Price were named All-State. This was a repeat honor for Price.

In 1998 Nick Linder and Tim Saehler led the team to 24 wins and an MVC title. A first-round District loss to Muscatine ended the season. Saehler was voted MVP.

The final year of the 90's saw another MVC title and a 33-6 record. Joe Colangelo, Nick Linder, Brian Furlong and sophomore Jeff Gilmore were the leaders. Furlong and Gilmore were named All-State and Nick Linder was named MVP.

## *2000's*

Coach Chelf's ninth and final season in 2000 as head coach saw the Little Hawks win their fourth straight MVC title and eighth in the last nine years. Brian Furlong repeated as All-State. The MVC record was 19-4.

Head sophomore coach Dennis Knoop was named to succeed Jay Chelf. His first year (2001) was a 36-2 season and the fifth consecutive MVC title (9th in 10 years). The 36 wins tied the school record. Jeff Gilmore and Matt Wooldrik were named All-State. The MVC title streak was snapped in 2002. Pitcher Zach Hammes signed a pro contract with the Dodgers and did not play in 2002. Matt Wooldrik repeated as All-State. Matt won his 13th varsity letter to become the all-time City High leader in varsity letters won - football (2), basketball (3), track (4), and baseball (4).

In 2003 Cody Smith and Drew Dunham were named All-State. The Little Hawks qualified for the State and beat Urbandale in the first round, but lost to West Des Moines Valley in the semi-finals. In 2004 Smith repeated as All-State and was named MVC Player of the Year. Nick Muhlenbruch and freshman Jon Gilmore were selected to the second All-State squad. The team

*2001 team - MVC Champs (36-2 record)*

did record another 30-win season (30-11). The 2004 season saw the relocation of the City High baseball field to Mercer Park due to construction at City High.

In addition to Ed Watt, City High had another graduate with major league experience. Bob Oldis, a 1946 graduate, played with the Washington Senators, Pittsburgh Pirates and the Philadelphia Phillies in his career. He played in the 1960 World Series with the Pirates and was known for being a great defensive catcher with an outstanding arm.

The Little Hawks have made five appearances in the State tournament. Second place finishes in 1959, 1992, and 1995 were the top finishes. There have been 35 Little Hawks named to All-State since the teams were first named in 1968.

# All-State Baseball Recognition

All-State baseball teams were selected starting in 1968.

| | |
|---|---|
| 1968 | Dave Wooldrik |
| 1973 | Joe Leone |
| 1975 | Glen Moss |
| 1979 | Tony Powell |
| 1982 | Jeff Canfield |
| 1983 | Scott Flynn |
| 1984 | Mark Lumpa |
| 1984 | Scott Flynn |
| 1985 | Mark Lumpa |
| 1992 | Adam Hanrahan |
| 1992 | C.J. Thielke |
| 1993 | Brian Mitchell |
| 1993 | C.J. Thielke |
| 1994 | Zach Grabinski |
| 1994 | Brian Mitchell |
| 1994 | Brad Seaton |
| 1995 | Pat Gavin |
| 1995 | Zach Grabinski |
| 1995 | Jeremy Loria |
| 1995 | Brian Mitchell |
| 1996 | Dan Heefner |
| 1996 | Mitch Price |
| 1997 | Mark Seaton |
| 1997 | Mitch Price |
| 1999 | Brian Furlong |
| 1999 | Jeff Gilmore |
| 2000 | Brian Furlong |
| 2001 | Jeff Gilmore |
| 2001 | Matt Wooldrik |
| 2002 | Matt Wooldrik |
| 2003 | Drew Dunham |
| 2003 | Cody Smith |
| 2004 | Jon Gilmore |
| 2004 | Nick Muhlenbruch |
| 2004 | Cody Smith |

*Bob Oldis - Pittsburgh Pirates*

*Ed Watt - Baltimore Orioles*

# Men's Baseball

| Year | W - L | Coach | Captains | Misc. Information |
|------|-------|-------|----------|-------------------|
| 1906 |  | A. F. Siepert | Lee |  |
| 1907 | 2-2 | "      " | Lee |  |
| 1908 | 1-4 | "      " | Don Crissinger | 35 practicing |
| 1909 |  | NO TEAM |  |  |
| 1910 | 2-1 |  | Grant Keppler | Rusty Gordon = 15 K's<br>Earl Sangster gets both wins |
| 1911 |  | NO TEAM |  | Baseball dropped in favor of track |
|  |  |  |  |  |
| 1921 | 3-0 |  |  | Beat St. Mary's, St. Pat's and U-High    (also had 2 more unreported games) |
|  |  |  |  |  |
| 1945 | 2-1 | Earl Sangster |  | First baseball team to represent I.C.H.S. since 1921,  Coach was player on 1910 team, 11 games scheduled,  35 players reported for team |
| 1946 | 2-2 | Gil Wilson |  | IHSAA started summer program |
| 1947 |  | Frank Bates |  |  |
| 1948 | 1-1 | "      " |  |  |
| 1949 | 20-5 | "      " |  | Dick Doran - 20 K's in extra inning game |
| 1950 | 5-14 | "      " |  |  |
| 1951 |  | "      " |  |  |
| 1952 | 8-8 | "      " |  | 4th in Little Six Conference |
| 1953 | 12-5 | "      " |  | Lost in District Finals in 10 innings |
| 1954 | 13-4 | Bill Holmstrom |  | 2nd Little Six Conference,   lost in District final |
| 1955 | 3-12 | "      " | Art Dunlap<br>Dave Monk | Lost to Van Horne in tourney |
| 1956 | 14-4 | "      " |  | 2nd Little Six, lost in District to Pella,, freshman Ed Watt had 13 K's |
| 1957 | 13-3 | "      " |  | 2nd Little Six (All losses to State champ Muscatine),  Ed Watt had 13 K's vs. Muscatine, but they lost the game. |
| 1958 | 14-4 | "      " |  | All losses to Muscatine, but did snap Muscatine's 40-game streak |
| 1959 | 17-2 | "      " | Bill Slaymaker<br>Ed Watt | State runner-up to Council Bluffs Thomas Jefferson 2-0,  Watt 15 K's, Watt's had 206 K's in 98 innings |
| 1960 | 10-5 | "      " |  | 3  losses to Muscatine |

# Men's Baseball

| 1961 | 11-6 | Bill Holmstrom | | John Oakes MVP |
|------|------|----------------|--|----------------|
| 1962 | 18-5 | "     " | | Lost to Williamsburg in State Tournament,  Donn Haugen 0.00 ERA,  John Rhoades 1.62 ERA |
| 1963 | 11-3 | "     " | Don Rhoades Ken Richard | (Don Rhoades later to return as head coach) |
| 1964 | 15-6 | "     " | Donn Haugen | Lost in finals of District |
| 1965 | 13-8 | "     " | Mike Wymore | 4th MVC,  lost in Sub-State Final, MVP Wymore |
| 1966 | 12-6 | "     " | Dale Hill | MVP - Rick Hahn |
| 1967 | 14-3 | "     " | Jerry Frantz | |
| 1968 | 15-2 | "     " | Gary Smothers | Dave Wooldrik All-State & MVP; After 15 years Bill Holmstrom left to be AD at Clinton, Iowa |
| 1969 | 10-9 | Ron Schnack | Ward Stubbs Dave Wooldrik | MVP - Wooldrik |
| 1970 | 10-8 | "     " | Bob Schultz | |
| 1971 | 12-12 | "     " | John Piro | MVP - Piro & Bill Fay |
| 1972 | 14-14 | "     " | Jim Kafer | MVP - Kafer |
| 1973 | 15-5 | "     " | Joe Leone | 3rd MVC,  Leone 1st team All-State |
| 1974 | 10-15 | "     " | | 8th MVC |
| 1975 | 18-11 | John Vanni | Mike Hoffman | 5th MVC, Glenn Moss All-State |
| 1976 | 9-17 | "     " | Tom Frantz Dan McKenzie | 8th MVC |
| 1977 | 6-12 | "     " | Doug Dunham Tim McDaniel | 8th MVC |
| 1978 | 12-12 | "     " | Mike Hoogerwerf Jerry Johnson | 7th MVC |
| 1979 | 11-11 | Don Rhoades | | 6th MVC, Tony Powell All-State |
| 1980 | 10-17 | Bob Rasley | Don Commings | 8th MVC (2-12 MVC) |
| 1981 | 13-16 | "     " | Mike Bogs John White | 6th MVC,  lost to Mason City in Sub-State (3-2) |
| 1982 | 15-16 | "     " | | 6th MVC, Jeff Canfield All-State |
| 1983 | 14-15 | Ron Adams | | 5th MVC,  All-MVC were Scott Flynn & Terry Allen, Flynn was also All-State. |
| 1984 | 24-8 | "     " | | 3rd MVC,  Scott Flynn  & Mark Lumpa All-State |
| 1985 | 19-14 | "     " | Mark Lumpa | 6th MVC, MVP - Mark Lumpa, also MVP in Iowa All-Star game and All-State |
| 1986 | 23-7 | Marty Lantz | Steve Bradley | 1st MVC,  Lantz MVC Coach of the Year |
| 1987 | 16-13 | Randy Norton | | 6th MVC |

# Men's Baseball

| 1988 | 16-16 | Randy Norton | | 6th MVC |
|------|-------|--------------|---|---------|
| 1989 | 22-15 | Marty Lantz | | 6th MVC |
| 1990 | 19-11 | "    " | | 4th MVC |
| 1991 | 21-15 | "    " | | 7th MVC |
| 1992 | 25-12 | Jay Chelf | | 1st MVC, 2nd State, Adam Hanrahan & C.J. Thielke All-State and MVP |
| 1993 | 24-6-1 | "    " | C.J. Thielke | 1st MVC (19-2-1), Thielke and Brian Mitchell All-State, MVP - Mitchell |
| 1994 | 31-9 | "    " | Brad Seaton | 1st MVC, Seaton, Zach Grabinski, Brian Mitchell, All-State, MVP - Mitchell |
| 1995 | 36-5 | "    " | Zach Grabinski Brian Mitchell | 1st MVC, 2nd State - Lost to WDM Valley in State Finals, Pat Gavin (P), Grabinski (1B), Jeremy Loria (C), & Mitchell (3B) were All-State, MVP - Mitchell, also MVC Athlete of the Year |
| 1996 | 21-16 | "    " | Dan Heefner Mitch Price | 5th MVC, Heefner & Price All-State, MVP - Heefner, |
| 1997 | 33-11 | "    " | Mitch Price Mark Seaton | 1st MVC, qualified for State and lost in semi-finals, Price & Seaton All-State, MVP - Seaton |
| 1998 | 24-12 | "    " | Nick Linder Tim Saehler | 1st MVC, lost in District to Muscatine, MVP - Saehler |
| 1999 | 33-6 | "    " | Joe Colangelo Nick Linder | 1st MVC, Brian Furlong & Jeff Gilmore All-State, MVP - Linder |
| 2000 | 29-10 | "    " | Brian Furlong Ryan Kindhart | 1st MVC (19-4), Furlong All-State and MVP |
| 2001 | 36-2 | Dennis Knoop | | 1st MVC, Jeff Gilmore & Matt Wooldrik All-State |
| 2002 | 24-15 | "    " | Conner Jostes Scott Willman Matt Wooldrik | Wooldrik All-State and MVP |
| 2003 | 28-14 | "    " | | Qualified for State, Drew Dunham & Cody Smith All-State, MVP - Smith |
| 2004 | 30-11 | "    " | | Cody Smith All-State, MVC Athlete of the Year, and team MVP, Jon Gilmore & Nick Muhlenbruch 2nd All-State |

# Women's Softball 1973-2004

Softball began with the 1972-73 school year. It was a summer sport with the first practices held the last two weeks of school and the season ending in mid-July with the tournament. As with most of the other women's sports added to the City High sports scene, the small towns of Iowa had already had softball for years.

Orrie Rew, who also would coach women's track starting in 1975, was the first coach of women's softball. Again because of spring deadlines for yearbooks, very few records are available for the first 10 years of the sport.

The first squad (1973) had a 10 game schedule and had 25 report for the team. The 1974 team had a 5-11 record. From 1975 through 1979 no records were found. Christine Skelly Weber, a softball standout in the late 1970's, mentions this memory: "I was fortunate to be a natural athlete, but unfortunate to be smaller and younger so as to merit only a track shirt and painter pants as a uniform when I first started playing softball at City High. Fortunately by tournament time the other coaches and umpires had persuaded Coach Rew that I should wear a real varsity uniform if I was going to play. I guess I never realized how much less we had in those early days until I see girl athletes these days."

## 1980's

The 1980 team had a 1-13 record and finished eighth in the MVC. The 1981 team was Coach Rew's ninth and last team and also his best team. The Little Hawks were second in the MVC with a 10-3 mark and Coach Rew was chosen MVC Coach of the Year. He retired following the season.

*First Softball team to qualify for State, 1982*

Peg Augsperger was named to succeed Orrie Rew in 1982. She coached for four seasons. Her best season was 1982 with a 31-10 mark. That team was ranked fifth in the state and qualified for the State tourney for the first time ever.

Melanie Ruth Alberts headed up the program for the next four seasons. Her teams got increasingly better each season, culminating in a 26-17 record in 1989.

# 1990's

Brad Randall was the next head coach (1990-1993). In Coach Randall's first season Nicole Steve was selected to the All-State team. Brad's last team in 1993 set a record for wins with 33 and were District Champs.

Jan Grenko was the next head softball coach and at six seasons has the second longest tenure as head coach. Her first team in 1994 tied the record for most wins with a 33-13 record and a third place finish in the MVC.

In 1995 Jann Duffy, Kathie Kempf, Jenny Stewart, and Julie Baker led the team to 24 wins. In 1996 Julie Baker won her second team MVP award.

The 1997 squad was MVC Champs and won 29 games. Abbie Rohert was the captain and sophomore Karla Hirokawa was the MVP. Jan Grenko was chosen MVC Coach of the Year by her fellow coaches. Hirokawa, Kami Berry, Tanya Hammes, Courtney Kowalke, and Sara Brummond were all named All-MVC.

*1997 MVC Champions - won 29 games*

The 1998 Little Hawks team repeated as MVC Champs and won a school record 38 games. That record remains at this writing. The team lost to Muscatine in the District tournament. Junior Karla Hirokawa hit .381 and was named first All-State. Kowalke was fifth All-State. Kami Berry, Megan Recker, Nicole Stockman, Sarah Julius and MVP Courtney Kowalke were named All-MVC. Jan Grenko repeated as MVC Coach of the Year.

The 1999 squad won its third consecutive MVC title with a conference mark of 23-1. The overall record of 36-9-1 is the second most wins in City High history. The team lost in the Regional semi-finals. Jan Grenko was named MVC Coach of the Year for the third consecutive season.

Kami Berry was MVP and Karla Hirokawa was named to the Elite All-State team. Shannon St. John hit .409 and was named to the second team All-State. Pitcher Courtney Kowalke was named to the fourth team All-State. Courtney's 22-6 record gave her 63 wins in her career. Coach Grenko resigned following the season. Her 183 victories is the most by any City High softball coach.

# 2000's

Gary Stamp was named to succeed Jan Grenko in 2000. He remained just one season. That team finished 34-18 and lost in the District to C.R. Jefferson. The MVC record that season was 19-7. Courtney Kowalke was named MVP for the second time, she now had 85 wins in her career. Shannon St. John was named first team All-State, hitting .329 for the season. Her battery mate Kowalke was named to the third team All-State. Sara Brummond, Stacey Senes, Katie Finn and Jess Elliott were all named All-MVC.

In 2001 Mark Tegals became the third coach in three seasons. The Little Hawks had a great late-season surge and were Regional Champions by defeating perennial state power C.R. Jefferson on their own field to qualify for the State Tournament for the second time ever.

*2001 team - 2nd team to qualify for State*

Courtney Kowalke capped a great four-year career by being named as one of the All-State pitchers, as her career win total topped the 100 mark. She was also named team MVP for the third time as she shared the honor in 2001 with Jess Elliott. The team lost in the first round at State, but did manage a regular season victory over Des Moines Lincoln, which won the State title.

In 2002 the Little Hawks were District Champs and won 25 games. Jess Elliott and Lindsey DeFrance were co-captains and Elliott was MVP for the second time. Elliott was also honored as the MVC Player of the Year. Elliott, Sally Wombacher, Megan Gatens and Kelli Paul were named to the All-MVC team.

In 2003 City High improved to 26 wins and lost in the Regionals to C.R. Jefferson. During the regular season the Little Hawks defeated West Des Moines Valley, who later won the State title. Jess Elliott matched Courtney Kowalke's honor by being named team MVP for the third time. Elliott, Wombacher, Paul, Erin Whiting and Katie Finn were named All-MVC.

The 2004 season was Coach Tegals' fourth and last season as head coach, leaving to take a position in Des Moines following the season. His final season saw the Little Hawks win 22 games. Catcher Alaina Neu was named first team All-MVC.

There have been 32 seasons of women's softball at City High. Because this is a summer sport, much of the early years do not have accurate records available.

The Little Hawks have had two State tournament appearances (1982 and 2001) and three MVC titles (1997, 1998, and '99). Seven coaches have headed the program through 2004 with Orrie Rew having the longest tenure at nine seasons.

# Women's Softball

| Year | W - L | Coach | Captain | Misc. Information |
|------|-------|-------|---------|-------------------|
| 1973 | | Orrie Rew | | First year for sport - 10 game schedule, 25 on the team |
| 1974 | 5-11 | "        " | | |
| 1975 | | "        " | | |
| 1976 | | "        " | | |
| 1977 | | "        " | | |
| 1978 | | "        " | Jackie Wright | |
| 1979 | | "        " | | |
| 1980 | 1-13 | "        " | | 8th MVC |
| 1981 | | "        " | Julie Kratoska Lisa Nicola Dawn Stutzman | 2$^{nd}$ MVC (10-3) Rew MVC Coach of the Year, also retires |
| 1982 | 31-10 | Peg Augsperger | Beth Lainson | 5$^{th}$ MVC, qualified for State - first time ever, Lainson and Connie Hargrave were All-MVC |
| 1983 | 9-20 | "        " | | 6$^{th}$ MVC |
| 1984 | 7-23 | "        " | | |
| 1985 | 9-27 | "        " | Kara Frantz Michelle Gehrke Amy Hagen Becky Troyer | MVC (0-14) MVP - Gehrke |
| 1986 | 10-25 | Melanie Ruth | | |
| 1987 | 21-24 | "        " | | |
| 1988 | 25-24-1 | Melanie Ruth Alberts | | |
| 1989 | 26-17 | "        "        " | | |
| 1990 | 15-21 | Brad Randall | | Nicole Steve All-State |
| 1991 | | "        " | | |
| 1992 | | "        " | | |
| 1993 | 33-15 | "        " | | District Champs |

# Women's Softball

| 1994 | 33-13 | Jan Grenko | | 3rd MVC |
|------|-------|------------|---|--------|
| 1995 | 24-29 | "        " | Jann Duffy<br>Kathie Kempf<br>Jenny Stewart | MVP - Julie Baker |
| 1996 | 23-28 | "        " | Julie Baker<br>Lisa Griffith | 4th MVC. Baker, Teesa Price, Kami Berry were All-MVC, MVP - Baker |
| 1997 | 29-20 | "        " | Abbie Rohret | 1st MVC (19-7), Karla Hirokawa was 4th All-State, MVC Player of the Year & MVP, Grenko MVC Coach of the Year |
| 1998 | 38-13 | "        " | Kami Berry<br>Megan Recker | 1st MVC (22-4), lost in District, Hirokawa 1st All-State, Courtney Kowalke 5th All-State & MVP, Grenko again MVC Coach of the Year |
| 1999 | 36-9-1 | "        " | Kami Berry<br>Megan Recker | 1st MVC (23-2), lost in Regional Semi's, Karla Hirokawa, Shannon St. John & Kowalke All-State, MVP - Berry, Grenko MVC Coach of the Year, 3rd year in a row. |
| 2000 | 34-18 | Gary Stamp | Sara Brummond<br>Hilary Hanrahan<br>Shannon St. John | Lost in District, St. John first All-State, Courtney Kowalke third All-State & MVP |
| 2001 | 29-27 | Mark Tegels | Katie Finn<br>Courtney Kowalke | 4th MVC, Regional Champs, State Qualifier; during regular season defeated D.M. Lincoln, eventual State Champs, Kowalke All-State Pitcher, 100 + career wins, Kowalke & Jess Elliott MVP |
| 2002 | 25-24 | "        " | Lindsey DeFrance<br>Jess Elliott | District Champs, Elliott second All-State and MVP |
| 2003 | 26-22 | "        " | Lindsey De France<br>Jess Elliott | Lost in Regionals (C.R. Jefferson), During regular season defeated W.D.M. Valley, eventual State Champs, MVP - Elliott |
| 2004 | 22-27 | "        " | Alaina Neu<br>Kelli Paul | Alaina Neu, catcher, 1st team MVC, Neu - MVP<br>Coach Tegels resigns to take a job in Des Moines |
| 2005 | | Jodie Scheetz | | |

# ATHLETIC DIRECTORS

Prior to the late 1940's, schools did not have a position of Athletic Director, as we know it today. The duties of scheduling contests, hiring officials and handling finances were the responsibility of the high school principal with the assistance of coaches.

The first individual to have the title of Athletic Director at City High was Howard Moffit and he held that position from 1947 through 1953. Moffit also coached numerous sports while at City High.

Bob White succeeded Howard Moffit. Like Moffit, White was a City High graduate. White was in charge of the sports programs at City High (and also West High for a period of time) for 34 years until his retirement in 1987.

Bob White and City High athletic successes are synonymous. From his days as an outstanding athlete to his overseeing of a 20-sport athletic program, he was Mr. City High. An entire chapter could be devoted to this man who put in 40 years of his life at City High, as player, coach and Athletic Director.

Some of the vast changes in the Iowa City athletic scene during White's 34 years as Director were the opening of West High and two junior highs, and the addition of 10 women's sports. There were also numerous changes in the make-up of the MVC. New facilities at City High included the new gym and the first all-weather track. A new men's sport, soccer, was also added during his tenure. For a number of years he led both the City High and West High programs until they were finally separated.

*Bob White - Athletic director for 34 years*

Bob White won numerous awards in his career including both State and National Athletic Director of the Year. He established the Iowa State Athletic Director's Association and was its first president.

Gary Hveem was hired in 1987 as successor to Bob White, upon his retirement. Hveem was a successful football coach in both Iowa and New Mexico, and most recently an administrator in the New Mexico High School Athletic Association. Hveem served City High for 10 years until the spring of 1997, when he resigned to take a position in New Mexico. More facility upgrades, an addition of the Little Hawk Club to the booster program, and an emphasis on the total program were highlights of the Hveem adminstration.

In 1997 Larry Brown, a Hall of Fame football coach and also a City High graduate, was hired to replace Gary Hveem. Brown remains the A. D. as of the 2004-05 school year. The replacement of the all-weather track, weight room upgrades as part of a new 15-classroom renovation at City High, and the moving of the baseball field to Mercer Park are some of the highlights of the Brown administration.

# MVC All-Sports Championships

The Mississippi Valley Conference started awarding an All-Sports trophy to the school with the best conference finish, in all sports, starting in 1985 for men and 1992 for women.

| MEN'S WINNERS | | WOMEN'S WINNERS | |
|---|---|---|---|
| 1986 | 1996 | 1994 | 2000 |
| 1989 | 1997 | 1995 | 2001 |
| 1990 | 1998 | 1997 | 2002 |
| 1991 | 1999 | 1998 | 2003 |
| 1992 | 2000 | 1999 | 2004 |
| 1993 | 2001 | | |
| 1994 | 2002 | | |
| 1995 | 2003 | | |

*MVC All-Sports Trophy*